The Church in China in the 20th Century

The Church in China in the 20th Century

Collected Writings

CHEN ZEMIN

Edited by
RUOMIN LIU
and
RICHARD J. MOUW

WIPF & STOCK · Eugene, Oregon

THE CHURCH IN CHINA IN THE 20TH CENTURY
Collected Writings

Copyright © 2019 Chen Zemin. All rights reserved. Except for brief quotations in critical publications or reviews, no part of this book may be reproduced in any manner without prior written permission from the publisher. Write: Permissions, Wipf and Stock Publishers, 199 W. 8th Ave., Suite 3, Eugene, OR 97401.

Wipf & Stock
An Imprint of Wipf and Stock Publishers
199 W. 8th Ave., Suite 3
Eugene, OR 97401

www.wipfandstock.com

PAPERBACK ISBN: 978-1-5326-3763-6
HARDCOVER ISBN: 978-1-5326-3764-3
EBOOK ISBN: 978-1-5326-3765-0

Manufactured in the U.S.A.   03/07/19

Contents

Preface by Richard J. Mouw | vii
Introductory Essay by Raymond L. Whitehead | ix

An Overview of the Theoretical Foundation and Practical Tasks of Building New China: The Contribution of the Chinese Church (Shanghai, 1939) | 1

Protestant Church in China Today (Tokyo, 1992) | 25

The Post-denominational Unity of the Chinese Protestant Church (Nanjing, March 21, 1998) | 33

Living as Christians Today: Biblical Insights (Nanjing, 1988) | 40

On Nanjing Theological Seminary (Beijing, August, 1986) | 47

Remarks at the Close of the Fortieth Anniversary Celebrations of Nanjing Union Theological Seminary (Nanjing, November, 1992) | 55

Speech Given at Commencement Ceremony of Central Philippine University Iloilo City, Philippines (March 26, 1995) | 60

The Heavenly Vision (Nanjing, 1987) | 66

Pastor and Priest (Nanjing, 28 April, 1991) | 71

Convocation Address Columbia Theological Seminary (September 11, 1996) | 77

Living is Christ and Dying is Gain (Nanjing, September 29, 2000) | 81

Sermon: St. Paul's Church, 2005 April 10—To Unite All in Christ, that We May Become One | 84

Montreat Conference Bible Study (in Outline) Montreat, N.C. (July 21–27, 1996) | 88

Intensify Theological Reconstruction in the Chinese Church:
  Address at the Jinan Conference (Jinan, November 20, 1998) | 97

Outline of Presentation: Candler School of Theology, Emory University
  (November 13, 1996) | 102

Inculturation of the Gospel and Hymn Singing in China
  (Oberlin College, Oberlin, Ohio, July 14–18, 1996) | 110

Reconciliation with the People (Montréal, 1981) | 121

Theological Construction in the Chinese Church (Nanjing, 1956) | 127

Christ And Culture in China: A Sino-American Dialogue
  (Columbia Theological Seminary, October, 1992) | 149

Self-Propagation in the Light of the History of Christian Thought
  (Nanjing, 1954) | 174

Y. T. Wu: A Prophetic Theologian (Beijing, November 27, 1993) | 186

Protestant Christianity in China: Facing the Challenges of Modernization
  (Beijing, April 1992) | 196

Faith's Journey: Foreword to *Love Never Ends* (Nanjing, January 1998) | 203

Address on the "Celebration of the First Publication of 'God is Love'"
  (Shanghai, December 14, 2004) | 210

Preface

Richard J. Mouw

THIS IMPORTANT BOOK OF essays makes a unique contribution to our understanding of the recent history of the church in China. The fact that the first essay was published in 1939—a decade before the Communists came to power— points to the importance of this collection as a documentary history of the life of the Protestant churches during seven decades of significant—and frequently turbulent—changes in Chinese life and culture.

What adds greatly to this book, however, is that the author, Dr. Chen Zemin, is a dedicated Christian leader who has experienced much of this history first hand, having celebrated his 101st birthday in October 2016. He has served as a pastor, a composer of hymns, a teacher, a theologian and a historian. And in all of this he has played a key role in church-state relations, as well as in representing Chinese Christianity in a global context.

I made the first of twenty-plus visits to China in 1994, shortly after being appointed to the presidency of Fuller Theological Seminary. I met Dr. Chen and became one of his admirers, and over the next decades I witnessed personally how Dr. Chen has mentored a number of scholars and church leaders who have themselves made significant contributions to the cause of Christianity in the Chinese mainland.

Dr. Liu Rumin, my fellow editor of this volume—who did the hard work of collecting and in several cases translating these essays for an English-speaking audience—is a prime example of how Dr. Chen's mentoring has borne much fruit in Chinese Christianity. He has taught systematic theology and New Testament at Nanjing's Union Theological Seminary, and is engaging in research and teaching in Germany, where he received his PhD degree from the University of Heidelberg. Like his mentor, Dr. Liu Rumin serves, through his own important scholarship, as an important voice for the Chinese church in global settings.

This volume also features an Introductory Essay by Dr. Raymond Whitehead, a distinguished Canadian theologian who taught for a number of years at the Nanjing seminary, where he was a colleague of Dr. Chen's.

In preparing this English translation of Dr. Chen's writings for publication, I have been able to draw upon support from Fuller Seminary funds specifically designated for partnering with China's "Three-Self" churches. I also received much technical help from several people, and I am particularly grateful to Shi-Min Lu, a PhD candidate in Fuller Seminary's School of Intercultural Studies; she supervised the final typing of the manuscript, with particular attention to the consistent use of Chinese characters throughout.

In 1984 my distinguished predecessor in the Fuller presidency, David Allan Hubbard, led a delegation of trustees and administrators to China, making direct contact with church and seminary leaders in the "Three-Self" churches. That pilgrimage was the beginning of an exciting learning experience for the Fuller community about how God has blessed Chinese Christianity's sustained efforts to be obedient to the Gospel. In that learning experience Chen Zemin has been one of our important teachers. The publication of these essays means that his teaching ministry can now be expanded in the English speaking world.

Introductory Essay

Raymond L. Whitehead

THE READER OF THIS important collection of papers of Professor Chen Zemin might well approach the book with some questions in mind. Does the Protestant Christian Church make a significant contribution to the people of China and beyond? What are the special characteristics of the theology emerging in China? How does Protestant Christianity relate to the official atheism of post-revolutionary China and where does Protestant Christianity fit in among the competing secular and religious world-views in contemporary China? How do Protestant Christian communities in China express themselves in the language and culture of their country? Insights on these and other questions can be found in these writings.

Chen Zemin has served the Church in China for over seven decades. His remarkable career spans a period of war, revolution and social upheavals. The first article in the collection was written in 1939, when Japan had occupied much of China and all out world war loomed in Europe and the Pacific. In the Pacific region the following decade witnessed the Japanese sweep into Southeast Asia and the Philippines, the bombing of Pearl Harbor, years of battle on Pacific Islands, the struggle in Burma, the airlift over the Himalayas into Western China, the atomic bombing of Hiroshima and Nagasaki, the Japanese surrender, revolutionary civil war in China and the establishing of the People's Republic in 1949 under the leadership of Mao Zedong.

Chen Zemin survived all this with a strong faith and a commitment to peace. He was already teaching at the Seminary in Nanjing when Bishop K. H. Ting arrived in 1952 to head up a reconfigured "Jinling Union Theological Seminary" or in its official English name "Nan Jing Union Theological Seminary" (NJUTS). He continued through the ups and downs of social and cultural revolutions and was on hand when the seminary, after a period of closure, re-opened in 1981. The reader may appreciate more deeply these works by Professor Chen keeping in mind this historic panorama as the context of his life's work.

A word must be said about "Protestant Christianity" for readers unfamiliar with Chinese Church history. The term "Protestant Christianity" appears numerous times in these articles. When Catholics and Protestants arrived in China (at different historical periods) questions of translation were of immediate importance. Terms for "God" and "Christ" had no exact Chinese equivalents. The Roman Catholic missionaries determined that the best translation for "God" was "Tian Zhu," "Heavenly Lord" or "Lord of Heaven." Catholic Christians became known in China as "Tian Zhu Zhao" ("Tian Zhu Jiao"), followers of the Lord of Heaven Religion. Later when Protestant missionaries arrived they chose other translations for "God"— "Shan g Di" ("High Ruler"), or "Shen" meaning "god or spirit." But Protestants called themselves by the transliterated word for Christ, "Ji Du Zhao" (Ji Du Jiao) followers of "Christ Religion" or "Christianity." To this day Tian Zhu Zhao (Tian Zhu Jiao) and Ji Du Zhao (Ji Du Jiao) are seen by many in China as two different religions. Ji Du Zhao (Ji Du Jiao) is often translated as "Christian" or "Christianity" but it can be unclear if the term is being used to refer to all Christians—Catholic, Orthodox and Protestant, or if it is intended to mean Protestant Christianity specifically. Therefore it is translated often in these writings as "Protestant Christianity" reflecting the context of the Chinese original.

The very first article in this collection speaks to two of the questions raised above. In 1939 Professor Chen writes of the contribution of the Chinese Protestant Church to the building of a "New China." From the Sun Yat-sen revolution of 1911 through the "May Fourth Movement" of the 1920s (1919) and succeeding years, in spite of foreign invasions and competing "War Lords" inside China, Christians were part of the struggle for social, political, cultural and spiritual renewal. (Sun Yat-sen of course was himself a Christian.) Chen affirms in this essay the Christian work for "peace, justice, purity and truth." This work is not narrowly confined to members of the church. The Christian understanding is that God is loving parent of all humankind, "so that all people on earth are compatriots, brothers and sisters. In this unified and great family, all of us as God's children should love each other and cooperate with each other in order to create a great fellowship. The construction of a new China should take such a view as its foundation." Certainly evangelism, sharing the Christian story and values, is a responsibility of the churches. Equally important, Chen wrote, is the work of education, healthcare, and social service in rural and urban areas.

The breadth of Chinese theological thought shown in this first essay is picked up again in the next two, but with a very great difference.

"Theological Construction in the Chinese Church" reflects the post-revolutionary context of the 1950s. The article here includes further comments written in 1991 when the article was republished. This essay along with "Reconciliation with the People" (his 1981 presentation at the Montreal world conference on "A New Beginning" for China and the churches) has quite a different flavor. The Protestant Church in China had moved forward on the "three-self principles" of self-support, self-administration, and self-propagation. Independent from western missionary budgets and oversight the Protestant Church in China emerged as a vital community participating in the cultural, political and social re-birth of China. Professor Chen writes about how weak the theological foundations in pre-1949 China were, but fortunately he and others were able to lay the ground work for a Protestant Church in China that could both affirm its patriotic Chinese heritage and confidently witness to a Christian faith that was true to the Gospel but no longer foreign to China.

Professor Chen's theology responded to the challenges presented by the triumph of a Marxist revolution that officially espouses scientific atheism along with socialism. The 1939 essay by Dr. Chen already expressed an approach for working with people of varying world views, seeing all humanity as one family. People do not need to agree in order to work together. Although some Christians in the West may see Christianity and American style capitalism as inseparable, others in China and elsewhere see socialism as more compatible with Christian faith and ethics. In "Reconciliation with the People" he writes: "Our point of departure is to opt for the people, to opt for the welfare of our country, and to opt for a social system that is more just and humane than anything the Chinese people have seen in our history of over four thousand years." (Of course he acknowledges that the social system in China has imperfections.) He states that God sides with the poor and oppressed, therefore all who side with people, atheist or not, side with God. Professor Chen also seeks to express Christian theology in a way that is congruent with Chinese culture and philosophy. He writes in this 1981 article that "to conceive of the cosmos as an evolving continuum of creation-evolution-salvation-consummation" under a Sovereign God of the universe and history, "would not prove too unacceptable to the Chinese mind."

In his 1956 essay on theological construction Dr. Chen suggests that one way to do theology is to see God and Humanity as two centers of an ellipse. Theology sometimes leans in a theocentric direction and at other times becomes more humanocentric. The dynamic interaction between these two foci has propelled theology forward. He notes that though this geometric metaphor is quite useful it also has limitations as do all metaphors.

Humanity and God are not equals. Also theology moves forward so cannot be confined to an elliptical pattern.

Interestingly, in a note to the republication of his article in 1992, Professor Chen comments that he was happy to see Karl Barth also use the metaphor of the ellipse with God and Humanity as the two foci (in Barth's 1963 book *The Humanity of God*). Professor Chen's original essay goes on to use the metaphor in dealing with several theological problems—God and humanity in religious thought, the relationship of revelation and reason, the Trinity and Christology. Chen finds the metaphor to be an especially helpful tool in relating theology to Chinese culture and thought.

It is necessary for Chinese theologians to do theology in their own context. Chen ponders the problem of how "theology can sum up the religious experience of the Chinese church." In the 1950s the Protestant Church in China had arrived at a new selfhood. It was as if the eyes of Chinese Christians were suddenly open. They began to look at their own religious experience as a starting point for theology. Chen first traces the tension in theology from the very early church on, between emphasizing the continuity or the discontinuity between humanity and God. At times God is seen as "Wholly Other" and humanity as totally fallen and depraved. In this view God is "unreachably high, inaccessible to reason, and infinitely exalted." At the other extreme is an easy flow between humanity and God that allows Christians to find God in nature, culture, and in the broad efforts of human beings to create a better world. In this view God "lives among us as an affectionate, loving and forgiving" parent.

After reviewing this theological struggle from the first century down to the twentieth century, Chen raises the question of where Chinese theology is in all this. The awakening of the Chinese theology in the 1950s came at a time when much of the theological world outside China emphasized a Neo-orthodox position that emphasized an extreme discontinuity between humanity and God.

Professor Chen notes that the two views are not entirely mutually exclusive. Christians in China however reject the extreme discontinuity and seek a way that is more open to understanding "God's creative wisdom and saving love" as "good news for all humankind." Just as the Bible announces that "the coming of Christ" means "the good news that the human race would exist in harmony and peace, making God's glory shine over the whole earth."

This theological attempt to express faith in terms relevant to the philosophical and scientific culture that emerged in China and encourages Christians to work for the common good with others regardless of their world views creates other challenges. The most difficult problem perhaps is that many Christians in China take a much narrower and exclusivist view. Especially poor and uneducated Christians often see the Christian community as over against a dark and evil world. Even many educated Christians are more comfortable with a fundamentalist world view where the church is seen as the only pure community. Outside the church, in secular society and in other religions, they see only darkness and evil. This makes it difficult for them to work with people of other faiths or world views.

On the one hand leaders such as Chen try to express theology in broad terms and affirm that Christians can work cooperatively with those outside the Christian community. But on the other hand they also try to avoid alienating the many Christians with a more narrow view of the world. The national church leaders work very patiently with those whose faith rests upon a limited set of fundamentalist doctrines, trying to bring them into dialogue so that there can be a mutual respect while working out their differences. In "Self Propagation in the Light of . . ." he explains how over a period of thirty years the old western founded mainstream denominations and indigenous but exclusivist and sectarian groups have been united. In the past some of these groups had fought each other and condemned each other. Now they have moved toward theological thinking that will "transcend denominationalism, promote church unity, mutual respect, mutual learning and mutual enrichment."

Chen Zemin comments on the interest in Protestant Christianity among university faculty and students in China. Some of these scholars developed an interest in Christianity from their study of history and philosophy, not from contact with the churches. The term "culture Christians" is used by some to describe those who adhere in varying degrees to Christian values and concepts. Some of these scholars have developed small communities that begin to function almost as house churches. No one can say how these communities may develop over time.

Several years ago one scholar from a Beijing university said that three main world views are interacting in the Chinese intellectual world. These are Marxism, Confucianism, and Protestant Christianity. Since then the national leadership in China has in fact started programs for the study and development of Confucian ethics and philosophy, while not abandoning Marxism. Protestant Christian thought is also developing both in university religious studies and in theological schools throughout the country. Chen Zemin and others have been active in the dialogue among these world views.

Professor Chen contributed much to the effort to expanding Christian forms of music and worship that arise out of Chinese culture. His essay on hymn singing in China reviews the historical and contemporary development of Chinese Christian musical forms. This effort has met resistance from many urban Christians who are accustomed to western hymns and gospel songs. They have a pro-western mentality he says. In the rural areas Chinese styles of music are more appreciated by Christian gatherings. Some Christians are afraid of music that uses Buddhist and Taoist musical forms. Chen points out that the Buddhist and Taoists do not seem afraid of Christian or western influences mixed with their traditional formats. He writes sometimes in their temple ensembles he detects "some resemblance to Western melodies and even phrases or lines of Christian hymns wrapped up in traditional instrumental accompaniments." Even though interfaith theological dialogue is lagging in China, Chen wonders if it "would be possible and profitable to begin right now to have some interfaith musical dialogue?" From all of the above we can see that Chen Zemin made and continues to make a vital contribution to the life and thought and work of the Protestant Christian Church in China.

At this point I will make some personal reflections about Professor Chen. I first met him in 1981 when he attended the international Montreal conference on China and the Churches. Then the next year I was privileged to have him serve as interpreter for a series of lectures I gave at Nanjing University on "Religion and Society in North America." Questions from students touched on a wide variety of issues. He handled the interpretation of the question and answer sessions with ease and charm. He and I privately continued the dialogue on a number of issues.

In succeeding years our paths crossed a number of times in China or in North America. From 2002 to 2007 I taught at the seminary in Nanjing and had many opportunities to see Professor Chen in action, and to talk with him privately and in small groups. I remember vividly when he, already an octogenarian, stood on a box on a front pew to conduct the Seminary Choir in front of him on the stage in several anthems. His musical gifts were obvious and his continued energy contagious. His teaching continued into his nineties. Many generations of students benefited from his wisdom, knowledge and spirit.

Professor Chen's office at the Seminary was next to mine. On many occasions we would sit in the morning drinking strong and flavorful Chaozhou style tea, a specialty of his native south China community. The tea is consumed in tiny cups with frequent refreshing of the pot. We talked about theology, China, the world. I learned a great deal in these informal conversations. Other professors especially those from south China dropped in from time to time enjoying the Chaozhou tea and talk.

Chen Zemin is an irenic person. He maintains his reserve and gentle humor and all the characteristics of a Chinese scholar. It has been a privilege and an honor to know him and work with him. A bit of his nature comes through in a hymn-he wrote in 1982 and set to an ancient Chinese tune. In the hymn he imagines the Creator as an artist with a paint brush. I will close with an English translation of some of his words in this hymn:

> Sunset hues light sea and sky, Wild geese return to rest.
> I'd like to be a free bird, to sight the earth from on high,
> View our country being touched, By the Creator's brush. . . .
> We strive to build a new world, of justice, love and peace,
> To raise the cross in witness, Christ's truth widely to spread.
>
> Raymond L. Whitehead, Toronto, Canada, March 2011

An Overview of the Theoretical Foundation and Practical Tasks of Building New China
The Contribution of the Chinese Church (Shanghai, 1939)

CHEN ZEMIN

INTRODUCTION

IF WE CAREFULLY STUDY and analyze all the great religious, political, or social movements of history, we will see that the substance of these movements cannot be separated from theory and practice. As to theory, philosophical foundations determine the basic meaning and directions of the entire movement, guide its practical work, establish its ideal goals, and serve as the springs of its power. As to practice, concrete plans and organization turn empty theories into actuality, turn faith into actual strength and work, and turn ideals into realities. Ideals that are divorced from reality become irrelevant abstractions and empty talk and offer no benefit to human life; practice that lacks theoretical foundation becomes blind and sluggish floundering that even at best can lead to only partial success. In the interaction of these two elements we can see the nascent form of a philosophy.

In volume 9, issue 2 of *Truth and Life*, Mr. Wu Leichuan's (吴雷川) article "What contribution can Christianity make to the renewal of the Chinese people?" seems intended to be the embryo of a philosophy. Many other important church leaders have also voiced similar calls. But these theories were all voiced some years ago, and were all focused on particular movements, such as those to improve life in the countryside, to build human character, and so forth. Today every aspect of life in China—political, social, and all others—is experiencing dramatic changes, and in this special and critical era, the mission and responsibility of the Christian church in building a new China has become great and pressing. Now we have special need for a theory of construction that is complete and suits this special situation, and that can guide us in this important task of construction. We have even greater need for a realistic and effective plan and organization that is both all-encompassing and concrete so that we can realize our hopes and ideals, so that we can bring this war of resistance to the completion of its mission, and so that the special hopes of Christians in this war—hopes for the full revival of China, the Christianization of China, and the arrival of God's kingdom in China—can be realized through the faith and efforts of compatriots in China.

The present article is the author's weak but heart-felt and sincere call, stimulated by the needs of these times. My hope is that it will bring forth a response from China's passionate and capable Christian compatriots, so that united under the banner of Christ we can complete this great task of building our nation, and bringing in the kingdom of God as it is in heaven.

THE THEORETICAL FOUNDATIONS FOR CONSTRUCTION.

In the Christian theory of building a nation, the most basic issue is that of faith. Within this issue, what we need to study is whether or not the Christian faith is suitable to the task of constructing China. Let us examine this first by looking at several basic Christian beliefs.

Christian faith in God is the foundation of Christian theology, and serves as the compass for all the work of the Christian church. As we Christians construct a new China, we should take this article of faith as a pre-condition. The God in the heart of Christians is an all-capable and all-benevolent God, the creator of all creatures and ruler of the entire universe, and for everything in the universe he has a wise and complete plan; the stars in the heavens and the creatures on the earth all move and exist within a great system of which he is the master. All the turmoil in the world is also under his supervision, and it is the lot of Christians to discover his great plan and will and act and live according to it; a meaningful life is one in which Christians do this to the utmost. This is the simple yet lofty Christian philosophy of life. Furthermore, while there are a great many unresolved disputes that make Christian philosophy complex and deep as theory, if we clean away all the loose ends and remove the disputed points, what remains are these essential truths on which the great majority agree. These are the truths that guide Christian act and thought, and they also serve as our goals in constructing a new China. If the Christian church is to fulfill its responsibility in the nation, faith in God is the starting point for all of our work. In our vision of the future, a new China is one part of the universal plan of a fully good and all-powerful creator, a part that is in harmony with the rest of creation; it is a country under the control of this all-benevolent God, and a channel through which the kingdom of heaven is realized on earth.

In Christian theology, God is a spiritual reality. This point of faith determines one important characteristic of our ideal new China. In this era of transition during which material civilization is developing and overtaking spiritual civilization, people sometimes come up with a mistaken understanding and estimation of material and spirit. One extreme development is materialist philosophy. Though this school of philosophy contains an element of truth in its reaction to older views' over-emphasis on spirit, it has missed the center and veered too far to the left. This is the basic reason why it opposes Christianity, and why Christianity opposes it. Here we do not wish to enter into the endless debate between idealism and materialism. We simply stand on Christian faith, and state that our ideal new China is not a materialist country that ignores spiritual life; rather, it is a country that emphasizes the spirit while not overlooking material life. It is spirit that drives the material, rather than the material governing the spiritual, because the entire establishment of the nation is built upon a part of the great plan of an all-sufficient God who is spirit.

The God of Christianity also loves peace, justice, purity and truth. The building of new China shall take these four virtues as goals. We must steer clear of the violent contention of fascist nationalism, rid ourselves of all material and spiritual impurities and immorality, and end hypocrisy and ignorance in human society. Establishing peace, justice, purity, and love of truth in new China may seem to be too idealistic, but this is in fact the goal of Christians. We should take that which is highest as the goal of our striving, rather than pursuing goals that are lower and easier to reach, and establishing a baser society and country.

Finally, the God of Christianity is love, and our method is to rely on this ultimate love to construct a new China. This idea—taking the establishment of a new China of love as our goal—will be explained in detail below when we discuss the spirit of Christianity. The Christianity understanding of God is as stated above, and the Christian understanding of everything else follows and develops from this understanding. The world is the garden in which God's plan is worked out, and the physical world is the outer shell through which the spiritual world is expressed. So the view of life of the citizens of a new China is definitely not a hedonistic view in which "the meaning of life is to serve the body, hedonistic view, nor is it a self-sacrificing stoic view; even less is it a totally materialist and mechanistic view in which the spirit is totally destroyed or denied." Instead, it is a view of life in which God's plan is realized, in which a proper relationship is established between the material and the spiritual, and in which true happiness is established. The ideal new China is a practical embodiment of the kingdom of heaven in which all kinds of conflicts are reconciled.

Christianity takes God as the loving father of the entire human race, so that all people on earth are compatriots, brothers and sisters. In this unified and great family, all of us as God's children should love each other and cooperate with each other in order to create a great fellowship. The construction of a new China should take such a view as its foundation.

Christian faith gives us proper guidance in building our nation, and gives us a nation-building goal. We also need the Christian spirit to determine our nation-building method and give us the strength for nation-building, so we should now discuss the Christian spirit.

The greatest aspect of the Christian spirit is love. Broadly speaking, love is the entirety of the Christian spirit. Here let us leave aside onerous discussion and take a passage from the Bible to serve as our explication of love.

"Love is patient; love is kind; love is not jealous or boastful or arrogant, nor does it do that which is shameful. Love does not seek its own benefit, is not quick to anger, does not keep track of the evil actions of others, does not rejoice in injustice, and loves truth. It bears all things, believes all things, hopes all things, and endures all things. Love never ends."[1]

If we analyze this passage of Scripture, we see that Christian love includes ten aspects: persistence, tolerance, kindness, grace, forbearance, humility, uprightness, sacrifice, love of truth, faith, and hope. If we analyze these ten virtues and seek general patterns, we find that they cover three general groupings of attitudes—those toward oneself, toward others, and toward God. With regard to self, there are four attitudes: persistence, tolerance, humility, and uprightness. With regard to others, there are three: kindness, forbearance, and sacrifice. With regard to God and truth there are three: love of truth, faith and hope. These constitute the core of Christian moral teaching, and serve as the driving force behind the development of the church today, and they should also be part of the spirit in which we build new China. These ten attitudes or virtues form a system that can be put into practice, rather than being empty phrases. The three attitudes toward God and truth serve as the foundation for the other seven, and the source of their strength. Love of truth gives birth to faith, faith gives birth to hope,

---

1. I have translated this passage from First Corinthians (13:4–8) directly from the Chinese text in Prof. Chen's article, using the NRSV translation as a point of reference. (Translator.)

and faith and hope give the birth to the strength for the carrying out of the other seven virtuous attitudes toward self and others. This is the foundation of the system of Christian love.

The four attitudes toward oneself involve an effort of cultivation, and are necessary conditions for strong character. In Mr. Wu Leichuan's article, "What contribution can Christianity make to the renewal of the Chinese people?" we find that his conclusion is that "[Christianity] can create all the leadership talent needed for the present times." In fact, in the movement to construct a new China that we are presently discussing, what we need is not only leadership talent; we need all kinds of talent for planning and building. We need leaders, but even more we need front-line talents who will follow the direction of leaders and carry out the actual hard work. The cultivation of such human resources cannot rely on the revival of old China's high civilization as called for by Mr. Liang Shumin(梁漱溟), because China's old culture and morality is only a product of the past and has the traces of feudal society. While it appears to have some points of similarity with Christian love, what Mr. Liang sees is the shell of a dead culture; in contrast, Christianity's spirit of love is vital and alive. This the key difference between the two. (For a more detailed critique of Mr. Liang's theories, see another article by the author, "A critique of Liang Shumin's theories of rural reconstruction.") Cultivation of human talent also cannot rely on the spirit of competition and progress of western material civilization and individualism for its nurture, because these are completely based on a system of individual profit. If this didn't lead to China's becoming even more divided, it would lead to imperialism. To raise up the talent China needs today, only the spirit of Christian love is suitable and efficacious. So we should expand Mr. Wu Leichuan's conclusion, and take the Christian spirit of cultivation of personal character as our principle for cultivating all the people for constructing the nation.

Building on the cultivation of personal character as mentioned above, we need to consider the attitude people take as they deal with each other. Kindness, forbearance, and sacrifice are virtues and terms distinctive to Christianity. Kindness leads to forbearance, leading to sacrifice as its highest point. This spirit of dying on the cross is a historically unique example of the highest expression of love, and is the most praiseworthy virtue of Christianity. The building of new China absolutely requires many people who are willing to cooperate sacrificially, and the cultivation of such character is a big contribution of Christianity.

In addition to the spirit of Christian love discussed above, there is one other absolutely precious and valuable asset Christianity has for the work of constructing the nation—a spirit of bravely entering the world and engaging in hard and difficult work. Perhaps this spirit can be included within that of sacrifice, but it is worth special mention because it is easy for people to overlook it among the other attributes of love. The greatest difference between Christianity and other religions is precisely this spirit of entering the world. Christianity is a practical religion and one that is fully one with life. If we discuss Christianity but ignore the world, it becomes the Christian metaphysics of the Middle Ages, and lacks meaning and value. We need only look at the words and actions of Christ's life, see how diligently and self-sacrificially he served among the people, see what he commanded his disciples when he left the world! We should use this kind of spirit to replace the Buddhist renunciation of the world and Confucian refinement that have influenced the hearts of Chinese people. The greatest mission of Christianity is to change society and the world, and in the special situation of China today, that means constructing a new China.

Above we have already briefly discussed Christian beliefs and the Christian spirit. Here we can conclude the theory section of this article by discussing how Christianity decides directions and methods for building a new China.

Christianity's direction and method for building a new China should be determined based on three criteria. These are: 1) Christian faith and spirit; 2) the conditions in China; 3) the past experience and accomplishments of the Christian church in China. We have already examined the first two of these above, so there is no need to examine them again. The third of these is the most complex and difficult, so let us give it special attention here.

Submitting all the past work of the Christian church in China to a detailed and penetrating review would be a very difficult task. Much would need to be based on specialized academic knowledge. The American *Layman's Foreign Missions Inquiry* is a work specifically devoted to such questions, but since its vantage point and goals differ from ours, it cannot fully meet our needs as a source of reference. All we have at present is a miscellaneous set of reports, incomplete statistics, and empty and uncertain superficial judgments. At present, all we can do is, on the one hand, gather these miscellaneous data and documents, make a tentative overall evaluation, and—to the extent possible—ascertain the directions and effectiveness of the church's past work to serve as a guide to our present nation-constructing efforts; on the other hand, we should actively urge the central organizations of all the nation's churches to quickly set up an investigative group to examine the work of the churches, a group which gathers especially qualified and experienced experts in all areas, including evangelism, education, rural construction, and literacy work, to produce a detailed and penetrating account of the past work of the church, and to investigate the actual situation

An Overview of the Theoretical Foundation and Practical Tasks   7

and challenges, the possibilities for future development, and best means of promotion for all areas of church work. This group should produce a concrete and definite overall plan for all the nation's churches to use and refer to. We shall come back to this idea later.

What the author wishes to do in the present article is the first of the two kinds of work mentioned above, that is, to do my best with the materials at hand to make a preliminary evaluation and examination of what our nation-building work and method should be. This is discussed in combination with the "practical work of constructing the nation" below, so here I will not discuss it separately.

THE PRACTICAL WORK OF CONSTRUCTING THE NATION.

Above I have discussed the Christian church's philosophical and theoretical foundation for building a new China. This serves as the basis and compass for the practical work discussed below. The explanatory notes to the title of the present article include the following words: "Emphasize the practical and avoid empty talk."[2] So, what follows is the most important part of the article, the part which the author most hopes fellow Christians will give their attention to, offering criticisms and corrections, and providing mutual encouragement in its implementation.

When examining the practical work of building the nation, there is one thing that we definitely should not forget—as we as the Christian church wish to construct a new China, we should stand on a solid and united foundation, and hold to a shared faith and goal in our efforts. So, this work is comprehensive rather than fragmented, and takes the Lord Christ as its head. While it has many facets, they cannot be separated from each other. For the sake of convenience, many people separate this work into spiritual and material work. This is correct if we see these as two different kinds of work within one unified plan and project, but it would be a great mistake to see these as two as separable and independent. Some people whose work focuses on the spiritual even go to the extreme of thinking that spiritual work is the entirety of Christian work, ignoring the link between religion and life. Overlooking the fact that human life cannot be separated from its material conditions leads to a decadent and narrow "personal gospel" in which individual spiritual cultivation is the only impact of religious faith. The result is detachment from the world, which threatens the nation and the entire world. On the other hand, some view the material work of Christians

2. 强调实践, 避免空谈

as everything, with the result that they lose the real meaning of the spirit of religion and fall away from religion, becoming materialist social reformers. This also is not what we should do. These two camps even attack each other and tear each other down, which is the most regrettable thing in Christian work. Now what we should see clearly is that spiritual civilization is the soul of material civilization, and material civilization is the body of spiritual civilization. These two are inseparable, and as we discuss various aspects of the Christian work of construction, this is a point we need to frequently remind ourselves of. Take, for example, the task of rural reconstruction. This task combines both spiritual and material work, and we cannot distinguish which takes the bigger part, so the epistemology of our philosophy of construction is not entirely idealist, even less is it mechanical dualism, and it is also not entirely materialist. Instead it is a Christian philosophy with love at its core that harmonizes the spiritual and material. We have discussed this above.

However, in practical terms, with a view toward making our work more convenient, we have no other choice but than to divide our work between separate departments, because the task is too great and this is not something that can be completed by an individual or small group working alone. So, in order to complete the task, we need an organization, and we need the work to be distributed appropriately by the organization. As we discuss this kind of work, we need to discuss according to how the task is divided according to the system of organization. But we should understand that what we are discussing is different aspects of one whole task.

Let us start by discussing the task of spiritual construction. With regard to this, there are at least five tasks the Christian church can do, divided according to their nature and degree of progress. The lines separating these tasks are not entirely clear, and they overlap each other to a considerable extent, as is often unavoidable with the social sciences. Now let us look at these five.

1. Evangelistic work.

In all work that is presupposed by the task of constructing the nation, evangelistic work should be distinguished to some degree from "preaching the gospel" in the ordinary sense in terms of their significance and methods. Here we are concerned with evangelistic work, in other words, active rather than passive evangelism. The purpose of this evangelism is to make people firmer in their faith so as to give correct guidance to their lives, so this kind of evangelism is not overly concerned with issues of sin and rewards, but rather with giving people a Christian love outlook in their daily lives, with giving them hope and creating proper and perfect ideals and—with such ideals as their goals—with helping them set high moral standards, build new habits of life, and prepare for the coming of the kingdom of heaven.

Here we should refer to the experience and achievements of past evangelistic work. In the past, evangelism made up most of the church's work, and in some places all of it. This is the work to which most church human effort and funds were devoted, and in which achievements were most evident and most worthy of our attention. But if we examine this carefully, we will see that in much past evangelistic work, most attention was given to teaching doctrine, the Bible, and church governance, and that less attention was given to the practical aspects of living out Christian doctrine in daily life and using Christian teachings to develop a progressive view of life. In other words, in the past evangelism was quite successful with regard to form and organization, but our ideal results—building a new view of life, setting new standards, and forming the basis of a new Christianized society—have not yet been reached. This is like the revival movement that has been popular in the last few years. Superficially it appears to be a very positive phenomenon, but in fact many wonder whether those who are moved have a fundamental change in the way they approach life or permanent changes in the way they live their lives. Various other kinds of traveling gospel teams, "boat and cart" evangelistic bands, "new spring" evangelism teams and so forth do only the work of introducing the gospel, but probably too few can thoroughly inject the Christian spirit into the lives of the audience. There are various kinds of fellowship group movements that have deeper impact, and such efforts are very hopeful, but because of issues such as geographic limitations, limited time, and narrowly focused interests such fellowships can rarely become widespread movements. Also, fellowships have a natural tendency to become cliques, which is an inherent feature of group psychology, and if we are not careful this could become an obstacle to evangelism efforts.

In general, it has been common for past evangelistic work to place too much emphasis on promotion and to neglect deeper study. Too many people only see the form of Christianity and the outline of its doctrine, but their real understanding of it is all too shallow, so Christianity doesn't have much impact on their lives or give them any strong guidance. This is a lesson from the past to which we should pay much attention in our work of construction.

In order to correct the mistakes of the past and make up for weaknesses, we should thoroughly re-evaluate our evangelistic work, and should invest a little more effort and time in ensuring that those who accept Christianity see the implications of Christianity for their lives. From the Christian faith, we should seek out truths that fit into our nation-building goals; we should hold onto Christian faith as the rudder of life, as the ideal for life in new China, and as our goal in living, so that out of this grows hope and strength. This is the most basic task in constructing a new China, and what is most effective in shouldering this task is not temporary evangelistic and revival meetings but rather a church that has become integrated with its society; the most essential people for this kind of work are pastors and evangelists because it is they who have the deepest interactions with both believers and the common people, and are hence able to show Christian spirit and faith through their lives and give the people a powerful challenge. What we should now give the most attention to is this basic construction, strengthening the evangelistic work of all the churches so that they may spread the spirit of Christianity at the most fundamental levels of society, building strong faith among the people and serving as a base for constructing a new China.

2. Educational work.

In the past the educational work of the church has been its most fruitful. From the perspective of the average person who doesn't pay much attention to evangelism, the educational efforts of the church have made the greatest contribution to China; church schools have made an undeniable contribution in China's modern cultural history. But in the past ten years, like other aspects of church work, church school work has been gradually giving ground to a trend to emphasize other church organizations. Educational institutions are among the most important institutions in society, and in the work of constructing a new China the use of education as a tool is very important. So we should research how to use education to best effect in this great movement to build the nation.

The noun "education" is very broad, so in order to avoid repetition for the moment we should narrow our definition. By the term "education," here we mean only three kinds—church schools, education in the home, and Christian education. Ten years ago, church schools were the leaders in contributing to education and cultural circles in China. They introduced Western academics and use of Western methods, establishing the foundation for a new culture in China. At that time, many of the schools in China with the best equipment and highest standards were church schools, and many outstanding people in cultural circles were graduates of church schools. If the same trend had continued to the present, the situation of churches in China today would probably be very different. However, the voices protesting the cultural imperialism of the foreign powers became louder, and people became more suspicious of Christian education and schools. Also, both private and public education in China advanced rapidly, and in many respects surpassed that of church schools, so now church schools are experiencing decline. This is something we should pay attention to and take seriously in our work of construction.

Church schools are the institutions through which the church cultivates talent for society, which is the greatest contribution of the church to society, something on which almost all both inside and outside the church agree. But the question now is, in the process of building China, what is the special responsibility of church schools? Now many state and private schools have disbanded or suspended their work, and temporary schools with special missions have sprung up in the rear areas of China. Those church schools which have not been ravaged by war should recognize the needs of the times and work effectively, so that the work of building the nation is not undermined by the closing of schools, and so that our nation building ideals are not diverted by the current special situation. Producing educated and talented people for the needs of constructing the nation is a most important work. But it is even more important to train such people so that they have noble ideals and goals, great character, and will definitely use their talents and learning to serve the nation and the people. In the past there was one failure of church schools that we must admit; many students who underwent "religious molding" were not obviously any better than students who did not undergo "religious molding," and some were actually worse. In this War of Resistance[3], many people see that China's past education was a failure and, in the past, most education was in the hands of church schools. Thus, the failure of Chinese education is the failure of church education, and as we undertake the task of constructing a new China this lesson of past experience is worth our attention. Therefore, in church schools, religious and character education plays a very important part.

If we tie the Christian spirit and faith to this question we are discussing, the contribution of church schools to constructing the nation is even greater. Church schools are the institutions that give the Christian spirit to the people to make them effective workers in constructing the nation, and are the places where Christian faith is passed on to most people. If they are well run, church educational institutions will be the places where personnel for the construction of a new China are produced.

The work of Christian education in the home is as important as the work of Christian schools. In the past, the achievements of Christian

---

3. Sino-Japanese War.

education in the home have not been so visible because this is a relatively personal matter. However, the Christian family movement flourished for a time, and this was a beneficial effort. In the process of building a new China, this is an indispensable link.

The family is the smallest among society's social units, and is the most important among society's primary groups. We cannot say that ideal individuals can form an ideal society, but ideal families are the main factor in organizing an ideal society. The Christian family movement is an aspect of social education—a very fundamental one—and is the foundation of a new China's society. For education in the home, there is no education that is more perfect and efficacious than education in Christian love, and this is also one of the greatest contributions of Christianity to the constructing of a new China.

Religious education is slightly different from the two kinds of education mentioned above. The religious education referred to hereconsists of the work of religious education groups other than schools and families. These groups are often attached to churches, voluntarily organized by children or young people and guided and trained by religious education staff of the churches. These are the best organizations for training young people for service work, and they include youth fellowships, YMCAs, Sunbeam Bands, and so forth. These are all bodies for after-school activities, organized around the interests of young people, and can help young people develop many valuable virtues, train their talents for service, and cultivate their spiritual lives. For some young people, the benefits they gain from these organizations are greater than those from school or family. The church can mold many precious workers in this way, and also give them religious training. The uncompleted work of realizing the kingdom of heaven in China is waiting in large part for such organizations. Such religious education fits people's lives, and is precisely the kind our churches should have.

3. Publishing work.

Christian publishing, like church schools, has contributed greatly to China's new culture movement. In a recent article, Zhu Weizhi (朱维之) of the University of Shanghai has discussed this point. In the past, Christian publishing was quite extensive. When the new culture was in its beginning stages, Christianity exerted no small efforts to cultivate and nourish it. But now we are falling behind. Every year the Christian Literature Society for China, the Association Press, and other such organizations produce quite a few new books, but in comparison to the total number of readers in China the numbers are too small, and most of these books tends to be relatively theoretical. In the constructing of a new China, we also need to start a new movement in publications. In bookstores there are too many books that obstruct the task of construction, and too little of practical value to constructing the nation is published. This is an opportunity for revival in Christian publishing, and this is the time for Christian writers to arise and make their voices heard. Just look at the confused state Chinese literature is currently in. In both its thought and form, time and again we can see evidence of naiveté and weakness. Occasionally a few writers strike out and call for raising the quality of literature or for other special literary movements, but among both opponents and supporters there is a lack of powerful writers and high-quality readers. So far there are few literary works of real value, and within Christian literature such quality works are even rarer. In the West, Christianity has an important place in literature. There are many famous works by Christian authors, and these have served as guides for many social reformers and inspired many valuable social movements. Our new China needs this kind of new and valuable literature, and in the process of constructing a new China we even more need such literature to inspire the enthusiasm of citizens in constructing the nation. Christian writers should view such a responsibility as very important. Christian publishing organizations should also make haste to encourage young writers to write. Among young Christians, there are many talents that have not yet been discovered, and churches and church leaders should take up the responsibility of finding and digging out such talents so that they are not buried and so that the garden of Christian literature is not neglected and barren.

Using Christian literature as a vehicle for evangelism is very effective if we can really produce good literature. This is a relatively new ministry, with a very bright future. The cultural climate and mood of a nation is sometimes greatly influenced by special literature of its age, and as we engage in the task of construction it is necessary to have several powerful literary works; we long for several new books that are filled with the spirit of Christianity. May the leaders of the church no longer neglect this kind of ministry, and may bright flowers soon spring up in the garden of a new China's literature.

Cooperative writing between Christian authors is another effective new ministry. A few years ago we had organizations like the association of young Christian authors, and this was a very hopeful development. We hope that the church can again encourage this kind of movement, so that Christian writers working toward a common goal can produce collective works, and works of genuine literary merit, to serve as a source of guidance and strength for constructing new China.

4. Medical work.

The "medical work" referred to here is quite broad. In the past the medical work achievements of the church, especially with the assistance of western mission agencies, have been considerable, and in medical circles in China they still play a guiding role. However, we believe that the church can do even more. Simply treating diseases is definitely necessary in a poor China, but we have even greater work and hopes, and medical work in future China has an even greater mission.

At present, nursing wounded soldiers and refugees is a task calling for all our efforts. Our nation has many inadequacies in medicine and medical equipment, and has experienced many serious losses, and this is definitely something that we should work on. But after the war, treating diseases and accumulating medical equipment and training is a big task in national construction. There are ways in which church organizations and people can presently make a contribution in this regard. We only need to unite our doctors and nurses together in a large organization, mutually encouraging each other with Christ's love, and working together to research, to plan, and to carry out plans, and the people of China will be spared many innocent deaths and much pointless wasting of strength in struggles with disease and weakness. An ideal healthy China depends much on our efforts!

5. Social work.

This is a relatively vague term because we use it to cover all the kinds of work not covered by the terms above, such as the work of the YMCA and other social service organizations. In the past Christianity has already invested much effort in such work. However, in this time when the old social system has been shattered by war and chaos and the new system is already under construction, the responsibility of Christian social service is even more pressing and urgent. Evangelistic, educational, publication and the other kinds of work mentioned above are all foundation-laying long term efforts, and the accomplishments we hope for do not depend on immediate realization. However, before these accomplishments materialize, tens of millions or hundreds of millions of our compatriots will have lost their social ties due to war. Amidst poverty and disorder, if there is no good way to provide relief to them and help them resolve the serious problems in their lives, they may well generate very negative consequences for society. These problems are very immediate, and pose a great challenge to us. While such work is not the basis on which to build a new China, it is the start of building a new China. These are not tasks that pre-existing social work organizations are capable of handling on their own, but rather a cross that the whole church needs to bear. Whether or not the church has the strength to contribute to the construction of a future new China will be seen in such work now.

So far our discussion has journeyed from spiritual culture to social life. Next we should examine what kind of contribution Christianity can make to the economic structure of a new China. From a materialist perspective, this would be most fundamental. Here we have placed it at the end not because it is secondary or unimportant. We acknowledge that economic organization is a most important part of society, and if Christianity only exerts itself with regard to spiritual culture and ignores material life, then our overall Christian theory of nation building cannot be put into practice and would instead be only empty imaginings.

Christian "economic construction" is a relatively new work, and many people have harbored doubts about such a term. This has been a mistake, one that we should now strive to correct. If our religion is one that is integrated into life—indeed, if our religion is life itself—than we should give attention to every aspect of life, and not ignore the material aspects of life. Dr. Stanley Jones' book *Christ's Alternative to Communism* is a powerful challenge to Christian over-emphasis on the spiritual. Christ's answer in the wilderness when tempted by the devil was "Man should not live by bread alone," not "Man does not live by bread." When Christ raised the widow's son from the dead, the instruction he gave us was "Give him something to eat." Furthermore, we can find much evidence that would lead us to believe that if Jesus lived in today's China, he would definitely call for more than what the church has done in the past. Real Christianity is a religion of life, and addresses every aspect of life.

So we need to raise the slogan of Christian economic construction, and let all the people of the nation know that we are not empty idealists. In the work of constructing new China, we need to strive to set up a new Christianized economic structure to serve as the foundation for the other kinds of construction.

However, the issue of economic construction in today's China is difficult and complex. There are many different views and parties, and many disagreements and conflicts. Even if we only look at rural economic construction, there are a huge range of divergent views among scholars. Now with the war, much is being heard of the so called Chinese Industrial Co-operate movement. Ultimately, faced with such the massive problem of economic construction, how much can our church do? What can we do? These questions go to the heart of what is discussed in this article, and are the questions to which the author wishes to call the attention of co-workers in Christ.

Let's start from rural reconstruction. If we remove the spiritual culture elements of the rural reconstruction movement, what remains is within the domain of economic construction. Above we have already briefly discussed spiritual culture construction, so here, in order to avoid repetition, we will focus on the economic aspects of rural reconstruction.

Over the last ten years, the call for rural reconstruction has been increasing daily, though it has fallen off somewhat recently due to the war. If we investigate the rural reconstruction work and theory of each place and organization, we will see that with the exception of the Rural Reconstruction Institute (乡村建设研究院) of Mr. Liang Shumin in Shandong, neither Christian or non-Christian rural reform has been tied to construction of the nation. Many who carry out this kind of work simply feel that in rural areas bankruptcy is too severe and life is too bitter, so that there is no choice but to provide relief. The successful cases of Ding County (定县) and the Mass Education Movement (平民教育运动), of the well-known Li Chuan (黎川) rural reconstruction project, and cases of bank loans to rural areas—all are related to concerns of relief. Only Mr. Liang Shumin's rural construction theory is a systematic and visionary nation-building philosophy. Even though his proposals and ours as Christians differ somewhat in purpose and principles, and we cannot fully agree with his epistemology and methodology, his rural construction philosophy definitely provides the nation constructing efforts of the church with valuable guidance and stimulation.

In the constructing of a new China, we should give much effort to rural reconstruction, and there is no need to spill much ink explaining the reasons why this is true. China's historical background, China's current situation, and China's geography all make the rural reconstruction movement the most pressing one in China. Even though rural reconstruction cannot solve all of the problems facing China at the moment and cannot achieve much on its own, and even though there are many other important tasks for us, rural reconstruction is without a doubt an indispensable part of constructing a new China. Most important is that the church should see this clearly, and place rural reconstruction and national construction together in a single unified plan, and also take this as a responsibility of the church.

Even though the rural reconstruction movement was a fairly late development, and most of its work has been experimental in nature, these experiments have already given us much important and valuable knowledge and guidance. Until the outbreak of the war there were already almost 200 rural reconstruction sites, and of these more than 20 were managed by churches or church organizations. Of these, the rural reconstruction project

An Overview of the Theoretical Foundation and Practical Tasks 17

in Li Chuan was the most successful. Also, many Christians have served at sites not associated directly with the church; Dr. James Yen (晏阳初) in Ding County is an important example.

In the past rural reconstruction organizations nation-wide held three conferences, leaving us with three thick and valuable books of conference reports. In 1933, the National Christian Council of China also held a rural reconstruction conference in Ding County, with more than 100 participants representing 14 provinces and 15 organizations, and this conference also published a rural reconstruction conference report containing many precious presentation papers, work reports, and practical work plan outlines. These events and records now provide us with at least the following points of guidance:

1. Christian rural reconstruction work is an important part of our work of constructing a new China, but this work is somewhat behind that of organizations outside the church, so we should quickly make efforts to catch up.

2. Christian rural development work should not be done for the narrow goal of evangelizing; the purpose is rather rural reconstruction work itself. This is part of building the kingdom of heaven on earth. So in planning such work, we should pay attention not to put evangelism in the domain of rural development work. It is best that evangelism and rural development work are carried out by two separate bodies, working in cooperation but without one being administered under the other. In other words, the church's social gospel and individual gospel should proceed parallel to each other, each supporting the other.

3. All previous rural reconstruction work has seemed to have an experimental flavor, or seemed to be a mix of relief work and experimentation. Now we should expand this work, turning the results of past experiments into a large-scale plan and carrying out positive construction work. Many of the inefficient methods tried in the past, such as excessive expenditure of money and human investment, should now be avoided, and we should use the Christian spirit to encourage many young people to undertake training and become directly involved in rural reconstruction.

4. We should set up national guiding and supervisory bodies to be responsible for overall management and planning of rural reconstruction work. This is a need that was felt commonly by several hundred representatives at the third national conference on rural reconstruction. In this conference that was not purely a conference, many complicated

relationships prevented a unified national plan from being realized. Even though Dr. XuBaoqian (徐宝谦) presented such a suggestion, and it received the sympathy of most of the representatives, in the end it didn't succeed. In the meetings called by the National Christian Council of China, such a proposal has also been made, but it has not been realized due to issues of personal relationships. However, as rural reconstruction work becomes increasingly developed, the need for such unity is increasingly pressing. Especially now as we need large-scale construction efforts to replace small-scale experimental projects, this unity is needed. It is easier to unify the work of Christian organizations working toward a common goal, rather than the current situation of different church organizations working toward different goals, so we should call on the sympathy of the existing experimental projects to work toward the achievement of a united rural reconstruction movement.

5. Improvement and sharing of technical skills is an important part of rural reconstruction work, and we should invest effort in this, rather than placing all of our efforts into organization and evangelism. Dr. XuBaoqian has noted that "We are putting ample spirit into evangelism but not enough into daily practical work." This is a serious indictment of our past Christian work. In the future we need to emphasize the improvement and sharing of techniques, and especially emphasize the effectiveness of practical working methods, so that the rural reconstruction work of churches will not consist mainly of research edited into reports.

6. With an eye to avoiding bureaucratization of rural reconstruction work and other malpractices, Christian rural reconstruction work should not rely on political support for its implementation. The only effective method in our work is the love of Christ. Relying on political power will result in rapid but temporary advances in the impact of our rural reconstruction work, but the need result is often that reconstruction work that was filled with vitality becomes rigidified with rules, killing our spirit of creativity. It is best if we cooperative with the government in a spirit of friendship, working toward common goals, but not be organizationally tied to the government.

7. The rural reconstruction conference report of the National Christian Council of China contains many concrete plans and proposals. While some of these have now lost their original value because time has passed and the social situation has changed, others can still be implemented, and we should do so promptly. Otherwise, we not only

An Overview of the Theoretical Foundation and Practical Tasks   19

disappoint the efforts and hopes of participants in the conference but also lose a ready-made source of assistance.

The above addresses rural reconstruction, one aspect of national construction that the church has already begun to recognize the importance of. Two additional aspects to be developed are industry and commerce.

With regard to the question of the church's work in constructing industry and commerce, many people would have doubts, because it seems more reasonable for the nation to develop industry, and more effective for commerce to be either private or a combination of national and private. After all, the church generally doesn't like to engage in material works for profit. However, we should note this: The task of the church in constructing industry and commerce is not direct management of industry or business by the church, but rather something different in purpose and method.

According to political economists, heavy industry should be managed by the state, and this is a principle we accept. However, in the past, for a variety of reasons, the church has taken an opposing stance toward the state (though not an antagonistic one), and had an attitude of unconcern for the government. In the past, the deepest involvement of the church with the nation and government consisted of prayer. So as soon as it is acknowledged that many kinds of work should be managed by the state, the church no longer talks about them and lets the state handle them by itself, as if such matters were completely unrelated to the church. This is an erroneous attitude that we should correct, and here lies the significance of our industrial work in economic construction.

At present, as everyone knows, China needs extensive industrial facilities. In the past because our economy was backward, even though China had rich natural resources we had no way to develop them. Every year we suffered great losses as they were developed by our low-efficiency labor under the dominance of the foreign powers. To rectify this situation, the most effective strategy is to develop our industry. However, in a country as large as China, even if the government had deep financial resources and the most effective administrative power, it would be hard to be successful in immediately starting a big project to develop industry without the devoted cooperation of most of the people. The responsibility of Christianity consists of calling on citizens both in and outside the church to respect the government's plans for industrial construction, and in every area—including human resources, capital, and administration—give the utmost cooperative support.

With regard to human resources the church can help more than in other areas. In the process of development industry, we need technicians who have good character, a spirit of sacrifice, and high degrees of professional training, and churches can serve as important bodies for training such people, especially with regard to spirit and character.

However, because in the past the church only paid attention to building character and the spirit, we seem to have neglected technical training to some extent. Here we only need to look at professional training bodies established by the church such as colleges and research institutes. Outside medical training, which is associated with charity work, achievements in areas of technical training seem relatively weak. This is a result of the incorrect attitude mentioned above, and something we should start trying to correct.

The situation described above is just a generalization. Amidst the special situation facing China, the government is occupied with prosecuting the war and maintaining social order, so the responsibility on the shoulders of the church for training specialized personnel is heavier. In this area the church must make greater efforts to move forward!

There is one more point we cannot overlook. In the midst of developing industry, China should avoid the dangerous road taken by capitalist Western nations. The taking of this road by China is something about which many people have doubts, and is something that we Christians should give special attention to. The dead end the industrial nations of the West have now reached is not an inherent result of developing industry, but rather represents an unnatural situation resulting from extreme individualism and liberalism. If we can use the Christian spirit and faith to drive the process of industrial development, keep watch at every step to prevent selfishness from seeping in, and take the realization of the kingdom of heaven as our goal, we can certainly avoid this unfortunate result.

Finally, the Chinese Industrial Cooperative movement which is currently being promoted is a plan that is worthy of study by the church. Here it is not necessary to provide a detailed introduction to this project. Our hope is merely that the church will pay a little more attention to industrial development. With regard to business, our hope is the creation of a new commerce system so as to eliminate the defects of the profit system. We should recognize the fundamental impact of commerce on society, and fill the majority of the people with the Christian spirit so that they realize the kingdom of heaven on earth in their commerce. Perhaps religious work, educational work, and social work are ways to realize this hope. In any case, at present we have no promising concrete plan, but through faith and hope, we feel that the establishment of this new commerce system is an area in which the church can contribute to China, and this is something which we should be able to achieve in the future.

Now we have already generally discussed all the kinds of work the Christian church can do for the construction of a new China. Here we should again state that these individual works areas are the individual parts of one large movement, driven by a single force toward one ultimate goal. This is one wholistic Christian movement to build the nation, one that draws on Christian faith as its strength and takes the realizing of the kingdom of heaven as its goal. This is because each of these parts are tied together to produce a complete overall impact. In order to reach our goal, we must have one central organization to serve as the overall plan designer and promoter of this movement. So the "overall mind" of Mr. Liang Shumin is a necessary part of this movement.

CONCRETE ORGANIZATION.

Above we have already seen that a unified nation-wide organization is greatly needed in the rural reconstruction movement, and lack of such an organization is a serious problem. Similarly, if we wish to promote our Christian movement to build a new China, we must also study how to create a well-structured and strong national organization, and also find ways to avoid or solve the difficulties and malpractices faced in past church unification movements. Here we need to understand a distinction. The unified national organization spoken of here is not the same as the united national church of which we often speak, in other words, the elimination of denominations. Instead, our purpose is, in the process of carrying out a responsibility shared by all churches in China, to establish one massive cooperative effort based on a shared mission, shared needs, and a shared faith. There have been many examples of this kind of thing in the past, but most relate to one particular area of work. These existing joint organizations could unite into the ideal large organization of which I speak, but they could not shoulder the heavy task of building a new China in its place.

In the past, the issue of church unification has given rise to a great deal of controversy. Because at present all the churches realize that the mission of the Christian church in China faces them with shared needs and a shared situation, the feeling is growing that the unification of the churches is an indispensable part of church progress. However, this is only a shared feeling. In practice, due to differences in mission agencies, economic support, faith, and organization, the church unification movement has encountered many difficulties. Now our Christian movement to build a new China is actually a vehicle for dissolving many of these differences. We are not advocating this movement of national construction in order to unify the church; however, for the sake of the nation constructing movement, we simply must have a considerable degree of oneness in spirit, work, and organization. In the process of advancing this movement, for the sake of shared work and a shared mission, the church is naturally uniting, so that the church in China is becoming one family in the Lord. This is a natural outcome, and a necessary aspect of the realization of the kingdom of heaven.

But what form would a unified organization for the building of a new China take? Given the present situation of the church, the National Christian Council of China would be an appropriate and solid organization to serve as a starting point, because it presently has the strength to call on all the churches of the nation, it has strong human resources, and is viewed as a leading organization by churches all over China. So we hope that the Christian Council can carefully consider this movement, and then summon representatives from church organizations and different churches to hold a large-scale conference to discuss an overall church nation-constructing body and also choose staff for the overall body (such as board members). It would be best if these representatives were leaders within different churches and church organizations in different areas so that they could represent the views of different churches, organizations, and regions, carry out the plan nation-wide, and recommend experts from different churches. This is the first step of organizing.

Next, the chosen representatives should set up a tightly structured central body according to the outline plan decided by the representative conference, and gather different kinds of experts from across the nation to serve as the staff of the central body. It would then be up to these experts in the central body to decide the next steps of carrying out this movement's plan. This is the second step.

The third step involves grassroots-level work. Under this unified organization, each church, church district, and church organization would, in the spirit of Christ, carry out the concrete work following the plan of the central body and—with strong faith and hope—complete the plan.

This organization and plan would not be experimental in nature. This would be a practical general mobilization so, in order to avoid large-scale mistakes, it would be very important for the central body to gather many specialists to carry out research and supervisory work.

This idea is only a very general opinion. Specific and practicable methods would need to be determined by those with special expertise who are in charge of administering and organizing. What is described above is only the author's ideal for the great movement; I also point out that the work of national construction cannot succeed without systematic organization.

Finally, within all the plans and work, the condition that determines the success or failure of the entire movement is the source of our effort and our strength. The entire work of Christianity is built on faith, and the source of strength for our work lies in our faith and in our leader Jesus Christ, to whom no one can compare. Why can't we achieve even greater works than others? Christ has already promised us that we can do even greater things than he did. Christ has already picked up the cross, blown the first trumpet call of the movement for the kingdom of heaven, and laid the foundation for this movement. Fulfilling the implications of his death on the cross falls to us as Christians. Completing the great task of building the kingdom of heaven on earth falls to us as Christians. Making China into a Christianized country and making it a model of the kingdom of heaven on earth falls to us as Christians!

CONCLUSION.

The plea above is not a new one. It represents rather the thoughts, desires and strength found in the heart of many Christians. I have already heard similar sighs, and sensed a similar growing of Christ's life in our hearts. In the midst of cruel war, in the midst of Christ's blood flowing on the cross, we need to gather such desires together, uniting scattered strength into a great movement, and bringing the spirit of the great movement Christ began in Palestine into the chaos of China today, to serve as comfort to those who are disappointed, to serve as a gathering of strength, to serve as a revelation of hope, and to serve as light in the darkness!

Watching the bodies of our compatriots shattered, watching the achievements of centuries torched into ashes in the blink of an eye, watching our burdened motherland gradually disintegrate, how can our young hearts be still? How can we keep our lips tight together? Watching the budding of new hope, watching the twinkling light in the darkness, watching the work of God's saving grace in this turmoil, watching the glory of the heavenly kingdom promised by Christ, how can we not call out the hope and passion in our hearts even more loudly!

This is but a weak call from the heart of a Christian, but I believe that in the hearts of many compatriots across the country it will find an echo, and my hope is that these echoes will combine into a loud roar calling forth the sympathy of Christians across the nation, inspiring great power, and bringing the hoped for heavenly kingdom into reality in China, so that all glory be given to the all-holy, all-powerful, and all-loving Father in heaven!

原本发表于《真理与生命》第12卷第5-6期， 1939年10月出版，(301-332页)。（"燕京大学宗教学院"？）

作者当时是上海沪江大学（社会学系）本科三年级学生。本人对此文的写作，早已忘记得一干二净。后来于2008年由北京世界宗教研究所的段琦教发现此文。我认为当时虽有一股热情，但思想还远没有成熟，极为肤浅；而且改朝换代，时政背景已经大为不同，现在不值得发表！承蒙刘若民老师恳请南京大学Don Snow教授译成英文，至为感谢！陈泽民谨识。2010年3月15日。南京。

Protestant Church in China Today
(Tokyo, 1992)

Chen Zemin

ONE WAY TO PRESENT a picture of the Christian church in China to our Japanese friends is to begin retrospectively and in comparison with Japan. There are many similarities between the Christian churches in the two countries.

First, in both countries Christianity had been from the beginning a foreign religion, imported from the west at about the same time. Catholic Christianity was introduced by the Jesuits during the period of colonial expansion of the so-called Christian powers in the 16th century. Francis Xavier came to Japan in 1549, and Matteo Ricci to China in 1583. Both used the colonial enclaves of Goa and Macao as their springing boards. Both succeeded in some measure in their inaugural attempts, then met with difficulties and suffered temporary decline due to the failure on the part of some earlier missionaries to take enough notice of the foreignness of their religion. Catholicism was almost exterminated under the persecutions in the 16th to 17th centuries and prohibition policy in the 16th to 17th centuries in Japan. Xavier had been rightly accused of his lack of understanding of oriental religions and civilizations. Matteo Ricci made some headway because of his policy of accommodation, but the Franciscans and Dominicans were banned by Emperor Kang Xi after the Rites Controversy in 18th century, as a punishment of the reluctance on the part of the Pope and his emissaries to realize the significance of Chinese historical cultural and religious forces, in sharp contrast to the wiser and more understanding Ricci.

Protestant Christianity came to Japan in the later half of the 19th century, and developed the Meiji period (1868–1912), through the efforts of denominational missionary organizations. In spite of the admirable anti-denominational "non-Church Movement" (Mykyokai) headed by Kanzo-Uchimura (内村鑑三), Protestant Christianity as a whole had been looked at with askance and suspicion by the people because of its foreignness. In

China, it was unfortunate that Protestant Christianity was forced upon China in the salvoes of gunboats and through the intrigues of merchants of Western imperialist powers, and missionary advances were flanked and protected by unequal treaties imposed upon the rotten Manchu Government in the 19th century. As a result Christianity, both Catholic and Protestant, had been long regarded by most patriotic Chinese as a tool of political, economical and cultural invasions of colonialism and imperialism. Until the last three decades Christianity had been stigmatized by the Chinese people, who were not particularly anti-religious at all, as yang-jiao (洋教, foreign religion), with justifiable sentiments of hatred, contempt and resentment.

Another similarity lies in the historical cultural and religious background of the two countries. In Japan, Confucianism, Buddhism and Shintoism have had deep and far-reaching influences over a thousand years. In China, Confucianism with its ethical, pragmatic and humanistic emphases, remained the main stream watering the national cultural soil, and together with Buddhism, which had been long indigenized, and Taoism, somehow fused with the other two, formed the triple roots of the national ethos. In both countries the traditional religious and cultural factors have been so strong and all-permeating that any imported religion that failed to assimilate or to accommodate with them, but claimed to be the sole and exclusive source of revelation, condemning dogmatically other affiliations to heathenism and damnation, would be sure to meet with suspicion and resistance. When it did make some success, as in pre-liberation China, it was at the cost of alienating its adherents from their compatriots. The terse acid saying that "one more Christian means one less Chinese" sums up the deplorable general situation.

A third point of similarity, as a consequence to the two pointed above, is that believers both in Japan and in China constitute a very small minority among the peoples. If I am not mistaken, they amount to only about one percent in Japan, although the influence and prestige of Christians are far greater than the numerical strength. In China, taking Catholics and Protestants together, the percentage is still lower, about 0.6–7. So we are both facing the task and challenge of how to bear witness to our faith and commitment amongst an overwhelming majority of fellow-countrymen of strong non-Christian cultural background and orientation.

Having made these comparisons, I presume it is easier for you Japanese Christians to understand the situation, endeavours, aspirations and problems of Chinese Christians than those from the so-called Christian countries in the West. We are near neighbours, and we have so much in common in our historical cultural heritage and experiences. We know that you have been grappling with similar problems. The well-known Japanese

Catholic novelist Shusaku Endo (远藤周作) likens being a Christian to having a wife chosen by his parents. He wrote "Many times I tried to make her leave, but this foreign wife called Christianity shook her head and refused to go. So I had to make her Japanese." This was what some conscientious Chinese Christians had tried to do before 1949 with little success. And this is what we have been laboring at since the liberation and the launching of the Three-Self Patriotic Movement in 1950. Three-Self means that the Chinese church must be self-governing, self-supporting and self-propagating. It means the church must not, as it had been before, be dominated by missionaries, supported with foreign funds, and run in patterns according to various denominational traditions, copying the culturo-theological thought-forms of the many so-called "mother churches." We must break the image of foreignness. In so doing, it is necessary to rediscover and realize our selfhood and achieve independence, so that we can have a full status in the mutual sharing and interdependence within the Church Universal. This is not anti-foreign. To adapt Endo's simile and dictum, "We must make her Chinese."

Yesterday, on September 23, Protestant churches in China were commemorating the 34th anniversary of the inauguration of the Three-Self Patriotic Movement. During the past thirty-four years, thanks to the blessing and the grace of our heavenly Father and the guidance of the Holy Spirit, we, holding fast to the biblical principle of Three-Self—for we believe that this principle is not an invention of our own, but has sound biblical and theological basis and has been ever at work throughout the historical development of world Christianity—we have made some headway for which we are grateful. The road has not been straight and easy. There have been zigzags and obstacles, and misunderstandings both among ourselves and from the outside. We have committed blunders and made corrections. During the chaotic decade called "cultural revolution," which was in reality culturally destructive and politically counterrevolutionary in nature and effect, almost all traces of organized religions, not just Christianity, seemed to be cleanly wiped out. But God works creatively even in the demonic forces. The purging turned out to be a fiery chastening process and had its educational effects. We have learned how to recognize and avoid the evils of ultra-leftism. Order was finally restored and the Party and Government returned to the right interpretation and implementation of the policy of religious freedom. The faithful and steadfast emerged afresh with rejuvenescent vitality and new visions. The year 1979 marked the beginning of a second phase of the Three-Self Movement. Since then we have been working on the holy task of rebuilding the house of the Lord. The heart-warming promise and mandate of Haggai that "the latter splendor of this house shall be greater than the former" (2:9) has been beckoning and prompting us forward.

Now, what have we done and accomplished in the last thirty-four years? Bishop K. H. Ting, Chairman of the National Three-Self Patriotic Committee and President of the China Christian Council, in his opening address before the Third Chinese National Christian Conference in September, 1980, summed up the accomplishments of the preceding phase of thirty years of endeavor in the following three points. I shall dwell but briefly on these.

First, we have accomplished in making Chinese Christians patriotic Chinese. Before and shortly after the liberation, many Chinese Christians had become victims to the alienating indoctrination and anti-communist propaganda of their Western "mentors," and took faithfulness to God and loyalty to the Church incomparably higher over against or even incompatible with the love of one's country. The contradiction had become more acute when they thought that the country was to be ruled by atheist communists, whom they took to be Satan, the sworn enemy of Christ. After liberation, however, innumerable undeniable facts and personal experiences convinced many honest Christians that under the leadership of the Communist Party new China is far, far better than it had ever been before; that the party was really working for the welfare of the people, with a spirit of self-sacrifice that put many a sincere Christian to shame; that the Party was advocating in theory and practice a policy of religious freedom. But some die-hard anti-communist Christians were still unreconciled and advanced theological arguments like posing "life," by which they meant a mystical, esoteric, undefinable "union with Christ," against the moral and rational discernment between good and evil, or right and wrong; or insisting upon the doctrine of total depravity of all men and the futility and sinfulness of any human effort towards betterment of human society; or interpreting premillennialism with an overtone that New China, however good and welcome by the Chinese people, was doomed to be short-lived and would soon be totally destroyed at the second coming of Christ. All these set the serious Christians to think and rethink. There arose a nation-wide mass theological movement involving both rank-and-file believers and church leaders. I shall not go into the loci theologici and arguments. Bishop Ting is making an analysis of this theological movement in one of his addresses here in Japan. The overall effect, in short, was that the contradiction or dilemma between love of the Church and love of the mother-land was resolved in a unity on a sound biblical and theological basis. Now a favorite slogan prevailing among Chinese Christians is "爱国爱教, 荣神益人." (Love the country and love the church; glorify God and benefit men).

Secondly, we have succeeded in changing the countenance of Christianity in China. With the withdrawal of missionaries and cutting off of foreign funds after 1950, the Chinese church was left to the Chinese Christians, to sink or swim, willy-nilly. So in a sense the necessity of Three-Self was forced upon us by the specific political situation. But it was through the persisting enlightening and endeavours of pioneering leaders like Dr. Y. T. Wu and others that it became a conscious and organized mass movement. The convening of the First Chinese Christian Conference in 1954, which gave rise to the National Three-Self Patriotic Committee, was an important milestone. Since then we have gradually changed the countenance of Christianity from yangjiao (foreign religion) into a church self-governing, self-supporting and self-propagating with more and more Chinese characteristics.

Thirdly, these two accomplishments had led to another, namely, a gradual change of public opinion and impression of the people regarding Chinese Christians and the church. We have identified ourselves with the people and taken part in the struggle of constructing an independent new socialist China, sharing the weal and woe in the vicissitudes of national development. We are taken in by our fellow-countrymen. Many church members have done good deeds and made outstanding contributions in their jobs. More and more people have realized that Christians too are good Chinese citizens and that Christianity is a religion which Chinese citizens are fully entitled to believe and uphold by their own choice. We have won the recognition, sympathy and respect of the broad masses of people as an autonomous Chinese church. Thus new and greater opportunities have opened to us to witness our faith and for the light of the Gospel to shine forth in this country.

Now, let me relate to you some features of the present-day Chinese Protestant Church.

First, there has been a remarkable church growth since the last five years. There is no exact statistics. A conservative estimate of church members and enquirers is over three million. It means an increase of about four times over the total before 1949. In September 1979 two churches were reopened in Ningpo (宁波) and Shanghai, the first to break the ice, about three years after the downfall of the "gang of four." Since then according to the latest report there are more than eighteen hundred churches reopened or set up anew. This amounts to an average rate of one church a day over the whole period. By a "church" here I mean a permanent church building set apart for worship services and other religious activities, with a fairly consistent congregation administered by one or more pastors or preachers. These churches are located mostly in cities and towns. There are sixteen churches in Shanghai including the suburban counties, and three in Guangzhou. The size of the congregation varies from a couple of hundred to several thousands, about one quarter to one third being young people. In larger churches it is often necessary to hold two or more sessions of Sunday services to avoid overcrowding. If we take the average size of a congregation as one thousand, it leaves more than two million Christians to handle. So there are thousands or maybe tens of thousands of what we call "assembly points" (聚会点), i.e., meetings held in homes or other places than a conventional church building. These "points" are mostly scattered in the rural areas, but you will often find some in cities also, distributed according to geographic accessibility. The size of a "point" varies from some twenty or thirty to several hundreds. They are usually administered by lay leaders, most of them depend upon the city or county churches for guidance and assistance, such as supply of Bibles, hymnals, Christian literature, and the administering of baptism and communion services, etc. In remote places they are left to their own discretion and devices. This explains the uneven development in the level of Christian nurture, and, as in some places, susceptibility to deviations, heretical contamination and anti-China infiltrations from abroad. These we lump up as "abnormalities." This is an understandable phenomenon when the rate of increase of believers outstrips the process of reopening churches, which involves much more than taking back and repairing church buildings.

How to account for this rapid growth? Many explanations have been advanced. I think, however, most basic of all it is due to: (1) the Three-Self Patriotic Movement with the three main accomplishments mentioned above; (2) the overall implementation of religious policy on the part of the Party and the government, though not without obstacles and problems. As to the latent and perennial spiritual yearnings and need beyond the material and mundane in man, I shall for the present leave to theologians and sociologists and psychologists of religion. The Holy Spirit is always at work and we can but offer our prayers and thanks to God for His blessings and guidance.

Secondly, we have entered into a post-denominational stage. This has come about gradually as a result of the Three-Self Movement and dissociation with foreign ecclesiastical organizations. We realize and respect the characteristics and particular contributions of various denominations that have evolved in the historical development since the Reformation. We have also learned the lesson of harmful dissensions and disruptive effects of denominationalism. We try to conserve the valuable heritage without being tied to the denominational structural network. So remaining true to the Apostolic faith and biblical tradition, we adopt a latitudinarian attitude and the principle of mutual respect concerning theological and liturgical variations. We take Ephesians 4 as our motto and believe that unity with variety, not uniformity, will more manifest the abundant grace of God. For instance, alternative co-existence of two ways of baptism by immersion or by sprinkling, and various forms of administering the Lord's Supper, proves helpful in maintaining a harmonious unity and enhancing mutual understanding. This modern adiaphorism seems to be conductive to building a united church instead of arousing unnecessary controversies.

This brings us to a third characteristic. At present we are not yet a United Church of China in the ecclesiastical sense. The China Christian Council set up in 1980 is more like your N.C.C., and functions as an associating and coordinating organization of a transitionary nature, concentrating in the work of pastoral care and ecclesiastical affairs. It works together with the Three-Self Patriotic Committee like two hands serving the body whose head is Christ, and musters all Protestant believers and communities to build a well-run United Church of China. There are similar twin-organizations on various levels, national, provincial and local. We have not adopted any particular ecclesiastical polity. Ordinations are often decided upon and carried out on the local level, assisted by provincial councils. The China Christian Council, in collaboration with provincial councils, has printed one million and three hundred thousand Bibles, of the "Union Version." In addition, there are versions in three minority nationality languages, Korean, Miao and Lisu. The printing of another edition of Chinese Bible using simplified characters arranged horizontally is in preparation. There were several hymnals published by provincial councils. Last year the C. C. C. edited and published a new hymnbook including four hundred hymns, one hundred of which written and composed by Chinese Christians.

The rapid church growth brings with it many problems. Pastoral care and Christian nurturing have lagged behind. This accounts for the poor quality and low level of religious life, especially in the rural areas. There is a gap of a whole generation between the aged ministers and the young. To meet the urgent need of providing leaders a program of pastoral and theological training is being carried out. On the bottom over a hundred short-term courses ranging from two weeks to four months are being conducted by local and provincial councils, mostly for lay leaders of the "assembly points" in rural areas. A "syllabus" published quarterly by the seminary in Nanjing is used widely for this purpose, with a total circulation of forty thousand. Then there are four centers of theological training offering two-year programs for senior middle school graduates. In addition, three or four more of this kind are being planned, to be located strategically to meet the needs of various regions. In Nanjing the Union Theological Seminary, with a four-year collegiate program and a graduate course, is open to the whole country, for training ministers, theological teachers, writers, church musicians and artists. There is an enrollment of one hundred and eighty students this year.

Before I conclude I may add that one characteristic of the theological climate in China today is that we have transcended the sharp fundamentalist-modernist contradiction through mutual respect and willingness to learn from each other. The picture drawn by Bishop Ting in "Theological Mass Movement" referred above portrays the general trends of Protestant thought endorsed or tolerated by most evangelicals and liberals, allowing some differences in emphases and exegetical treatment. In trying to sum up the theological situation in China, I think of Dr. YoshinobuKumazawa's description of the Protestant theological construction in Japan as "biblical, missional, national and free in emphasis and orientation,"[1] and I see another parallelism between the churches in our two counties. My description of the Chinese theological picture is: biblical, evangelical (in the classical sense of the word), national, but not nationalistic, keenly concerned with the church's relation to the construction of a modern socialist China, and latitudinarian. Once I was asked by a British theological educator as to what is the theological theme that we think most important. My answer was the doctrine of Incarnation: the God who forever creates, reveals, redeems, sanctifies and leads us all into His final glory has become flesh and dwells among us in the world, "full of grace and truth; we have beheld his glory, glory as of the only Son from the Father." (Jn. 1:14) Allow me to quote Kumazawa once more: "Indigenization does not mean establishing a colony of Christians in the secular or pagan world. It means identifying what God is doing in the secular world and finding out what we can do to participate in his work."[2]

We are a very small and young church. We have come to share with you our experiences, understandings, aspirations and problems, and to learn from you. Now I must hold my tongue and use my ears and heart. Thank you.

---

1 *Where Theology Seeks to Integrate Text and Context*, in *Asian Voices in Christian Theology*, ed. By G. H. Anderson, 1976, p. 181.

2 Ibid., p. 205.

The Post-denominational Unity of the Chinese Protestant Church

(Nanjing, March 21, 1998)

WHILE I WAS PREPARING for this conference, two topics on the list of presentations attracted my attention: "Recent Trends in the Study of New Religious Movements" by Armin W. Geertz of the University of Aarhus, Denmark, and "The Post-Denominational Unity of the Chinese Christian Church—Dream or Reality?" by RostislavFellner of the Oriental Institute, Czechoslovakia.[1] The first involves the emergence and spread of new sects and cults, which in the Chinese context pose some threat to church unity, and the second seems to call for an apology.

Religions are like trees. As they grow they bifurcate or trifurcate and branch out into a number of organized groups that bear some resemblance to, and preserve their identity with, the mother trunk, and yet keep on differentiating until in the end they tend to become mutually exclusive or antagonistic to each other. Attempts at reunion often seem difficult, if not completely fruitless. Is the experiment which aims at the post-denominational unity of the Protestant church in China today a dream that can never be realized? Is it, as the Chinese saying goes, navigating upstream against the current?

This perennial phenomenon of the differentiation of religions has been long observed and studied by historians and sociologists of religion. The classical Weber-Troeltsch church-sect dichotomy and their analyses have been generally accepted, and further developed and elaborated by H. Richard Niebuhr, Howard Becker, Liston Pope, Milton Yinger, to mention just a few representative figures amongst a host of scholars. The end result may be summarized into the following typological schema, which I have found very useful:

ecclesia—the church

---

1 In the event, neither Armin Geertz nor RotislavFellner were able to attend the conference in Beijing.

denomination—class church

established sect

sect

cult

new religion.²

Applying this schema to the Christian churches in China in the second half of the twentieth century, we find that there were three churches (ecclesiae) in 1950:

1) the Catholic Church, about 3.5 million members strong;

2) the Russian Orthodox Church, with about 300,000 members; and

3) the Protestant Church, with approximately one million church members and enquirers.

In the Catholic Church and the Orthodox Church there were no denominations, and their sub-divisions are beyond our present interest. But with the Protestant Church the situation was more complicated. Protestant Christianity had been introduced into China for about one and a half century, and on the eve of the revolution there were at least twenty denominations supported and dominated by twice or three times as many foreign missionary societies.³ Their ridiculous geographical distribution, and competition and contention among themselves, was seen as a scandal and won the disrepute of "imported foreign religions" as a tool of "cultural invasion" by Western Powers. Then there were a number of church groups that fall into the category of "established cults," such as the True Jesus Church, Seventh Day Adventists, the Salvation Army, Assemblies of God, The Pentecostal Church, and the Little Flock (Christian Assembly). Some of them were of foreign origin and others of indigenous origin. The only known group that I would classify as a sect or cult was the Jesus Family in Shandung.

Religious traditions are differentiated by nation, class, educational level, patterns of secular conflict and other non-religious variables. As Richard Niebuhr observes, variations in the ethics, polity and theology among various denominations "have their roots in the relationship of the religious

---

2 For detailed descriptions of the schema, see Michael Hill, *A Sociology of Religion*, pp.47–94; J. Milton Yinger, *The Scientific Study of Religion*, pp. 224–28.

3 In 1920, fifty-five missionary societies sent more than six thousand missionaries to China. These belonged to the following seven major denominations: Anglican, Baptist, Congregational, Lutheran, Methodist, Presbyterian, and the China Inland Mission. See *The Christian Occupation of China*, 1922, Chinese transl., vol. III, p. 1190.

life to the cultural and political conditions prevailing in any group of Christians . . . The exigencies of church discipline, the demands of the national psychology, the effect of social tradition, the influence of cultural heritage, and the weight of economic interest play their role in the definition of religious truth."[4] All denominations have a *raison d'etre* for their emergence and transmission. The evolution of each denomination, in the final analysis, is the result of processes of contextualization. All denominations introduced into China during the nineteenth century missionary movement brought with them particular valuable legacies and contributed to the enrichment of the churches in China. But they failed to make the Church Chinese, partly, I would say, by their persistence in denominationalism. Each denomination has its roots in the soil of its origin, and when transplanted to the Chinese soil *in toto* it became stunted and failed to grow. Naturalization was needed. In the political and social changes of the early fifties the roots of the imported denominations were cut off and the "trees" began to wither, trunk and branches. The churches had become so weak by 1957 that they had to be reorganized and merged to hold "united services." (It must be pointed out that during the period from 1949 to 1957 the implementation of the religious policy of the Party was, taken as a whole, as good as could be expected, or at least much better than in the succeeding years. The dwindling of the Christian Church in this period has been wrongly attributed by many Western observers to the supposed stringency of religious policy on the part of the Party and People's Government. This is entirely groundless and based upon biased presuppositions.)

It is not my intention here to dwell long on the launching and development of the Three Self Movement. Suffice it to say that one of the purposes of the Three Self is to make the Church in China really Chinese, just as the Church in England was made English or the Church in Germany German. In the early nineteen-fifties when the Three Self Movement was launched, to safeguard solidarity and smooth cooperation, a principle of mutual respect was proposed and adopted. This meant that in matters of doctrinal differences, of liturgy and church policy (these three often being the causes of controversies leading to schism and splits), one should be patient and tolerant toward those who hold different views because of different denominational backgrounds, by "seeking common ground in major matters and preserving trivial differences." This policy of mutual respect proved very effective in preparing the way for the churches to merge and hold "united services" in 1957.

---

4 H. Richard Niebuhr, *The Social Sources of Denominationalism*.

When the "cultural revolution" was over, religious activities began to surface again. The China Christian Council was established in 1980. This marked the beginning of the post-denominational stage. The old roots of imported denominations having been cut off, the churches began to take root in the Chinese soil in a new social context. One observed an unexpected, rapid Church growth. In the course of the following twelve years (from 1980 to 1991), the total number of church members and enquirers increased to about 6.5 million, more than six times the pre-1950 total. Churches (local congregations with church buildings and leaders) are being reopened or built anew at the rate of three churches every two days. (Only two churches were reopened in the fall of 1979.) Now there are more than seven thousand churches and over twenty thousand assembly points (congregations without regular church buildings, also known as "home meetings"). There are no denominations. Church members under the age of forty have little or no knowledge of denominations, and mostolder Christians are quite satisfied and happy with the non-denominational pattern of services and church organization, and have no desire to return to the old path. With the exception of three groups of "established sects," namely the Little Flock, the Seventh Day Adventists, and the True Jesus Church, an overwhelming majority of Protestant congregations are determined to consolidate around the China Christian Council and locally around the provincial and municipal Christian Councils. Strictly speaking, the Christian councils are not churches in the ecclesiological sense. So we may say that the Chinese Protestant Church is still a uniting church, not quite a United Church of Christ in China. We are advancing toward church unity in the sense that we have forgone denominationalism. It is a new model of conciliar unity. The China Christian Council is different from National Christian Councils in many other countries in that the latter presuppose the existence of denominations or other church constellations. The CCC is not quite a United Church of Christ, for it still lacks a well defined church polity. On the local level the many congregations are represented in the local (municipal or county) Christian councils which serve as coordinating and advisory committees but do not have administrative authority. It is not like the Presbyterian synod. The relations between the China Christian Council and provincial councils, and those between the provincial and the local councils are not very clearly defined either. Councils of "higher levels" do not "direct" or "order" but advise or summon councils of "lower levels" and local congregations, offer help and exercise "leadership" through consultation and persuasion, not coercion, and by organizing cooperative activities and enterprises such as running leadership training classes etc.

One can sense that this is a rather loosely organized unity. At the Fifth All-National Assembly held in January in Beijing, a document entitled "Provisional Regulations on Church Order and Ministry" was adopted. Basic rules concerning Church Membership, Ordinance, Church Council and Offices were laid down and recommended for trial practice. A new clause was also added to the Constitution of the China Christian Council to emphasize the obligation on the part of provincial local councils to implement pertinent resolutions and recommendations of the CCC. These are some of the attempts to strengthen the solidarity and unity of the church.

The idea and ideal of church unity have been the subject of arduous studies and heated discussions for almost a century. Various models of church union have been conceived and attempted. The experience of the Chinese church is unique in that it is based on a particular socio-political context. The roots of denominationalism had never gone deep enough in the soil of Chinese culture. So once we have come together and done away with denominational barriers, we are on cleared ground to experiment in building an edifice to enfold and give shelter to multitudes who hold the Christian faith, and to bear witness to "the unity of the spirit in the bond of peace, that there is one Lord, one faith, one baptism, one God and Father of all, who is above all, and through all, and in all" (Eph. 4: 3-6).

We realize this is no easy task. We have learned to move carefully and slowly onward, and to guard against hastiness, coercion, artificial uniformity, proselytism, and schismatic division. The cardinal virtue, the essence of Chinese culture, is the "peaceful unity of opposites." We are endeavoring to achieve church unity through this virtue.

****

I can only be brief in the second part of my paper. Is not the development of religion like the tree of evolution, always divergent *ad infinitum*, as shown in the post-Reformation development of the Protestant churches into numerous denominations, and the sudden flowering and proliferation of hosts of cults and new religions in the second half of this century? Humans are alike in being religious, but very much different from one another in their ways of seeking spiritual satisfaction. Will the incipient centrifugal tendency of the three "established sects" I mentioned above, namely the Little Flock, the Seventh Day Adventists, and the True Jesus Church, escalate and grow into new denominations and eventually break the fragile unity of the Chinese church? Perhaps possible, but unlikely. First, as the "Conciliar" Church (I use this to denote collectively the churches within the fold of the Christian councils, often also called the "Three Self Church") has a respectful attitude towards these groups and takes thoughtful measures to accommodate their specific requirements or requests (like welcoming the Seventh Day Adventists and the True Jesus Church members to hold services according to their customs on Saturdays, and offering conveniences to the Little Flock members to have their bread-breaking meetings wherever they like), most of them are quite willing to maintain friendly ties with the Conciliar Church rather than breaking away. Secondly, as regards the minority of these groups who are not ready to cooperate, the Conciliar Church is willing to wait with patience and love, and not to put pressure on them. In history, church unity has never been complete and "pure" without dissenters. Small numbers of dissenters do not precipitate the formation of schismatic splits.

Lastly, there remains the question of sects, cults and new religions. As the Protestant church in China is making rapid advances in the increase of the number of adherents, there arise a multitude of sects and cults that style themselves as "Christian churches" and proliferate in wide areas, especially in more backward rural communities. Many of these bear some resemblance to the Pentecostals in their meetings, for example in singing "spiritual songs," spending long hours in prayer accompanied by weeping, crying or howling, dancing "spiritual dances," speaking in tongues, and invariably practising "spiritual healing." Some of these are eccentrically apocalyptic, believing in the imminent Second Coming of Christ. Most of these groups gather around some charismatic leaders who demand absolute loyalty and blind obedience from their followers, and usually take a hostile attitude toward or stand aloof from the Three Self or Conciliar Church, which in turn regards them as aberrant or heretical in their beliefs. Their activities are often clandestine and occult, and it is difficult to gain access to them and to assess their numerical strength. It is believed that they account for the rapid growth of Protestant Christianity in some way and to a certain degree.

I cannot go into detailed description of such groups. Our present concern is whether these will become a threat to the church unity leading to its eventual dissolution. Plausible answers to this question require more comprehensive and intensive studies in the theology, psychology and sociology of cults. This is why I am looking towards learning from the wisdom of Prof. Geertz and his presentation. But many believe that in the processes of modernization, with improvements in mass education, medical care and cultural activities, most of the sects and cults will lose ground and gradually die out. New ones may emerge. They come and go, and most probably will remain marginal. Their effect on the main stream of Christianity can only be negligibly small.

The unity of the church in China started as a dream; it is now being realized. We are realistic and aware of the difficulties and barriers on our path. We are striving forward until the uniting church will become a United Church of Christ, and spell out the present CCC (China Christian Council) as the Church of Christ in China.

Living as Christians Today
Biblical Insights
(Nanjing, 1988)

> Behold, now is the acceptable time;
> Behold, now is the day of salvation.
>
> (2 CORINTHIANS 6:2–10)

THE HISTORY OF PROTESTANT Christianity in China begins with the arrival of Robert Morrison at Guangzhou in 1807. The first part of the story covers about one hundred and fifty years. Many volumes have been written on this period with various descriptions, conclusions and assessments from different angles. Some are helpful, some are not quite so. Now we have turned to a new chapter. As regards the relationship with Christians of other countries in the future, we are looking forward to a new era of brother and sisterhood and being fellow-workers in Christ, of genuine mutual understanding, concern and respect. We have come to share with you some of our experiences and reflections of how Christians are living and witnessing for Christ in China today, in the post-Cultural-Revolution period of rebuilding and rehabilitating the Christian Church. Let me first give you a brief sketch in figures as a background of my presentation.

As you all know, the Christian Church in China underwent a total "blackout" of about fifteen years. Then, beginning from 1979 there came a "recall-to-life" and recuperation. The changes have been stupendous. According to our latest survey and estimates (1987) there are now more than 4,700 churches and 16,600 "meeting points."

This means we have been re-opening or building anew at a rate of more than one church a day. The total number of Protestant Christians, including church members and inquirers, is over four million. (This may be a conservative estimate. But I would rather be a bit conservative on this than exaggerate, as some people like to take pleasure in making sensational news with scanty factual support.) As compared with 700,000, the pre-liberation total, the result of one hundred and fifty years of missionary efforts, this means an increase of about five times in a period of three decades. This is really miraculous, taking into consideration the rugged roads of hardship and trials we have trodden. We praise and thank God for His guidance, protection and blessings.(There are many factors contributing to this rapid growth, which I shall touch upon a little later, and there are also many problems and difficulties calling for immediate attention and further endeavouring.)

But the Lord has led us to walk through the valley of the shadow of death, and makes us lie down in green pastures, leading us beside still waters and restoring our souls (Psalm 23, See also Ezek. 34:11–16). "Thus says the Lord: Come from the four winds, O breath, and breathe upon these slain, that they may live." And lo, "the breath came into them, and they lived, and stood upon their feet, an exceedingly great host" (Ezek. 37:9–10). Now we are facing the task of rebuilding the Lord's house. "Take courage, all you people of the Lord, says the Lord; work, for I am with you." "My spirit abides among you, fear not . . .The latter splendor of this house shall be greater than the former, says the Lord of hosts; and in this place I will give prosperity, says the Lord of hosts" (Hag. 2:4,5).

It is through these experiences that the message and force of the Resurrection of our Lord Jesus Christ, and the Great Commission and promises given to the apostles in the first century, and the stories of the Pentecost and afterwards, recorded in the first chapters of the Acts of the Apostles, have become all the more real and vivid to us during these years. And we have been talking about, and meditating on a Theology of the Resurrection in our church a great deal. The little (?) book by the Rev. Professor Rowan Williams, whom I had the privilege to meet in person in Oxford, becomes more revealing and thought-provoking to us, in developing a theology of Resurrection in the context of present-day Chinese church and society.

But the growth of the church is faster than we can keep up with. There is a grave shortage of pastors, preachers and church workers. At present there are only about six thousand pastors and preachers in the whole country, most of them in old age, and others rather young and without adequate training and experience. There is a wide age gap among the practising ministers. Most of the rural churches and assembly points have only lay workers who have little or no training at all. The quality of spiritual nurture and pastoral care is very low, and in some places this breeds disorders and deviations. "When Jesus saw the crowds, he had compassion for them, because they are harassed and helpless, like sheep without a shepherd. Then he said to his disciples, the harvest is plentiful, but the laborers are few; pray therefore the Lord of the harvest to send out laborers into his harvest" (Mt. 9:36–37). The Nanjing Union Theological Seminary was reopened in 1981. Altogether 150 students have graduated over the past three years. And since 1984, eleven theological schools and colleges or training centers at regional or provincial levels have been set up. A Bible school of junior standard was opened in Shaanxi (陕西) Province last year. Heilongjiang is preparing to set up another. Last year a one-year training course was started in the Nanjing Seminary for the province of Henan, where there are over 830,000 Christians with less than 100 pastors and preachers. It is hoped that from the 50 trainees many may be ordained to take up ministerial responsibilities in that province. Over 700 regular students are being trained in these colleges. Many church councils at provincial or municipal levels are also running short-term courses of one to four months to train lay workers. A correspondence course is published bi-monthly and has over 33,000 subscribers. These and other measures are what we have been taking to meet this number-one need in building the church in China.

Shortage of Bibles was also a problem, and caused concern to many Christians abroad. The shortage has been due to, not just the devastating "Cultural Revolution," but also the growing needs of new converts and inquirers and an increasing interest in (and demand for) the Bible among non-Christian students and intellectuals. In the past five years three million copies of the Bible have been printed and distributed. The Amity Printing Press in Nanjing, thanks to the assistance of the United Bible Societies, gives priority to printing the Bible and other religious literature. We have compiled and published a new hymnal for national distribution. Ms. Cao Shengjie (曹圣洁), Associate General Secretary of the China Christian Council and Executive Secretary of the Committee on Church Music, who is here with us today, is the chief editor of this hymnal. Under the guidance of the Holy Spirit many other things are being done in meeting the many needs of the growing and thriving church.

Another feature of the Protestant Church in China I want to stress is that in response to the intercessory prayer of our Lord (Jn. 17), we are striving to realize the unity of the church, following St. Paul's admonition: "with all lowliness and meekness, with patience, forbearing one another in love, eager to maintain the unity of the Spirit in the bond of peace. There is one body and one Spirit, just as you were called to the one hope that belongs to your call, one Lord, one faith, one baptism, one God and Father of us all" (Eph, 4:2–6).

We have outgrown former denominational structural patterns which often brought about splitting, competition, waste of personnel and financial resources and disharmony. Adhering to the principle of mutual respect regarding matters of faith (theology), spiritually (ways of devotion and forms of service and liturgy) and church polity, we are reorganizing our congregations into local churches under "Christian Councils" at municipal, provincial and national levels. Most of the meeting points are associated with churches, and the ministers and preachers stationed at the churches go around to serve and help the assembly points. We seek to preserve the valuable historical heritage and contributions of the various denominations but try to guard against the evils of denominationalism and sectarianism. The China Christian Council is not like National Councils of Churches in other countries, nor yet is it a united Church of Christ in China, but is something somewhere between the two. Your experiences and efforts in seeking a new pattern of "ecumenical instrument" that will embrace not just Protestant denominations, Anglicans, but also Catholics are something beyond our grasp and hopes yet. But we can learn from you in this aspect. We are waiting for the Holy Spirit to lead us a step forward toward our aim, which is to achieve real unity but with variety, not uniformity.

You have heard of the consecration of two bishops in Shanghai on June 26. They will be bishops without dioceses. The title of bishop will mean a recognition of their spiritual excellence and being model pastors and teachers of the Word of God, and will not add any additional administrative responsibilities to what they have now. Both of them are already serving the Church in Shanghai in distinguished positions. Bishop Shen Yifan (沈以藩) (of Episcopalian background) is the resident Vice-president of the China Christian Council, Chairperson of the Commission on Theological Education, as well as senior minister of the Community Church in Shanghai. Bishop Sun Yanli (孙彦理) (of Methodist background) is the President of the Shanghai Christian Council and also Principal of the East China Theological Seminary in Shanghai. He is also senior minister of the Mu'en (沐恩) Church. Some have commented that the consecration of bishops may signify that the Protestant Church in China is intending to carry on the Apostolic Succession in the history of the Christian Church, and may prove to be a positive step in the Ecumenical movement. It is also significant to point out that in addition to the three bishops of Episcopalian background, there were three elderly pastors of high esteem participating in the laying-on-of-hands in the Consecration. These three are of Baptist, Presbyterian and Methodist background respectively.

You all know that all these experiments and achievements have been made under the guiding principle of three-self: self-government, self-support and self-propagation. The main purpose of this movement is to change the old image of a foreign religion into one that is authentically Chinese, to sow the seed of the Christian Gospel in the soil of Chinese culture and let it grow and bear fruits in a Chinese climate for the Chinese people. As primitive Christianity with its Jewish origin and background grew and developed into Hellenistic, Latin, Byzantine, Coptic, and later into the multifarious ethnic and national forms and patterns of churches, there is a real necessity and rationale for the existence of a Chinese Church. It is not at all anti-foreign, nor will it alter or dilute the essence or weaken the power and uniqueness of the Christian Gospel. Indeed, a message, in order to be meaningful and to be responded to, must be interpreted into national tongues. The Word must be made flesh and dwell among the people, so that the people can see that it is full of grace and truth (Jn. 1:14). This is what we understand by incarnation, to bring Christ into humanity and to live in blood-and-flesh reality among the Chinese people in order to win the people. The three-self principle is indeed not something of our own invention, not something new under the sun. I think Christians in Britain are among those who understand most readily and easily the Biblical basis and theological rationale and historical necessity of this principle. Six years ago when we had the honor and privilege of welcoming the Archbishop of Canterbury, Robert Runcie, at the Nanjing Seminary we heard the Right Reverend comment that the reformation in Britain in the sixteenth century and the establishment and development of the Church of England (and may I add, the Church of Scotland) could be taken as an example of "three-self." This is a most encouraging and complimentary statement concerning the Three-Self Movement, and we shall never forget it.

I think this is one very important factor that accounts for the rapid growth of the Chinese church in the last decades.

For the Chinese Christians this also means identification and reconciliation. In the first place, this is a process of seeking realization of the authentic self-hood of a Chinese church, not a shadow or copy of outstations of any foreign church body or missionary organization. It means independence. Only when we have become independent are we able to enter into interdependent relations in the Church Universal. It also means identification with the Chinese people, sharing with them the struggles, sufferings and aspirations, in weal and woe, indeed sharing with them the same fate, and struggling with them in building a new, socialist China. This is all the more necessary and significant because in the pre-revolution days we were alienated from the people by identifying with a "foreign faith," in various ways and degrees. To counteract and recompense for this wrong identification we have read in the gospel of reconciliation in 2 Corinthians Chapter 5 a wealth of meaning: to be reconciled to God in Christ, to be reconciled to the world (in this case to our fellow-countrypeople) in Christ, and to be reconciled to our alienated self-hood in Christ. These three dimensions of being a Christian today in China all hinge upon "in Christ" and are geared to a right relationship with our fellow-citizens. We have found Paul's experience most illuminating as he writes in 1 Corinthians 9:22 on "becoming all things to all people so that by all means I might save some." Translated into Chinese within the Chinese context it reads, "to the Chinese we became as Chinese." In what way? Again, Apostle Paul is the teacher. "Take thought for what is noble in the sight of all. . . rejoice with those who rejoice, and weep with those who weep" (Rom. 12:9–21). "Whatever is true, whatever is honorable, whatever is just, whatever is pure, whatever is lovely, whatever is gracious, if there is any excellence, if there is anything worthy of praise, think about these things . . . and do" (Phil. 4:8–9).

Through identification, reconciliation, and taking thought of and doing "whatever is noble in the sight of all," we are changing the concept and image of being a Christian in China. I could cite a long list of examples of Christians awarded with titles as model teachers, doctors, engineers, workers, peace-makers in neighborhoods . . . etc., and numerous anonymous "good people doing good things." As I understand it, Mr. Zhang, is going to elaborate this in his presentation. The first of the three goals of the Amity Foundation in Nanjing is to make the Christian presence more widely known and felt in our country through education, social welfare, services and philanthropic work. It is well-known to public security authorities that Christians are a rarity among delinquents and law-breakers. That Christians are living up to a higher moral standard than most others has become common talk. There is an awakening of interest in religions in general and Christianity in particular among young people and university students today. The contributions of Christian intellectuals among academic circles are being more and more recognized. There is a noticeable increase of the proportion of young and middle-aged people among those who come to church. The general attitude of Chinese people towards Christianity is gradually changing in a positive direction with more understanding, sympathy and appreciation. This in turn also accounts for the rapid growth in the last decade. We have not only been preaching and hearing the Gospel in words, but also trying to live out the gospel of reconciliation and service in love. The new commandment given by Jesus Christ in John 13:34–35 and 15:12–17, and the teaching in James 1:22–25 on being doers, not only hearers, are leading us to develop a diaconic theology and a synthesis of faith and works (James 2:14–26), and to see the importance of orthopraxis as a necessary accompaniment of orthodoxy.

But still we are a young, very small and weak church. There are many problems and difficulties and weaknesses and we need God's guidance and power to help prepare us for the task of building the house of the Lord. We have come to share with you our experiences and to learn from you, with the hope that the ties that bind us together as children of God in the love of Christ be strengthened.

In conclusion I would like to read a passage from the Second Epistle of the Apostle Paul to the Christians in Corinth, which sums up and depicts in a very vivid and realistic way what we Christians in China have been going through in the last thirty to forty years.

> "For he says,
> At the acceptable time I have listened to you, and helped you on the day of salvation.
> Behold, now is the acceptable time;
> Behold, now is the day of salvation.
> We put no obstacle in anyone's way, so that no fault may be found with our
> ministry, but as servants of God we commend ourselves in every way:
> Through great endurance, in afflictions, hardships, calamities, beatings,
> imprisonments, tumults, labors, watching, hunger;
> By purity, knowledge, forbearance, kindness, the Holy Spirit, genuine love,
> truthful speech, and the power of God;
> With the weapons of righteousness for the right hand and for the left;
> In honor and dishonor, in ill repute and good repute.
> We are treated as impostors, and yet are true;
> As unknown, and yet well known;
> As dying, and behold we live;
> As punished, and yet not killed;
> As sorrowful, yet always rejoicing;
> As poor, yet making many rich;
> As having nothing, and yet possessing everything."
>
> (2 Corinthians 6:2–10)

May the grace of God be with us all, children of our one Heavenly Father, both in China and in Britain. Amen.

This article has been slightly shortened.
Address given at a joint conference of the China Study Project of the British Council of Churches and the Friends of the Church in China (UK) 8–10 July, 1988.
China Study Project Journal, Vol.3, No.2 (August, 1988), p.4.
Reprinted by permission.

On Nanjing Theological Seminary
(Beijing, August, 1986)

Chen Zemin

THE FOLLOWING ARTICLE IS *a report on the work of Nanjing Theological Seminary during 1986 and was presented at the Fourth National Chinese Christian Conference, August, 1986. Data cited in the report are relevant to the year 1986 and may no longer be accurate.*

The Third National Chinese Christian Conference held in October, 1980, marked the beginning of a new era for Chinese Christianity. In order to train young people to take up the work of establishing and governing well a church based on three-self principles, the Conference decided that Nanjing Theological Seminary should resume classes as soon as possible. Under the guidance of the Three-Self Patriotic Movement Committee and the China Christian Council, with Party and government assistance, and supported by local churches, Nanjing Seminary convened classes in February, 1981.

Five and a half years have passed since that first group of post-Cultural Revolution students were recruited. During this time, we have enrolled more than 280 students from 26 different provinces, municipalities, and autonomous regions. By the grace of God, in the past two years, we have had 188 graduates: 64 in the four-year course[1] and 7 who have completed their studies in the graduate division. Of the 117 students in the two-year course, 67 have switched to the four-year course to continue their studies, while graduates of the four-year course have been accepted into the graduate program. This means that more than one hundred graduates will be going out to work in churches. Fifteen of these will be employed as teachers in other seminaries. In the past five years, only 12 students have had to leave school. For the Fall semester this year (September, 1986), we will have

---

1 The basic two-year course equips students to work as pastors in local churches. Graduates of the four-year course may continue for further study or specialized training.

177 students: 83 in the two-year course, 77 in the four-year course and 17 graduate students.

Nanjing Seminary's goal is to train young people who love China and the Chinese church, who believe in the truth of the Bible, who maintain the three-self principles, and who are well-rounded spiritually, morally, intellectually, and physically. We hope to mold them into dedicated servants of God who can meet the needs of our growing church. That is to say, candidates for theological training should: love socialist New China, accept the Party's leadership, have purity of faith, adhere to the teachings of the Bible, love God and love humankind. They should also be spiritually and morally mature, in good physical health, have a college education and a definite level of Biblical and theological knowledge. Students must also possess the ability to unite their colleagues and fellow Christians, to encourage and lead believers along the three-self path so that together we may establish a church suited to the greatness of the new era, a church which is uniquely Chinese. Through their words, faith, love and action, they will spread the Gospel. Together with the people of the whole nation, they should contribute to the four modernizations and to world peace, to the betterment of humanity and as witnesses to the glory of God. Besides meeting the urgent needs of the present however, we need to train qualified people in all specialities for the future, people who will assume responsibility for theological teaching and research, publishing, church art and music, and relations with Christians overseas.

Many obstacles still stand in the way of these goals. The foundation of the Chinese church is still somewhat weak. After the Cultural Revolution, the educational level of many of the incoming students was low, and the basis of their faith shallow. This caused problems in student selection and in teaching. Our faculty is limited. They did not have a great deal of prior experience in training students according to the aforementioned goals and requirements. For this reason, we were often unable to fulfil our goals in the last few years, and many problems still remain. As an expression of your responsibility for this holy task and of your care and concern for the seminary, we would appreciate the opinions and positive suggestions of our colleagues throughout the country to help us improve our work in the future.

(2)

In what follows, I would like to discuss the problems of the last few years and the work we have done.

(1) *General Classes and Religious Classes.* In order to insure that students have an adequate knowledge of Bible and theology, and practical

training in church work, and at the same time raise their cultural level and political awareness, and at the same time raise their cultural level and political awareness, an appropriate balance of religious and general classes needs to be attained. On the whole, religious classes comprise 70% of our curriculum, while general classes make up the remaining 30%. Most of the general classes, such as political studies, are in line with the common curriculum for institutions of higher education. In the politics course, we use the materials used by most colleges in addition to emphasizing patriotism and current political studies. However, we do not offer a course on dialectical materialism.

(2) *Relationship between Spiritual Training and Knowledge.* The seminary is neither a monastery nor a centre for religious studies. We want to help students combine spiritual nurture with the study of the Bible and theology. To aid in this, we encourage each student in the habit of morning and evening devotions. In addition, we arrange public worship services, morning and evening prayers, and a variety of prayer meetings and Bible-study groups. Still, we don't want to de-emphasize knowledge and study. Some of our newer students seem to regard growth in the spirit as antithetical to academic work. For such students more knowledge means less love of God. Religious pedagogy must combine every type of knowledge and spiritual growth with the real needs of the church. Thus, we also stress practical areas such as preaching and pastoral work. We must avoid establishing an "ivory tower" divorced from reality. Ideally, we would like to provide a lively study environment with an atmosphere of genuine piety compatible with spiritual growth. We would also like to impart a sense of sacrifice and devotion to the students.

(3) *Unity and Diversity.* The Chinese church has done away with denominational differences and pursues unity. Still, the seminary must maintain the principle of mutual respect toward different points of view with regard to matters of faith, liturgical traditions, and spiritual practices; and promote understanding and a willingness to learn from others. In this way, we can work toward harmony while avoiding fruitless arguments.

(4) *The Old and the New or Tradition vs Modernization.* We preserve the truth of Scripture and adapt from tradition what is true and valuable. At the same time, we should be open to the revelation and light of the Holy Spirit in the new era, especially that rich spiritual experience of our Christian people since the founding of our new nation. We should examine and evaluate our experiences. Our traditions have been tainted by the old society. In this new era, we should allow the Holy Spirit to guide us in judging, testing and correcting. The Holy Spirit will lead us "into all truth." Under the Spirit's guidance we will find the rich truth of the Bible and come to a new

awareness of God's grace in the present. We should not become complacent and conservative. Rather, we should resist uncritical acceptance of the old.

(5) *Relations with Christians Overseas.* We base ourselves in China, but embrace the whole world. We must understand, respect, absorb and digest what is of value in Chinese tradition, for we believe that it is a gift given to us by God. In modern China too, all that is true, good and beautiful is a gift from God. From our contemporary experience, we can begin to appreciate God's magnificent grace and revelations. Only when the seed of the Gospel has been planted in the fertile soil of our nation's culture and has taken deep root there, will it grow and bear fruit that many people may come to understand and accept it.

Of course, this does not imply a closed-door mentality or blind anti-foreignism. We acknowledge that there is much valuable fruit to be found in Biblical and theological study done overseas. We should gain an understanding of it, absorb it and use it to our own enrichment and improvement. But we must be able to discriminate among foreign things those which are wrong or which are not suited to China. An understanding of the world is helpful in broadening one's vision and knowledge and in developing one's critical faculties.

At Nanjing Seminary, we have the opportunity to meet many friends and scholars from overseas. Such contacts promote mutual understanding and friendship. However, we must guard against the tendency to worship foreign things. We must first gain self-respect and self knowledge by seeking truth from facts. We must also publicize our three-self stance and help to implement religious policy. We should, for instance, emphasize Chinese church history as a means of understanding our own past and present. This would also aid in the development of uniquely Chinese teaching materials for all our classes: Bible, theology, doctrine, pastoral care; even church music and art. The Nanjing Seminary library is relatively better than those of our other theological schools. But we must learn to use selectively and critically many of the books and materials from Hong Kong and abroad which it contains.

(6) *Improve Three-Self Studies.* Three-Self studies should be emphasized, especially study of the principle of self-propagation. The seminary itself is an important instrument for the success of self-propagation, so the spirit of three-self should inform all facets of our curriculum. We should begin a special class focusing on Three-Self *per se*. We have offered a class in Three-Self Theology in which a number of professors explored with the students all aspects of the subject from various angles. In addition, another course in Three-Self utilizing Three-Self documents will allow students to understand the history, significance and necessity of the Movement. There

is still much work to be done in this area, and we welcome the opinions and suggestions of our colleagues.

(7) *Theological Education for the 1980s.* We are now educating a new generation of theological students who differ in many ways from their predecessors. These new students were born and grew up after Liberation or during the Cultural Revolution era. They have no experience of life in Old China with which to compare life in New China. The chaos of the Cultural Revolution dominates their memories. They do not have sufficient knowledge of the superiority of socialism and have only superficial views on the problems of reform. They have also been influenced by unhealthy currents of thought that have recently infiltrated from abroad. At the same time, the rapid growth of science and technology and the information explosion have instilled in them a desire for freedom, a thirst for knowledge and intellectual openness. They may easily become skeptical and resistant to old rules and customs. The faculty will have to discuss how best to train these students.

At present, in addition to spiritual growth and course work, we encourage a wide-range of extracurricular activities from special interest groups to discussion groups and student meetings. Through these organizations, we attempt to cultivate responsibility and love for school, church, and nation. Although our dormitories are reasonably comfortable, we try to stress a simple life that is built on hard work and mutual help. We feel that seminary students ought to avoid a life of excessive comfort or a life-style above that of ordinary church workers. Rules and regulations are a necessity of campus life, but at the same time a sense of self-responsibility must be engendered. Each class has a faculty advisor and mature students are chosen to serve as advisors for class organizations. A student committee coordinates all aspects of these extracurricular programs. In this way, we are attempting to instill a sense of discipline and order in the seminary, but we still have much to learn.

(3)

The following are some areas in which further improvement is necessary.

(1) *Recruitment of Students.* Students at Nanjing Seminary have been recommended to the municipal and provincial levels of the two national bodies by churches all over the country. Many of these churches take this responsibility seriously and take pains to choose carefully. In some areas preliminary training is conducted before a student is recommended for the examination. Students chosen in this way are generally good. But we have also found that some students have little background in the faith or

the church and are ill-prepared to study theology. To train these students often proves to be a waste of effort and money and results in a loss to both church and seminary. Thus, it is important that we have the cooperation of all churches in the conscientious recruitment of qualified students.

(2) *Establishing a Curriculum.* In 1983, we considered establishing an intensive short course to train church workers more quickly. At that time, our first- and second-year classes became components of this specialized program. We also planned to select some members of this group for continued theological study. Thus, the second year of the shorter course had to be self-contained and practical while also providing a foundation for those students who would continue in their studies. But there is a contradiction between these two goals. The difficulty impinges on the ratio of regular courses to theology courses for these two second-year groups and on problems of continuity in moving from a superficial to a deeper level in the theology courses.

The second year of the two-year course must both raise the students' general educational level and provide them with sufficient ability in Bible, theological knowledge, preaching and practical church work. In such circumstances it is difficult to avoid spending too much time in too many classes, placing a great burden on students and faculty. The second year of the four-year course (and the third and fourth years) must continue to build on the foundation laid in the two-year course, expand the students' knowledge and at the same time avoid repetition. It thus becomes necessary to offer some new courses. Unfortunately, attempting to achieve these two goals in one year has proved to be an unacceptable burden on both the students and the faculty. We have also considered accepting graduates from the two-year courses in other seminaries into our four-year course, but this involves additional problems.

At present, our graduate students are selected mainly from graduates of the four-year course. Their four years of theological training prepare them for specialized research. From this group will come the seminary teachers of tomorrow. Another group is comprised of students who have graduated from a regular college or university, but who lack Biblical and theological knowledge and church experience. There should be a systematized course for these students, but such a two-track system would entail other contradictions and difficulties.

(3) *Relations with Churches and Pastoral Fieldwork.* Our students come from all over the country but because they spend a long time at seminary, it is easy for them to lose contact with their home congregations. We would like to see local churches have more frequent contact with the students they have recommended and show their care for them. Formerly, we permitted

the student to return to his or her home church for one semester of practical work. This was helpful, but had the disadvantage of interrupting the student's academic work. Now, thanks to the cooperation of the Nanjing churches, we plan to have most of the students work in local congregations during the academic year. When they return home for vacation, we hope that their home church can provide them with further opportunities for practical experience.

In other ways, too, we feel the churches have responsibilities and rights with regard to the continuing education of seminary graduates. We would like to suggest the need for a probationary period after graduation in which the student would continue the training process under supervision. Thus, all graduates of our two- and four-year courses and graduate students would receive a certificate on the completion of their seminary program, and then would return to their home churches for a period of one year. If the congregation approved of the student's work after that time, a diploma would be issued. We hope this new policy will be supported by the churches.

(4) *Placement of Graduates.* Placement is primarily the responsibility of the provincial or municipal branches of the two national bodies which recommended the students in the beginning.

One-hundred-five students from our last two graduating classes have gone into church work, while the rest have remained for further studies. A small number of these could not, for a number of reasons, find an appropriate position. This is a loss both for the students themselves and for the church. In addition to training pastors for all parts of the country, Nanjing Seminary prepares teachers for the other seminaries and supplies specialized personnel for the national church bodies. We hope that each of these organizations will take our nation-wide responsibilities into consideration in their requests for personnel. We also ask that the provincial and municipal organizations discuss the apportioning of students among themselves on the basis of their real needs.

(5) *Teaching Materials and Teacher Training.* Like the other seminaries, we have had trouble finding suitable materials for our religion classes. Old books or those from abroad can only serve as references. We need materials that are based on the unique characteristics of the Chinese church and its needs. Representatives from all the seminaries will need to cooperate in the development of these materials and solve questions of editorial rights and copy right.

Qualified teachers are also needed. Nanjing Seminary has more than ten teachers for its theology classes, but many of these are growing older and have too much to do. Because they are stretched so thin, the quality of teaching has suffered and we have been unable to offer some necessary classes. Thus, we have to pay attention to training a future generation of seminary professors. Of course, we will have to regulate the number of professors in conjunction with the other seminaries.

We thank God that there are now ten seminaries in China. This year, we will be able to accommodate 500 students. Thus we can speed up the task of training pastoral workers and promote research into self-propagation.

Nanjing Seminary has a sisterly relationship with the other seminaries, and we should humbly seek to learn from their experiences. After all, we have the same mission and confront the same problems. Last summer at the Mo Gan Shan Conference on theological education, we discussed our problems and pledged future cooperation under the guidance of our two national bodies. We agreed then on some concrete measures to improve theological education and to advance the church in China. I pray that we can continue to build on this foundation by openly sharing our experiences and mutually supporting one other.

Collected Documents of The Fourth National Chinese Christian Conference,
p.100.
Translated by Craig Moran

Remarks at the Close of the Fortieth Anniversary Celebrations of Nanjing Union Theological Seminary

(Nanjing, November, 1992)

REV. CHEN ZEMIN SPEAKS *of the Seminary's fortieth anniversary not only as an occasion for nostalgia, but as a time of summing up and gathering strength for greater achievements in the future. He stresses the contribution of the older generation and the assurance of young people to take their place. In the words of Rev. Wang's poem: "God's mercy abounds, from generation to generation passed."*

The exciting activities to mark the Fortieth Anniversary of Nanjing Union Theological Seminary's founding are about to end. For the past three days, some three hundred alumni from over twenty provinces, municipalities and autonomous regions, representing the more than one thousand who have studied at their alma mater over the past forty years, have happily come together to celebrate the school's founding.

In this fine golden autumn, while the seminary grounds are ablaze with beautiful flowers and colorful lanterns, we have sat in the auditorium and classrooms cherishing fond memories of past activities there. On the dry lawn in front of the newly constructed dormitory and tall general purpose building, we have become reacquainted amid happy laughter. The passage of time is merciless, and so many of us have changed, grown greyer, more wrinkled. But as we take a closer look — that youthful vigor of ten years ago and more, the candid, friendly glance, the hearty laugh — is still familiar. We meet, clasp hands, exchange a few words, or gaze wordlessly. After lunch everyone gathers in front of the classroom building for photos, mementos of affection between teacher and student, and the friendship of classmates.

There are so many feelings to express, but too many people. There is so much to say, but too little time. Three days have flown by. There are so many old friends still to greet. So many hands yet to shake. So many inner feelings still to share. In brief, this big family filled with Christ's love, this gathering of sisters and brothers, aunts and uncles, and grandparents, will stay with us as a beautiful memory to savor forever.

Looking back to the past and anticipating the future, this meeting is highly significant. Under the Lord's guidance, it will push us forward, working together with one heart and mind to complete the tasks God has given us: to implement the "three well," that is, to make the church well-run, well-supported and well-propagated; to put all our effort and energies into further strengthening the church in China, and to have even greater faith, hope and vision.

Forty years ago ceremonies commemorating the opening of this Seminary were held here at MochouRoad (莫愁路) Church (formerly Hanzhong 汉中 Church). At the time over one hundred students and fifty-some faculty from East China's twelve seminaries attended the grand opening ceremony presided over by the late Y. T. Wu. LuoZhufeng (罗竹风), former Director of the East China Religious Affairs Bureau, attended on behalf of the Party and Government, giving his personal attention and guidance. Time passes and "places remain though people move on," but Mr.Luo's concern for us remains fresh and vivid in our memories.

Principal Ting, Vice-Principals Cheng Zhiyi (诚质怡) and Ding Yuzhang (丁玉璋) and numerous faculty joined together for that significant ceremony. That union marked a new beginning for theological education in the church in China. Later, in 1961, Yanjing Union (燕京协和) Theological Seminary also joined the new Seminary, becoming part of our family along with its more than ten faculty and eighty students. So in fact, today's anniversary includes two seminaries, Nanjing and Yanjing.

During the past forty years, Nanjing Union Theological Seminary has braved many trials and hardships, closing twice and reopening twice. But through the difficult years, along the bumpy paths, the Lord has been our Guide. Thus, we have passed through the valley of the shadow of death, coming once more to lie down beside still waters in green pastures, where our cup overflows.

During the past forty years, previous generations of teachers and alumni traversed this long and winding road. They made many contributions, completed their mission, and have returned to the Lord's arms. On the occasion of this fortieth anniversary celebration, we especially honor and cherish their memory.

We give profound thanks for Vice-Principals Cheng Zhiyi and Ding Yuzhang, and numerous faculty such as Prof. Zhao Hengxiang (赵鸿祥), Bishop T.K. Shen (沈子高), Jiang Yizhen (蒋翼振), T.C. Chao, and others who contributed much to this Seminary and now rest forever with the Lord.

Remarks at the Close of the Fortieth Anniversary Celebrations   57

We remember the many alumni who have gone before us, giving their all for the church in China, who now rest their labors in the Lord.

We especially thank God for Bishop Ting's leadership during the past forty years. With God's blessing, he has helped the seminary to continuously move forward. We are all pleased to see him with us today. His report on the development of the church in China has greatly inspired and helped us. We pray God will continue to give him good health and long life.

During these forty years, countless brothers and sisters have received the call, given themselves to the Lord and come to this Seminary to be trained. They have given their best years to work full time for the Lord's church. After forty years of trials and tribulation, they have enabled the church in China to reach today's level of restoration. We give thanks and praise God for all their contributions.

At the opening ceremony the day before yesterday, my heart was deeply moved as I looked out over an auditorium filled with alumni and many friends. Although I feel she has faced many difficult twists and turns and presently still faces many problems, the church in China has hope. During these forty years many alumni sitting before me have served the Lord with devotion. Although they have faced severe difficulties, they have not wavered from their earlier commitment, and have given their all for the development of the church in China. Truly, this is the source of our hope.

In recent years, the faculty has been replenished with new blood and new faces. This truly makes us feel a new generation has come forward, and in future the faculty will be greatly strengthened. This will also help train up many more young sisters and brothers, adding to the vast array of our alumni who will contribute to the development of the church in China.

Before I conclude, the Anniversary Preparatory Committee has asked me to express thanks to all. We are grateful to all levels of the National, Provincial and Municipal United Front Works Department and the Religious Affairs Bureau, who have shown their attention and care, even giving up their personal time to attend these events. Everyone has overcome assorted difficulties and come long distances to join this celebration. For this we are deeply grateful. Many colleagues from various Seminary departments and the students have done much and taken great pains to assure the success of these events. Thank you. We also want to thank the churches of Nanjing and colleagues from the Mochou Road Church for all their efforts. Thanks also to the comrades from several hostels for their assistance. Also, our heart-felt thanks to many colleagues, coworkers and friends.

You all have come a long distance, but for various reasons, our hospitality has not been fully satisfactory. You have not complained but rather have returned warm appreciation. We apologize for our shortcomings and thank you for your understanding.

During our reunion, we have heard a number of very good reports, especially this morning's very moving one from Bishop Ting, from which I am sure we have all gained a lot. In our plenary sessions and small groups as well, you all have offered extremely valuable comments and suggestions. I think this is very good. Following our celebrations I am sure our seminary colleagues will give serious consideration to these opinions, thereby enabling our work to improve further in future. This will also enable our alumni work to improve and I hope everyone will offer even more and better ideas to develop our alma mater.

When you were all students here, some were probably unhappy with this idea or that problem. Others probably argued until they were red in the face. But during this gathering everyone has met cordially, forgetting any past unhappiness. I believe people are all like that. In our work we may have faced this or that problem, and had various shortcomings, but following the Lord's guidance we've been able to develop the church in China. In love, we've been able to totally forget about these small matters and work hard together to develop Christ's church.

At this fortieth anniversary celebration, we have not only looked back and remembered the past, more importantly, we have looked at the present and towards the future. Forty years have passed. Before us we still have ten, twenty, thirty years — much time.

In 1952, before Nanjing Union Theological Seminary was founded, the old Nanjing Seminary already had a forty-year history. I am happy to have come to the Seminary in 1950. In 1951 I attended the old Seminary's fortieth anniversary celebrations. Another forty years have passed since 1952 and during these forty years the church in China has experienced the most change ever. Now we see that we have already entered the beautiful land of Canaan. The next forty years will be the time to build the Lord's temple. So the mission before us is even greater, even better.

Before Prof. Wang Weifan (汪维藩) and I made our visit abroad, Prof. Pengcuian (彭萃安) gave us an assignment. Since Prof. Wang is a poet, she hoped he would write a poem to commemorate the Seminary's fortieth anniversary during our trip, and that I would set it to music, so we could sing it together as a fortieth anniversary hymn. Unfortunately our trip was very busy and I did not complete my assignment.

On the plane, just two days before returning to Nanjing, Prof. Wang was suddenly moved by the Spirit and he wrote a few verses, but I didn't finish the music. During our time in Hong Kong we awakened very early one day and he helped me with it, but though I looked at the words and had a little inspiration from the Spirit, I still did not complete the music. I'm terribly sorry not to have completed my task, but Prof. Wang's poem is ready and I would like to read it as the conclusion to my remarks today:

> Beneath Purple Mountain, on the Yangtze's shores
> God's mercy overflowing, forty autumns, forty springs.
> Weak vessel that I am, God casts me not away,
> Returning now, I'm washed in grace anew.
> Streams of the Spirit billow, fragrant grasses spread
> God's mercy unfailing, generation upon generation.
> Beneath Purple Mountain, on the Yangtze's shores
> God's mercy abounds, from generation to generation passed.

Nanjing Theological Review, No. 18 (1/1993), p.36.
Translated by Ewing W. Carroll and Janice Wickeri.

Speech Given at Commencement Ceremony of Central Philippine University Iloilo City, Philippines

(March 26, 1995)

FIRST OF ALL I want to thank President Agustin Pulido for his kind invitation to bestow upon me the honor of being with you here this afternoon, to congratulate you at the Commencement Ceremony of about eight hundred graduating students of CPU. On behalf of China Christian Council and Nanjing Union Theological Seminary I bring greetings in the love of God and in the name of Christ, to you, Mr. President, and to all the faculty and staff members and students of CPU.

Eight years ago, in 1987, Bishop K. H. Ting, President of China Christian Council and Principal of Nanjing Union Theological Seminary, led a delegation of six people to visit CPU. They were deeply impressed by the warm welcome and kind hospitality you had shown them, and were moved by the heart-warming "Central Spirit." Now I come to follow up this tie of friendship. May I use the metaphor of a septuple ligature, a cord of seven strands, to further strengthen the brotherly relationship between us. In so doing, I wish to introduce to you briefly the history and present situation of the Chinese Protestant church, and try to make some comparison between us, so that we can learn from you on how you are promoting the Christian cause through education and active social involvement to serve the interests of the people in your country.

First and foremost, geographically and culturally, China and the Philippines are Pacific countries. We are "near neighbors" in the western part of the Pacific Ocean. As some futurologists forecast, in the 21st century the focus or center of gravity of world politics, economy, social development and spirituality will fall on the Pacific Basin, and more specifically, the Asian rim of the Basin. We are both facing the challenges of this historical task and responsibility. There is much that we can do and cooperate and learn from each other in finding ways for establishing a new world order, at least in this part of the world, in safeguarding justice, peace and the integrity of creation, both on the domestic and international arenas.

Secondly, there is also a historical blood relationship between our two peoples. About one thousand years ago merchants and seafarers from mainland China began to settle in the Philippine archipelagoes and resulted in a group of mixed Filipino-Chinese. These, together with later immigrants, now account for about ten percent of your entire population. Of course they have been assimilated culturally and become citizens of the Republic of Philippines, and are contributing in various ways to the building up of your Common Wealth. So we are, so to speak, neighbors plus relatives.

Thirdly, the peoples of both countries have gone through similar experiences in struggling against dominating foreign Powers and fighting for independence and democracy in the past centuries. We Chinese people know from our own bitter experiences how to value such struggles, and we admire your staunchness in fighting against foreign aggressors, first the Spaniards, then Americans and Japanese, and lately internal dictatorship under the martial law. We are comrades-in-arms in our endeavoring to build our countries respectively into modernized, well developed, independent, democratic and peace-loving countries according to the will of our peoples to promote and safeguard their interests and welfare.

Fourthly, both CPU and Nanjing Union Theological Seminary belong to a minority group of Protestant Christians in our countries. As I understand, in the Philippines as well as in China Catholicism and Protestantism are regarded customarily (but wrongly) as two different religions. I think this is due to the historical fact that Catholicism was introduced into the Philippines in the 16th century and had become a state religion for over three hundred years. The Philippines is known as "the only Catholic country in Asia." Over 85 percent of the population are Catholics. Protestantism came to your country in the wake of the Spanish-American war of 1898 and has a history of only little over one hundred years. Under American domination Protestant churches grew rapidly and now account for about 5 percent of the population. In China Catholic Christianity was introduced in the fourteenth century, and through a long history of zigzag and retarded development was reported to have only three million believers before 1949. Protestant Christianity was introduced by Robert Morrison in 1807. In the course of one and half century, as the World's largest Protestant "mission field," with the largest "investments" in funds and personnel, was able to reap only less than one million converts in 1949. Unfortunately, the introduction of Christianity, both Catholic and Protestant, in the nineteenth century had been accompanied by merchants, diplomats, opium, gunboats and unequal treatises. It was regarded by the Chinese people at large as foreign religions and met with hostility and resistance. It is only since 1979, fifteen years after the disastrous "cultural revolution," that one observes an unprecedented church growth. Now the estimated total of four million Catholics and nine million Protestants only amounts to a tiny one percent of the entire population. Now the question is: as minority religious groups, what can we Christians do for the modernization and social progress in our countries? I think there is much that Chinese Christians can learn from our Philippine fellow Christians in meeting this challenge.

Fifthly, with this brief historical analysis in mind, it is obvious that Christianity in the Philippines is playing a far more important and effective role in the modernization of your country, especially in education and social progress, than in China. I am not belittling the contributions of Christian universities and schools to the modernization of educational system, propagation of scientific knowledge, and cultivation and nurturing of Christian leaders. There were thirteen Christian (Protestant) universities and hundreds of middle schools in pre-liberation China (before 1950). In 1951 all the Christian educational institutions were taken over by the government and became state universities and schools. Part of the indemnities for the properties of the thirteen Christian universities is being used to support universities in Asia under the United Board for Christian Higher Education in Asia. CPU is one of the recipients of the United Board grants. I mention this because we may take it as one of the "invisible" fibers connecting our two institutions. But in China now there is no Christian higher education as such. There are thirteen Protestant theological seminaries. Nanjing Union Theological Seminary is the only one among them that is open to the whole country and has a four year undergraduate program and a three year graduate program. The purpose of theological education is mainly for the training of pastors and church leaders, not Christian education in the general sense. This is not to say that Christianity has no influence among the intellectual circles. The impact of the Christian gospel is mainly through the activities and witnesses of the ever growing churches, through personal contacts, and their social involvement. It is encouraging to notice that in the last decade there emerge a group of so-called "culture Christians." They are intellectuals in all walks of life who have become intensely interested in Christianity and yet are not ready to join the church as confessing members. 【I may cite as an example, "Christianity and Modernization"—International Consultation Marks Fresh Start For Academic Dialogue—see *Amity New Letter*, Spring 1995】 In this period of "Open-up and Reform" Christianity in China is facing many challenges and new opportunities. The influence of Christianity in China is exceeding its numerical-proportional strength.

Sixth, I greatly admire CPU for your achievements in gaining independence and national identity. Founded by American Baptist missionaries in 1907, you had installed the first Filipino president in 1966, with the entire university property turned over by the ABFMS to the Filipino corporation of CPU in 1968, and all members of the Board of Trustees and administrative officers of the University had become Filipinos in 1973. (I learn of this historic progress of achieving independence from a flyer President Pulido kindly sent me.) You still maintain a fraternal relationship with the Board of International Ministries, ABCUSA, but you are essentially a Filipino Christian university, of, by and for the Filipinos. I think this is of paramount significance against the historical background of over three centuries of foreign domination, first Spanish and then American. This is a new pattern of relationship that combines complete independence with international cooperation. I believe this is according to the long standing policy and aim of ABFMS, of initiating, establishing, developing, and eventually letting-go and letting-be. Incidentally, (please excuse my bringing in a little personal note), in my early years I happened to be brought up in American Baptist missionary schools and university in China, and have made many ABC missionary friends. Perhaps it is through this coincidence that I am honored with being invited to be here today. And I am grateful for the kind suggestion from the Baptist World Alliance and Asian Baptist Federation. May I take this as another invisible fiber of the sevenfold cord.

But what I want to stress here is the importance of achieving national selfhood with ecumenical consciousness. Let me share with you our experience of the Protestant church in China. As I said above China had been the largest of mission fields in the world. But the church in China was no more than just a tiny dot on the map of global ministries. Christianity in China was looked down upon as foreign religions and Christians had a hard time in getting rid of the stink of "running dogs of imperialism." It was through the Three-Self Movement, (a movement launched in the early fifties with the slogan of "self-administration, self-support and self propagation") that we were able to change gradually the image of foreign religion into one that is really Chinese and Christian. The emphasis is on building the church as a Chinese one, just as the churches in America American. The Chinese church must be of, by and for the Chinese people. There is no necessary anti-foreignness in it. Only when we have achieved this national identity that our Christian witnesses can become understandable and acceptable to the Chinese people, and become a member in the ecumenical household of God. Of course this requires a long process of hard work in education and experimentation. Another result or achievement is that we have conquered, to some extent, the evils of divisiveness and splitting effects of denominationalism and entered into a post-denominational stage, with the China Christian Council as a working ecclesiastical structure of a *uniting* Church of Christ in China. We realize we still have a long way to go. In this we need the understanding, encouragement and prayers from our Philippine Christian friends.

Now to my last point, the seventh strand: I have noticed from the flyer that CPU "is a Christian institute of higher learning where a well rounded program of education is offered under the influences that strengthen faith, build up character and promote scholarship and research. Its motto is *"Scientia et Fides"* ("Knowledge and Faith"). On the cover of the flyer is well-chosen text from Proverbs 2. Compared with the commonly accepted guidelines for theological education in China, namely, to cultivate and nurture all-round and balanced development in "spiritual formation, character building, intellectual and physical growth and social involvement," (in Chinese we use five characters 灵, 德, 智, 体, 群 to express the five areas of training), I see there is much in common between our objectives in our educative work. The common ground is well defined in your motto *Scientia et fides.* As theological seminaries we put spiritual formation first, which as many Chinese Christians understand, includes faith (*fides*). But this is not the kind of faith that merely means intellectual assent to or acceptance of certain credal statements, doctrines, or conventional rituals or practices, which may sometimes lead to dogmatic conservatism or religious fanaticism with *spirit* (*pneuma*) writ larg. It is a more dynamic religious conviction or commitment open to new insights, understanding and development. As to the relation of faith and intellect we follow the Anselmic teaching *fides quaerensintellectum* (faith seeking understanding). Here we come to the important understanding of *scientia* (knowledge). "Knowledge is Power," as Francis Bacon had well said. As an institution of higher learning, your motto rightly puts knowledge first. At a time when the whole world is crying for modernization, knowledge is the all important factor. But there are all sorts of knowledge. Knowledge needs sound faith as its guidance. Your quotation from Proverbs provides a fuller interpretation of the motto. Let me read six verses beginning from your quotation:

> For the Lord gives wisdom,
> from his mouth come
> knowledge and understanding;
> he stores up sound wisdom for the upright;
> he is a shield to those who walk blamelessly,
> guarding the paths of justice
> and preserving the way of his faithful ones.
> Then you will understand righteousness and justice

and equality, every good path;
for wisdom will come into your heart,
and knowledge will be pleasant to your soul;
prudence will watch over you;
and understanding will guard you.

Proverbs 2: 6–11

Let this be my congratulation and prayer for you who have assembled here at the Commencement Exercise of CPU today. May this mark a real commencement, a new beginning in your life and career, to contribute your wisdom, knowledge, skill and understanding, and in good faith, to the building and development of a strong and prosperous Philippines, and a new world order of justice and peace, and the integrity of creation. Our friendship, symbolized by this cord of seven stands, our, good wishes and blessings will be always with you.

Thank you.

Rev. Chen Zemin
Vice Principal
Professor of Theology
Nanjing Union Theological Seminary
Nanjing, P. R. China

The Heavenly Vision
(Nanjing, 1987)

Chen Zemin

"Wherefore, O King Agrippa, I was not disobedient to the heavenly vision" (Acts 26:19).

Acts 21–26 records the events following Paul's seizure by the Jews during the disturbance in the Temple in Jerusalem. Tried and imprisoned in Palestine for three years, he was finally brought before King Agrippa to plead his defence.

This section is one of the most vivid and reliable historical narratives in the Bible. It takes place about 58–60 AD, after Paul has experienced his vision on the Damascus Road which led him to believe in Christ and changed him from a zealous persecutor of Christians to a loyal and devoted witness who preached the gospel for thirty years. Ten years after this event he died a martyr in Rome. The author shows a superb talent for chronicling events: the account is detailed, accurate, suspenseful, descriptive narrative presented in five main sections of first-person self-defence and other historical material. With its complicated twists and turns and leaps in time, it makes a vivid and fascinating dramatization. If we read it straight through as a story, we have the feeling that we are actually there at the scene, witnessing with our own eyes those profoundly moving events. Therefore, it also makes an excellent resource for Biblical research. In this historical drama there are several moving scenes which build, one by one, to the climax:

1. Chapters 21–22: Paul is seized by the Jews who caused the disturbance in the Temple; he makes his defence before the Tribune and spectators.

2. Chapter 23: He stands trial before the Council, using the dispute over resurrection of the body between the Pharisees and Sadducees as a divisory tactic to extricate himself from a difficult situation.

3. Chapter 23 (second half): Forty Jews swear an oath and plot to ambush and kill Paul. Paul's nephew hears of the plot and goes to the army barracks to tell him. The tribune sends Paul to Caesarea to be handed over to the Governor, Felix. The author quotes the Tribune's letter concerning Paul here.

4. Chapter 24: The High Priest, Ananias, the elders, spokes-men and other Jews arrive in Caesarea to state their case against Paul. Paul stands trial before the Governor, Felix, and conducts his own defence.

    N.B.: Felix was a wily Governor. He neither charged Paul nor set him free, but procrastinated, hoping that Paul might offer him a bribe. Paul was imprisoned in Caesarea for two years and used this opportunity to preach and witness to Christ.

5. Chapter 25: Two years later Festus replaced Felix as Governor. The Jews took this opportunity to demand that Paul be sent to Jerusalem and prepared to murder him en route; however, Festus refused.

6. Paul is brought before the court in Caesarea. Festus can see that the accusations against Paul cannot be proven, yet at the same time he does not want to put the blame on the Jews. Paul speaks in his own defence and requests to be allowed to make his case before Caesar (since he was a Roman citizen). He would use legal tactics to defeat the Jewish plot.

7. The final scene: the climax: Agrippa II and his wife Bernice visit Festus, who brings the case before the King hoping that this will please the Jews. Festus therefore called a "tribunal" composed of himself, King Agrippa and Agrippa's wife, Bernice. To a packed public court the defendent, Paul, pleads his own case (it seems there was no prosecutor).

In Chapter 26 Paul makes his defence to the tribunal. It is a remarkable and brilliant piece of testimony. He not only pleads his own case but also witnesses and preaches the Gospel. This is the climax of the whole drama, and in it there is one outstanding sentence — the climax of the climax so to speak: "Wherefore, O King Agrippa, I was not disobedient to the heavenly vision."

If we want to understand the full weight of the meaning of these words, we must take the whole drama together.

What follows the scenes described above is a brilliant epilogue, also very vivid and endlessly fascinating (verses 24–39), after which we are suddenly brought up short, a device to keep the readers' attention engaged.

I seem to be contravening the principles of sermon organization in spending so much time introducing this account; perhaps trying to cover too much. This is because I am reluctant to leave out any of the circumstances of this story. In fact, my aim is to bring out more forcefully today's text:

"I was not disobedient to the heavenly vision."

From the time of his conversion until his martyrdom, Paul experienced many difficulties and setbacks, yet he stood firm and unswerving, resourceful and courageous, in order to proclaim the good news to the gentiles and to attack the narrow ethnocentrism of the Jewish people. Herein lies the crux of the matter, his motive: that he did not disobey "the heavenly vision."

The Bible is a vision-filled book, it is the word of God. It is both "revelation" and "inspiration." But a "vision" is more vivid, more palpable than language. For example, in Genesis, Jacob dreams of the ladder to heaven, and wrestles with the angel; and Joseph has a dream. In Exodus, Moses on Mount Horeb saw the burning bush and heard God speak. In the books of the prophets, Isaiah saw a vision in the temple and received the divine command (Isa. 6:); Ezekiel saw the four living beings and the four wheels, and also the dry bones come to life again (Ezek. 37:); "visions" are the major content of the book of Daniel; Joel Chapter Two prophesies about the last days when "I will pour out my spirit on all flesh; your sons and your daughters shall prophesy, your old men shall dream dreams, and your young men shall see visions. . ." Proverbs says "Where there is no prophecy the people cast off restraint" (29:18). In Acts 2, Peter quoted the scene at Pentecost from the Book of Joel to explain that the Holy Spirit coming down from heaven was the fulfilment of the words of the prophets, and also that visions are from God. In Revelation, John, on the island of Patmos, saw many visions which carried in them the final promises.

The Patriarchs, prophets and apostles all received the revelation and command of God, the talents bestowed by God, and also were touched by the Holy Spirit in visions.

The church of the Apostolic age was a church which relied on visions for guidance and power. Over the past 2000 years, the Christian Church has developed a mission to the whole world. We, part of the history of the church and its mission, have also seen many visions.

The word "vision" is rendered in Hebrew as *hazon*. Sometimes it can be translated as "revelation" but more accurately, the meaning is closer to "apparition" which has a direct connection to the act of seeing, often translated in English as "vision" and in modern Chinese, is rendered very well as "distant image." This, "distant image" points to a sight which appears before our eyes or to an experience. It also refers to the future, and includes the meaning "ideal" although it is even more concrete, more palpable and vivid than ordinary ideals; its origin, moreover, is God.

According to the principles of Biblical exegesis, a text may have several levels of meaning. If we use the analogy of the three-fold nature of man, that is, body, mind and spirit, Biblical texts can also be interpreted on several levels:

1. The lexical (body): an interpretation based on the surface meaning of the text — taking the writings at face value as an accurate depiction of historical fact.

2. The psychological or ethical (mind): the vision or dream is explained as a psychological state, an interpretation favored by modern psychology.

3. The spiritual interpretation (soul; sometimes known as the allegorical method, promoted by the Alexandrian school): Although such an interpretation easily becomes arbitrary, resulting in a subjective judgement and skewed interpretation, yet its value lies in indicating that the Bible is a book of the Spirit, inspired by God. Consequently, the spiritual exegetical method is highly important and cannot be denied, but it is a method which should be employed with great caution.

No matter whether we speak from the standpoint of 1., 2., or 3., above, "vision" is still that "distant image which comes from heaven," from the revelation of God. That persons, events and concrete situations differ, is not important. If each instance of "vision" in the Bible were to be translated, "distant image from heaven," the message would be clearer and more easily understood, and this would not detract in the slightest from the authoritative and prophetic nature of the Bible.

Whichever of the above meanings we apply, each of us who serves the Lord has, at sometime in our lives, seen visions and distant images, has had various spiritual experiences, has had ideals; some have been very clear and concrete, others could not be confined to a specific time or shape. In the Book of Joel it is written, "Your old men shall dream dreams, and your young men shall see visions." The Three-Self Patriotic Movement, too, is a heavenly vision seen by some progressive servants of God. Today, as we build up the new Chinese church in this very important time, as we meet each challenge and test, we must ask ourselves: "Have we strayed from that heavenly vision?" You have come to theological college because you have seen some distant vision from heaven. You have returned from local churches all over the country for the start of a new semester. In your churches you have seen many things, some greatly inspiring, some perhaps arousing misgivings, as though we, like Paul, are facing the tribunal in the public court. But can we bring to mind at this time the loving heart and resolution we felt when we heard the divine call? Can we say "We have not set aside the distant image from heaven?"

In days to come, no matter whether it be in private meditation, during class, worship or church work, wherever we come into contact with other people, I hope we will remember that "heavenly vision."

O Lord, help us that we may be able to rely always on that "heavenly vision." Guide us, strengthen our resolve, invigorate us, that following in Paul's footsteps, we may go courageously forward. Enable us, in any place, at any time, to witness to the Gospel and be loyal servants of God with unswerving faithfulness. Amen.

Nanjing Theological Review, Nos. 6 and 7 (September, 1987), p.50. translated by Jill Hughes

Pastor and Priest[1]
(Nanjing, 28 April, 1991)

CHEN ZEMIN

Text: 1Pet. 5:1-4

THE APOSTLE PETER WRITES in First Peter, "Now as an elder myself and a witness of the sufferings of Christ, as well as one who shares in the glory to be revealed, I exhort the elders among you to tend the flock of God that is in your charge, exercising the oversight, not under compulsion but willingly, as God would have you do it — not for sordid gain but eagerly. Do not lord it over those in your charge, but be examples to the flock. And when the chief shepherd appears, you will win the crown of glory that never fades away." In the same letter he also says, "You are a chosen race, a royal priesthood, a holy nation, God's own people, in order that you may proclaim the mighty acts of him who called you out of darkness into his marvelous light."

Today, the Jiangsu Three-Self Association and the Jiangsu Christian Council are holding a solemn ceremony to ordain six brothers as ministers. What we call "the ministry" in our churches is based on the teaching of the Bible as well as on church tradition. In the churches, we ordain selected people and appoint them to propagate the gospel well, to run the church well, and to fully commit themselves to the task of caring for the believers and serving God. In the history of Christianity, there are, roughly speaking, two different systems of ministries. One has three ranks which include bishops, pastors and deacons. For "bishop," the Bible sometimes uses "overseer;" a "pastor" is a local church leader and can also be called "father" or "priest;" "deacons" see to the management of church affairs. Even now, the Catholic Church and the Orthodox churches have preserved this ministerial

---

1. Sermon preached at an ordination service held by the Jiangsu Christian Council in St. Paul's Church, Nanjing, 28 April, 1991.

structure. The other type consists of only two ranks: pastors and deacons, with elders and overseers sharing the same rank with pastors.

Most biblical scholars who have examined the book of Acts and the letters of Sts. Paul and Peter are convinced that the New Testament churches had only two ministries, namely elders and deacons, and that the titles of "overseers," "elders" and "pastors" referred to the same ministry.

As it is recorded in Acts 20:17; 28, Paul "sent a message from Miletus to Ephesus, asking the elders of the church to meet him." And when they met, he said to them: "Keep watch over yourselves and over all the flock, of which the Holy Spirit has made you overseers, to shepherd the church of God . . ." And in 1Pet. 5:1–4 (which we have just heard) it says, "As an elder myself, I exhort the elders among you to tend the flock of God that is in your charge. . ." In Tit. 1:5, 7 Paul writes, "I directed you to appoint elders in every town," and, in the same context, "a bishop is God's steward . . ."

These passages, together with many others, clearly identify elders as overseers and bishops and describe their task as tending the sheep, thereby characterizing them also as pastors. In the New Testament, the terms "pastor," "bishop," and "elder" all refer to the same ministry. It was not until the third century that the church developed the ministry of bishop ranking higher than pastors and elders. As a result, the Catholic Church and the Orthodox churches have a three-rank system. In our Protestant churches in China, we have bishops as well, but they are different from Catholic and Orthodox bishops. Our bishops have a special call and spiritual standing, they enjoy high spiritual authority and great prestige among the believers. But they have no diocese, and are therefore for all practical purposes pastors, with no extra rank in the hierarchy of ministries.

A conceptual difference between elders and pastors emerged only with the reformation in the sixteenth century. Based on 1Tim. 5:17, Calvin distinguished between elders "who rule well" and elders "who labor in preaching and teaching." Consequently, the Presbyterian churches have special elders for administration and leadership, mostly appointed by ordinary believers, but usually not in full-time positions. Only their elders who "labor in preaching and teaching" are actual pastors.

In the Bible, the term "pastor" is used only once. This is in Eph. 4:11, where a distinction is made between "pastors" and "teachers." In the original language, the expressions "pastor," "tending the sheep," and "shepherd" are all derived from the same root word. In the Old and New Testaments, this form of address appears more than a hundred times, in reference to the shepherd who tends the Lord's flocks. This same word is behind our term "pastor," which is therefore a fully appropriate and biblically based title.

Our Protestant churches in China have no unified ministerial system yet. Some local churches have established even more ministries; besides pastors, elders and deacons they have evangelists and teachers. Some have no pastors but only elders, while differentiating between elders and pastors, with "elders" referring to those who rule and administer a church. Deacons are usually those who assist pastors or elders in handling the church's finances and other business matters. All in all there are no strict and unified regulations. We follow the principle of mutual respect and wait for the Holy Spirit to guide us towards greater unity in the future.

According to the Bible, the special task of a pastor is the tending of God's flock. This implies that a pastor follows God's will in "looking after" the believers and acts as their "overseer." These terms connote concern and love, as well as leadership and organizing work. Our word "overseer" is reminiscent of a superior person exercising control over others, as for instance a government official does. But I don't think this is meant in the original. The point is that a pastor must follow the will of God and apply God's guidance and love as his standard. He cannot simply follow his own personal wishes and impose them on the believers. Most important, however, is the expression "tending the flock;" this is a very suitable metaphor. A shepherd, in caring for his sheep, first of all feeds them, which means supplying them with spiritual food. He also tends them, protects and consoles them, gives them medical care and all forms of guidance. One who is ordained must also be a good leader to the believers, just as Jesus is our "chief shepherd" or as Yahweh is our shepherd.

Such a heavy responsibility shall be exercised "not under compulsion but willingly." What is meant here, according to the original, is a committed and unreserved enthusiasm. Also, it shall be done "not for sordid gain but eagerly." Becoming a pastor means to respond to a call from God, to happily say: "Here I am, use me!" Who would fuss about any disadvantages emerging from such a self-sacrificing commitment? Who would care about personal ambitions like career, reputation or financial reward? St. Paul writes in 2 Cor. 6: "We work together with God and do not accept his grace in vain; in every way we have commended ourselves as servants of God." "I disregard honor and dishonor, ill repute and good repute; I am unknown and yet well known; dying, and yet alive; punished, and yet not killed; sorrowful, yet always rejoicing; poor, yet making many rich; I have nothing, and yet possess everything." Such inner freedom and greatness belongs to an abundant life.

A pastor must not strive for power. "Do not lord it over those in your charge, but be examples of the flock." The power held by pastors is entrusted to them by God, they must not abuse it. Much may be entrusted to them: the flock of believers, all church property, administrative leadership, teaching authority, and so forth, yet they cannot behave like dictators, although some church leaders unfortunately do make a fetish of their power. Peter says: "Be examples to the flock!" The power of an example is most persuasive: it has the authority to sincerely convince others. A pastor must therefore, as St. Paul says in 1Tim. 3: "be above reproach, be temperate, sensible, respectable, an apt teacher . . . a worker who is reliable before God and has no need to be ashamed, rightly explaining the word of truth." Pastors must make themselves examples and influence others through virtue.

So far I have been talking about the biblical demands on a pastor as a shepherd. But apart from that, a pastor is also a priest. As priest, he represents the community of believers when he brings the offering to God, he intercedes, presides over the worship and administers the sacraments. As time is limited, let me simply make a few points:

1. (1) From the entire Old Testament to the four Gospels and the book of Acts in the New Testament, the word for "priest" occurs more than three hundred times. In most cases it refers to religious professionals in Israel or other nations who are assigned to represent the believers in the communication between God and humans. In Israel, they are descendants of Aaron and Zadok or Levites. They hold an almost hereditary office, though one should still see it as a voluntary commitment. By the time of Jesus, the priests, just like the Pharisees, clung so obstinately to the letter of the law, that they missed the spirit of it and became an obstacle for the direct communication between God and people. Hence they faced condemnation from Jesus.

(2) When the Catholic and Orthodox churches developed their three level ministerial hierarchy, priests became a privileged class monopolizing divine power and separating God and the masses of believers.

(3) Only much later, during the Reformation did Martin Luther propagate the priesthood of all believers. As a result, the concept of priesthood was blunted in the Protestant churches. Some Christians are even hostile to it. However, what Jesus and Martin Luther actually opposed was only the abuse and misunderstanding of priesthood. They never denied that a pastor can represent the believers and has the special commission and capacity to guide the believers in worship and in their sacramental dedication to God.

(4) Our great pastor and chief shepherd Jesus Christ holds a threefold office: In one person he is king, prophet and priest. The book of Hebrews refers to Jesus as priest or High Priest over a dozen times. According to the order of Melchizedek, he puts himself in the place of all believers, and gives himself up to God, atoning for our sins with his own precious blood. Just like our great shepherd, an ordained pastor holds the office and capacity of a

priest. The liturgical texts we are using in our ceremony today frequently use the word "priest", and so it is clear that a pastor is also a priest.

2. First Peter 2:9 also makes reference to priesthood at one point: "You are a chosen race, a royal priesthood, a holy nation, God's own people, in order that you may proclaim the mighty acts of him who called you out of darkness into his marvelous light." Included in the "priesthood" mentioned here are all believers who have received baptism, entered the church and accepted salvation. Those who are addressed by Peter as priests are clearly named at the beginning of the letter (1 Pet. 1:1–2): "the exiles of the Dispersion in many places, who have been chosen and destined by God the Father and sanctified by the Spirit to be obedient to Jesus Christ and to be sprinkled with his blood." Biblical scholars tell us that these phrases refer to the entire body of believers. The same is true for the worship of the church; it is a collective dedication. In the New Testament churches, the title of a priest is never applied to overseers, elders or pastors as individuals.

In the Christian teaching, the word "priest" therefore has a fourfold implication: It refers first to Jesus (Hebrews), secondly to the community of believers (Peter), thirdly to individuals ordained as pastors (church tradition), and finally to every single believer (Martin Luther). Martin Luther, however, never denied the priestly function of a pastoral ministry, especially not where the administration of the sacraments is concerned.

These four implications do not actually contradict each other, but are rather mutually related and complementary. The priestly function of a pastor is first of all derived from the atonement achieved for us by Christ, the High Priest (with Christ's priesthood having nothing in common with that of the priests in the Old Testament). Also, the priestly function of a pastor as a chosen, ordained and spiritually empowered representative of the believers is strongly related to a Christian community and can only be understood in this context. If he leaves the church, he loses this capacity. As an individual believer he would still be a priest in Martin Luther's sense, but no longer in the sense of a representative. In order to be a priest in the latter sense, a pastor needs to be ordained in a church if he or she is to be qualified to represent the church and its members. To be ordained means that one recognizes before the assembly, that authority comes from Jesus Christ and expresses the power of the Holy Spirit. This understanding is based on the Bible and is also very important in theology.

Finally, let me once again cite the apostle Peter: "You have been chosen and destined by God the father and sanctified by the Spirit to be obedient to Jesus Christ and to be sprinkled with his blood, to be "a royal priesthood,. . .to tend the flock of God that is in your charge . . .willingly . . .and eagerly, . . . to be examples to the flock. . .to proclaim the mighty acts of him who called you out of darkness into his marvelous light. . ...And when the chief shepherd appears, you will win the crown of glory that never fades away."

Nanjing Theological Review, No. 14/15 (1–2, 1991), p.132.
Translated by Gotthard Oblau.

Convocation Address
Columbia Theological Seminary
(September 11, 1996)
Pastors and Teachers
Ephesians 4:11–13

I FEEL GREATLY PRIVILEGED and honored to be invited to be with you this morning at this important occasion of convocation of Columbia Theological Seminary. I want to avail myself of this opportunity, on behalf of China Christian Council and the faculty and students in Nanjing Union Theological Seminary in China, to bring you greetings and congregations.

My text for this morning is prompted by three questions in the Book of Judges. In the 17thand 18th chapters of Judges we find a very interesting episode about a certain man whose name was Micah. There are no fewer than six Micahs in the Old Testament. This was not the canonical prophet Micah of the eighth century. He was just anobody living in the hill country of Ephraim. He was a very religious person. He believed in Jehovah, but was also practicing idolatry. He had an idol made of silver that he had stolen from his mother, set up a shrine, and installed one of his sons to be his priest. But he was not quite satisfied with this because his family was not of the tribe of Levites. It was believed that Levites would make good priests. It happened that a certain young Levite was wondering about looking for a job and a place to live. Accidentally Micah hired this young man to be his family priest, and gave him a reasonable salary and subsistence. We do not know whether this young man had any special training as a professional religious worker. Perhaps there was no organized theological education at that time. Anyway he seemed to be happy with his work and pay. Then one day five valiant men were sent by the tribe of the Danites to prowl the land and to explore it, seeking for some place where they could make their territory. When they came to the hill country of Ephraim, to the house of Micah, they incidentally met the young priest. They recognized in his voice as a Levite. Perhaps he spoke with a peculiar ethnic or local accent, or possibly it was his artificial priestly tone or manners that belied (or betrayed) his identity. The five Danites were surprised, and put to the young priest the following three questions: "Who brought you here? What are you doing here? What is your business here?" In the Chinese Bible the last question is translated as "What have you gained here?," which may be understood as "what have you learned here?" or "what do you expect to learn here?" These are three pertinent questions often posed before seminarians in China. The first question seems rather objective and matter-of-fact that requires not much self-examination for the answer. But if we change the "who" into "what": as "what brought you here?," then these three questions are very important indeed for al theological students to ponder throughout the whole course of their seminary lives. They remind me of a Chinese proverb attributed to Zhengzhi (曾子), the closest disciple of Confucius: "I examine myself every day with three questions: Have I been unfaithful to my commitment? Have I been untruthful in dealing with my friends? Have I not learned what is taught?"[1]

I am not going to dwell on the story, nor on the three questions. It is the answers to them that deserve our attention this morning. The answers are not far to be found. When I first came to Columbia Theological Seminary in March I asked President Oldenburg, "Is there a motto for the seminary?" "Yes," he said, "we have two words in Greek on our seminary seal." I looked up in your *Catalogue* and found the two words: "*poimenoskaididaskalous*," taken from Ephesians 4:11–13. This is our text today. Let me read the passage in full:

"*The gifts he gave were that some would be apostles, some prophets, some evangelist, some <u>pastors and teachers</u>, to equip the saints for the work of ministry, for building up the body of Christ, until all of us come to the unity of the faith and of the knowledge of the Son of God, to maturity, to the measure of the full stature of Christ.*"

To single out *pastors* and *teachers* does not mean to belittle the gifts of apostles, prophets and evangelists. There is some overlapping in these gifts. Apostles are supposed to be sent with authority, as the word originally implies. Prophecy, if we take it to mean *speaking forth for* or *on behalf* of God, is included in the office of the pastors and teachers. If we think of it as foretelling about the future, then it may not be the chief purpose of theological training, if it can be trained at all. As to evangelism, telling the good news, it is also among the chief functions of the pastor. So as I understand it, your motto underlines the importance of pastors and teachers, not to the exclusion of other gifts. And the final aim is "to equip the saints, (or

---

1. Chinese text, Confucian Analect 1: "吾日三省吾身-为人谋而不忠乎？与朋友交而不信乎？传不习乎？"-《论语-学而》

seminarians) for the work of *ministry*, for building up the body of Christ, until all of us come to the unity of the *faith* and of the *knowledge* of the Son of God, to maturity, to the measure of the full stature of Christ."

In essence, this is the same as what we have in the *Statement of Commission* of the Committee on Theological Education in China. The purpose of the thirteen existing theological colleges in China is to train first of all ministers or pastors, and, not less important and urgent, to train theological teachers and Christian educators. About eighty percent of over one thousand five hundred graduates from these thirteen schools are serving as preachers or ministers in the churches, and over eighty graduates from the Nanjing Seminary are teaching in all these theological schools. They are so badly needed in the rapidly growing churches in China. The total number of Protestant Christians is conservatively estimated as over fifteen million. There are about ten thousand "churches" and thirty thousand "meeting points." But there are only a little over two thousand ordained ministers. Many congregations have lay leaders who do not have any theological training to speak of, and many flocks are without shepherds. "The harvest is plentiful, but the laborers are few." The dangers of disorders, deviations and aberrations are real and grave indeed. Hence the urgency and importance of theological education in China: to train more pastors to meet the needs of the churches, and at the same time to rain more qualified teachers for the theological schools, which will in turn produce more and better-equipped pastors to serve the churches in more efficient and better ways. In this way the Church as a whole may steadily grow quantitatively and improve qualitatively in a "benign circle," so to speak.

But to many people there often seems to exist some contrasting difference and even tension between pastors and theological teachers and in their training. The work of pastors is thought to be more practical in nature, in seeking to meet the spiritual and practical needs of church members, in emphasizing on "spiritual formation," which, in the Chinese context, is mainly of a pietistic and revivalist type that appeals more to the emotions and the heart than the mind. A good pastor often means one who can preach long and "moving" sermons, one who is able to "confirm and strengthen the faith" of believers, who are predominantly fundamentalist and conservative in their belief. (Only recently have some preachers sensed that "fundamentalist and conservative" may convey a derogatory nuance, and are happy to use the more fashionable term "Evangelical" instead.) On the contrast, theological teachers are often thought of as those who put knowledge above faith, who may excel in academic studies but are weak or faltering in their faith. The aftermath of the "fundamentalist-modernist controversy" in America in the early decades of this century seems to be still lingering in China now. Many young people are warned against the dangers of being led astray in their faith in the seminaries. The conflict between faith and knowledge, the contrasts between Jerusalem and Athens, the church and the academy, practical ministry and intellectual pursuit, bearing witness and critical reflection, and the ghost of *Credo quia absurdum est* are still breeding mutual distrust and disdain among pastors and teachers. How is it possible that the seminary can train both types of Christian leaders together at the same time and in a same campus—to equip them "for the work of ministry, for building up the body of Christ, until all of us come to the unity of the faith and of the knowledge of the Son of God, to maturity, to the measure of the full stature of Christ"?

This is why and how I, as a theological educator from China, and perhaps for the same reason many of you, who, having answered to the call of the Church, and committed yourselves to the work of ministry, have come to Columbia Theological Seminary. Little as I dare to pretend to say I have known your seminary, I am deeply impressed, with admiration, by the wonderful work you have been doing in integrating the training for these two types of church leaders under the one same goal of "building up the body of Christ." There may be different emphases in the various programs leading to two types of degrees. There may be some tension between the two. But as they are properly coordinated, the tension can be resolved into a dynamic, through some sort of *entelecheia*. I am thinking of the tenets of one neo-Confucian scholar Wang Yangming (王阳明) of the sixteenth century, who advocated the unity of knowledge and action (知行合一). "Knowledge is the beginning of action and action is the completion of knowledge." We begin with action from faith, a faith seeking understanding (*fides quaerensintellectum*), and use theological knowledge to serve the church in actual ministry, and so forth in an upward spiral way to achieve advancements both in action and knowledge, "until all of use come to the unity of the faith and of the knowledge of the Son of God, to maturity, to the measure of the full stature of Christ."

We are grateful that your seminary has established a cooperative exchange program with our Seminary in Nanjing. I need not go into the details of our past cooperative actions. We hope and pray that such sororal relationship be continued and further developed. We anticipate with hearty welcomes the visit of the fourth delegation from CTS to Nanjing next year, under the leadership of Dean James Hudnut-Beumler, to further strengthen the cooperation and mutual understanding, and to help NTS in integrating faith and knowledge in our work for the service of the church.

Thank you for your attention.

Chen Zemin
Nanjing Union Theological Seminary

Living is Christ and Dying is Gain
(Nanjing, September 29, 2000)

Chen Zemin

My text for this memorial service for our colleague, LuoZhenfang (骆振芳), is taken from Philippians 1:21. Paul included in his letters many teachings on life and death, and the Christian understanding of the meaning and value of life. The attitude one should have in the face of death is summed up in the well known verse which is my title for today. We can say this is Paul's guideline for the Christian life and death.

Paul wrote this letter while imprisoned in Rome, awaiting judgment. There were two possibilities before him: to be exonerated and released, able to continue to be present to the churches in every place and the brothers and sisters there, serving the church and spreading the gospel of Christ; or to be sentenced to death, which was his fate at the end of his life. As he faced life and death, he had the feeling of being between a rock and a hard place, with no control over the choice. "It is my eager expectation and hope that I will not be put to shame in any way, but that by my speaking with all boldness, Christ will be exalted now as always in my body, whether by life or by death." (v. 20) He went on to say, "For to me, living is Christ and dying is gain." (v. 21) On the face of it, this sounds a bit arrogant, putting oneself on a par with Christ. "Death is gain" is also very hard to understand. Most people see death as the completion of human life and work, as the end: how can there be gain?

In the original, these words are full of passion and the sentence is not very complete grammatically. The verb we use in Chinese is not in the original. A direct translation from the original would be "for me, living . . . Christ, dying . . . gain." To make the meaning clearer in Chinese, we add verbs. (It is customary in Chinese at times to omit the verb as well, to give more force to the sentence.)

Since seeing Christ on the road to Damascus, being called, and gaining new life, we could say that for Paul, living *was* Christ. Barclay says that

Christ was indeed the beginning, continuation and end of Paul's life; its encouragement and the source of its power. We can say that Paul's living was all for Christ, to show forth Christ and so we can say, "living is Christ." We are not Paul, and would not dare to say this, but we should take Paul as our model, learn from him, and strive to make our lives, our all, for Christ, learn from Christ, witness to Christ, and preach Christ. At the least, we should say, "living is for Christ."

Human life is a gift from God. Psalm 90, which we just heard read, tells us that though life is short, like a dream or a breath in comparison to the eternity of God, those who believe in Christ should learn well to number their days. We are told to have a heart of wisdom, to be satisfied with God's steadfast love, to rejoice and be glad all our days. A person's life is usually seventy years; "or perhaps eighty, if we are strong." Rev. LuoZhenfang was blessed by God with eighty years. He began to study theology in 1946, graduating from seminary in 1949. He served the church seven years, then joined the seminary, teaching, and doing research and pastoral work for forty-four years. Of his eighty years, fifty were given in the Lord's service. He worked conscientiously right up until the end. I won't forget his teaching and research (in linguistics), his translation of James D.G. Dunn's *Unity and Diversity in the New Testament*. He supported the TSPM through its fifty years, taking an active part in it, and bearing beautiful witness to Christ in Chinese church and society. We can say that he "lived for Christ, that all was for Christ." He embodied the teaching "living is Christ."

"Death is gain." If we apply common knowledge, these words are very hard to understand. Death is a sad thing. Why say it is gain?

1) Human life and death are in the hands of God, and are according to God's will. We cannot prolong our lives by a single moment. Medicine has advanced to reduce suffering and push back the moment of death, but in the end, people do die. How to treat death is an important part of how we treat life.

2) What happens when people die? There is no precise answer, but several hypotheses:

   - It is the end of everything, everything is extinguished. If this is so, there is not much meaning in human life. This is not Christian faith or teaching.

   - We go immediately up to heaven, or down to hall. We gain reward or retribution for our lives. This is what many Christians and worldly people think, but there is no evidence for it.

- We fall asleep, waiting for the final resurrection and judgment. Many Christians believe this, and there is some biblical evidence for it. Paul sometimes appears to believe this.
- We go to some "in-between" place and time, and continue to wait and train. This is the Catholic purgatory.
- Paul says, "my desire is to depart and be with Christ, for that is far better." (v.23) "To be with Christ," to be with other Christians who have died. This is a "spiritual fellowship."
- Revelation 14:13, "...blessed are the dead who from now on die in the Lord . . . they will rest from their labors, for their deeds follow them."

"Blessed," "rest from their labors,"—cast off the weakness of the flesh, the suffering, all the cares of the world . . ., and be with Christ. After death we continue to serve the Lord in some fashion and to live in some way forever. "Living is Christ (or, for Christ) and death is gain." It is without fear or trembling, to continue in the spiritual realm that work which went unfinished in life, with Christ and the other Christians, to enjoy the complete sweetness of spiritual fellowship. So it is called "far better." We believe that Rev. LuoZhenfang is now in such a place. We, the living, if we attain "living for Christ" will one day leave this world and be together with all the saints, continuing to serve the Lord. This is Paul's view of life and death, and the view of us Christians.

Finally, Rev. Luo left us just as we were about to celebrate the 50th anniversary of the Three-Self Movement. He had been part of the Three-Self Movement for the whole 50 years. In the commemorative photo album published for the anniversary were many photos of those from the older generation who have gone before us, who contributed to the Chinese church and the Three-Self Movement. They did not make it to the celebrations either, but we remembered them. Now Rev. Luo is part of their glorious ranks, serving with them in heaven. We the living must urge ourselves on, so that in the new century, in the new phase of the Chinese church that we have already entered, we continue to progress and to engage in theological reconstruction. As teachers, we should strive to complete Rev. Luo's unfinished work; as students, we should study hard, and realize his hopes, so that we the living live for Christ, fulfilling this glorious task. One day, we the living will follow them, but the Chinese church will, with God's blessing and under God's leading, continue to build itself up even better.

May God bless these God's words. Amen

Nanjing Theological Review, 4 (2000): 66–67.
Chen Zemin is Vice-Principal of Nanjing Seminary.

Sermon

St. Paul's Church, 2005 April 10.
To Unite All in Christ, that We May Become One (同归于一) Text: Eph. 1: 9–10; 4:13

"With all wisdom and insight he has made known to us the mystery of his will, according to his good pleasure that he set forth in Christ, to gather all things in him, things in heaven and things on earth." (同归于一)

(EPH.1:9–10)

"Until all of us come to the unity of the faith and of the knowledge of the Son of God, to maturity, to the measure of the full stature of Christ." (同归于一)

(EPH. 4:13)

[INTRODUCTORY GREETING]

IT IS MY PRIVILEGE and pleasure to be worshipping with you this morning. St. Paul's is "my old church." I had the honor of being the pastor of this church since its reopening in 1985, for a period of ten years, until I retired from the office in 1995. We thank God that under His guiding and blessing the work and ministry of St. Paul's has developed immensely in the last twenty years. The congregation has increased from about four hundred at the beginning of reopening into today's constituency of over three thousand, with a vibrant program of many activities. For instance, this Sunday Morning Service in English is a new adventure that I had never had the courage and ambition to think or try. As I have heard, and as I see it now, this is a program very much welcome by intellectuals and educated church members, and in God's good pleasure will attract more and more people to worship here. I am sure it will prosper and add to His glory for a long time in the future.

[THE SERMON]

The topic of my sermon this morning is "To Unite All in Christ, that We May Become One," or in Chinese, "同归于一." It is a sermon that I had preached in America, about nine years ago, when I was invited to attend a Global Mission Conference. The focus for the conference was on the church in China. The planning committee had chosen Ephesians for the Bible study sessions. At the end of the Conference I was asked to preach at the Auditorium of the Conference Center, and I tried to share our experience in Bible study in China to our American friends. The text of the sermon was taken from Ephesus 1:9–10, and 4:13.

[I] I began my preparation by first studying the Epistle in Chinese, and then compared with several English versions with the help of some commentaries. I used the Chinese Union version of 1919, which has been accepted as the "standard" version and used by almost all Chinese Christians. One expression in four Chinese 同归于一 appearing two times in the Epistle struck my eyes standing out conspicuously. The translator of the Chinese Bible in 1919 chose to use this phrase to express the idea of "[all] returning into one" in a way that is easy to understand to every reader. It has an allusion to one of the Chinese Confucian tenets of "天下大同" (Universal harmony), first recorded in the *Book of Rites*, (《礼记-礼运篇》 c. 300 B.C.), and reiterated and developed by the reformist-scholar Kang You-wei (康有为 in his《大同书》1897), and then by Dr. Sun Yet-sen, the founder of Republic of China (1924). I have been pondering on this idea of "coming into one" as a theological theme in Bible study. By comparing with various English versions, I noticed that this particular Chinese expression, found only in the Epistle to the Ephesians, is used to convey two different aspects or dimensions of "unity" in the Pauline teaching on the mission of the church.

[II] The first occurrence of this Chinese phrase 同归于一 is in 1:10, used to translate the Greek word *anakephalaiothasthai*. This is an infinitive meaning "to sum up", as in arithmetic or in rhetoric. In the English Bible it is translated in a number of ways: "to gather together in one" (AV), "to unite" (RSV), and "to gather up" (NRSV).

In the Anchor Bible Markus Barth suggests another, as "to be comprehended under one head" (Vol.34, p.89). To me it is still hard to comprehend.

Many exegetes think it is difficult to bring out the full force of this verb by translation. In the second century the Greek church father Irenaeus of Lyon had elaborated this verse theologically and developed a "theory of recapitulation" (from *capitulatio*, which is a literal translation in Latin), and imbued this difficult word with rich Christological and soteriological contents. It comprises both the restoration of fallen humanity to communion with God (reconciliation) and the consummation and completion of the entire salvation history, until according to God's good pleasure and plan in the fullness of time, all the creation, including all things in heaven and things on earth, are "summed up in unity with Christ as the head." Perhaps this is what Teilhard, de Chardin calls the **Omegas Point**! This is how some Christians in China, including those we call "culture Christians," have been trying to understand by the expression 同归于一 in this passage. I propose to translate it more literally in Chinese as 复归于元首 (to return to the prime head). The Chinese character 元, like the English "prime," expresses the ideas "the chief" and "the original." Both are compatible and suitable to translate the meaning of *anakephalaiothasthai*. [*ana* means again, *kephalaios* means head, or chief, or the first or original, and *-iothasthai* is a grammatical construction to express a verb in the infinitive.] Understood in this way, it helps us to see, tiny and mean and weak and ignorant as we are, somehow there is meaning and purpose in the whole universe and in the history of humankind, and that we ultimately are to be summed up and subsumed under the prime head. To take the whole divine cosmic unfolding of creation, redemption, sanctification and final consummation as according to the wise counsel and plan of God gives **meaning** to our own lives. That there is a divine *telos*, an end and purpose, in the whole universe, and that we all have a part to play in the fulfilling of this final end in Christ, gives **value** to our lives. "In Christ we have also obtained an inheritance." (同得基业 v.11) It gives us a sense of responsibility, honor and hope. Although our lives are short and trivial, we will be gathered up into One in Christ, cosmologically and eschatologically.[1]

[III] This same phrase 同归于一 appears again in 4:13 in a different context, and refers to a unity of a different order, but is closely connected with the previous one. It is about the unity of the church. According to the theology of Ephesians, the divine melodrama (传奇剧) described in the first two chapters is to be unfolded and realized in Christ, embodied in the Church, as is continued and developed in the following chapters (chs. 3–6). One American writer has explicated this theme under four theses: (1) the mission of the church as God's mission, (2) the church as the goal of the

---

1. 从宇宙论和从末世论的角度, 在基督里"同归于一"

mission (3) the church as the instrument of the mission, and (4) the eschatological fulfillment of the mission. As the final fulfillment of the mission, or the plan of God, is to "gather all things into one," the church, as the goal and instrument of the mission, **must also be one**.

From the Apostolic Age in the first century the church had begun to "split", not just by geographical dispersion, but unfortunately by doctrinal and practical or constitutional differences. Soon cultural and socio-political factors came in and intensified and aggravated the division. It is a scandal that now the *Church Universal* (which, means "the one whole church") is divided into an increasing number of churches, denominations, sect, cults, etc., in defiance of the Biblical commandment that the church should become one. In the Intercessory Prayer Christ prays "that they may all be one" (Jn. 17:20–21); and Paul had admonished us **to become one** repeatedly in this Epistle. In 3:6, which the English translation reads "the Gentiles have become *fellow heirs, members of the same body, and sharers in the promise* in Christ Jesus through the gospel." The Chinese version brings out the force in the original Greek by thrice repeating the adverb 同[2]. It is in this context that in 4:3–6, the second 同归于一 is used to sum up "the gifts given to equip the saints for the work of ministry, for building up the body of Christ." (从教会论的角度, 同归于一)

[IV] This is not the time to go into the past history of the divided churches in China, and how we have been striving to achieve unity through the present so-called "post-denominational stage." Many foreign visitors and observers have expressed, in guarded tones and perhaps with some misgivings, their sympathy, appreciation or even admiration for the preliminary and experimental steps we are taking towards church unity. We must be frank to say that we have by far not yet come to the unity as taught by Christ and Paul in the Bible. Ours is in a precarious situation. We are aware of the difficulties and testing challenges facing us. This is how the texts I have taken from Ephesians are being read and studied by Christians in China, as illumination, inspiration, admonition, warning and challenge. May God bless us and guide us, and help us in our common prayer that we will be coming into one.[3] Amen.

---

2. Which means "together" or "in the same way," as "同为后嗣, 同为一体, 同蒙应许。" In 4:3–6, the idea of oneness is more emphatically spelled out by repeating the character 一 (one) eight times: (合而为一, 一个身体, 一个圣灵, 一个指望, 一主, 一信, 一洗, 一上帝.)

3. 从中国教会的现实和未来, 反思同归于一

Montreat Conference Bible Study (in Outline)

Montreat, N.C., July 21–27, 1996
Ephesians Chapter 2

I. GREETINGS AND INTRODUCTORY REMARKS

Greetings

Very appropriate to take Ephesians for Bible study in a Global Mission Conference. Six chapters in this Epistle, given to five leaders for five sessions. We have not discussed among us to compare notes. There may be repetitions or overlapping and omissions in presentations.

There is a book published about thirty years ago, entitled *God's Mission—the Epistle to the Ephesians in Mission Perspective*, (by Edwin D. Roels, Eerdmans, Grand Rapids, 1962). Topics of the four chapters of the book give an overall yet concise analytical description of the Epistle:

Ch. I: *The Theological Basis of the Mission*

Ch. II: *The Church as Goal of the Mission*

Ch. III: *The Church as Instrument of the Mission*

Ch. IV: *The Eschatological Fullness of the Mission*

I am not going to follow this book and reproduce the contents. But it helps us "to determine the significance of the Epistle for the theory and practice of the Christian mission." (p.11?)

A few words in general introduction of the epistle as a whole may be in place. (Prof. Greer Ann Ng may have talked about it already, and I am running a risk of being redundant). For our present purpose we will bypass some historical critical questions.

[For further study: some important books of reference:

The Interpreter's Bible Commentary, Vol. 10, on *Ephesians*, by F.W. Beare, 1953

The Anchor bible, Vol. 34, *Ephesians*, in 2 Vols., by Markus Barth, 1974 (<u>the best</u>)

Bonnie Thurston, *Reading Colossians, <u>Ephesians</u> and 2 Thessalonians— A Literary and Theological Commentary*, 1995, Crossroad, New York (<u>small, the latest</u>)]

1. *Authorship and authenticity*: **Four schools of thought**[1]:

1) Affirmed Pauline authorship (traditional view, including Barth himself),

2) Based on original script dictated by Paul, augmented by interpolations of an editor, (IBC, Beare, and most modern Bible scholars),

3) Unable to accept Paul as the author (Goodspeed and many modern scholars),

4) Unable to pass any judgment for or against Pauline authorship and authenticity.

"Regardless of who wrote Ephesians, it represents the apex of Pauline thought," "It is an original, brilliant composition in the Pauline manner,"[2] "the greatest piece of writing in all history," "the supreme Christian document"[3]. The writer "has attempted to reduce Paul's bold and brilliant ideas to a system, to correlate them one with another to bring them under the dominion of a single ruling theme—the eternal purpose of God to unite all things in heaven and on earth in Christ; and so to demonstrate their significance, not alone for the particular social situation which first called forth their expression, but for the life of the church in all ages. "[4]

---

1. Bauth, Markus. The Anchor Bible . . ., 1974.p.37–38.

2. Thurston, Bonnie. Reading Colossians. . ., 1995, p. 87,89.

3. Carver, W.O.*The Glory of God in the Christian Calling, a Study of the Ephesian Epistle*, Broadman Press, 1949.

4. Bearne, F.W. *The Interpreter's Bible Commentary*, Vol.10, On *Ephesians*, 1953, p.604.

2. **Relationship of Ephesians to Colossians** Remarkable similarities between the two letters.

(Compare: Col. 3:12–13 to Eph. 4:1–2; Col. 3:16–17 to Eph. 5:19–20; and Col. 4:7–8 to Eph. 6:21–22.)

Statistically, about a third of the words in Col. are found in Eph; 73 of the 155 verses in Eph. have parallels in Col. (almost half of the book!) The two letters are stylistically similar and follow the same general structure. Various theories to account for the similarities and relationships, the best known is that of Goodspeed (1933) and G. L. Mitton.[5]

3. Theme, style and structure

Ephesians sets forth the divine plan of God, accomplished through the death and resurrection of Jesus, to reconcile Jews and Gentiles to God. God's final purpose is unity and harmony in the universe, and the church with Christ as its head is the instrument for accomplishing that purpose. The unity of all things is found only in Christ. It asserts the cosmic dimension of Christ's power and of the church's destiny. Because the letter speaks in cosmic terms, it exhibits a certain speculative tone. Stylistically, it is prayerful, liturgical, "doxological." In structure, it follows the pattern of a Pauline letter: beginning with an address (1:1–2) and closing with a blessing (6:23–24). It may be divided into two main parts. Chs. 1–3 are doctrinal or dogmatic, and chs. 4–6 didactic and practical. An analytical outline of the first three chapters may be helpful to us to have an overall idea of the doctrinal part, although I may be held guilty of transgressing on other's territory (mainly following Thurston.)

Ch. 1 What God has done in Christ

vv. 1–2 The Salutation

vv. 3–14 The Blessing—Doxology

vv. 15–22 Prayer of Thanksgiving

Ch. 2 The Mission of the Church in Jesus Christ

vv. 1–10 Saved by Grace through Faith, (individual)

vv. 11–18 Reconciliation in Christ, (community)

vv. 19–22 Construction of the Church, the Body of Christ

---

5. *The Epistle to the Ephesians: Its Authorship, Origin and Purpose*, by G. L. Mitton, Oxford, 1951, see Thurston, p. 84.

Ch. 3 The Mystery of God's Plan

vv. 1–13 The Mystery

vv. 14–21 The Summary Prayer

II. A STUDY OF CHAPTER 2

Having described what God has done in Christ in chapter one, now Paul, (or whoever the writer is), in the second chapter continues to explore what God has done in the redemption of humanity through the church, or the "redemption of the church." The chapter begins with the startling "And you!" In Chinese we say 笔锋一转, 直指向我们读者 (with a sudden turn of the point of his pen, directing to us readers) with a force of emphasis. Here "you" refers to the Gentile, including us who formerly were unbelievers. The following two sectionsvv 1–10 and 11–22, are organized in a similar pattern: the writer uses a "before and after" format to contrast conditions before and after the redemptive work of Christ. In vv 1–10 the focus is in the experience of the individual in Christ and the salvation Christ brings to her or him. Vv. 11–18 move to the wider area of the reconciliation of communities. The adverbs of time denoting the past used in these passages are striking: ("once" in vv. 2,3, "at one time" in v. 11, "at that time" in v. 12, and again "once" in v. 13. In Chinese we have "那时"or "从前" repeatedly for five times. The particle *de* (*but*, 然而, in v.4 and v.13), introduces the *turn* and links what follows with what went before, with a strong effect of contrast.

(1) Verses 1–10 Saved by Grace through Faith

Life before redemption is depicted as "following the course of this world," a "following the ruler of the power of the air, (the spirit that is now at work among those who aredisobedient)," "living in the passions of our flesh, as *by nature* the children of wrath." [Thurston points out that this is another Hebraism indicating that the human tendency is toward evil. No one is "*naturally*" reconciled to God.]* With the "but" (*de*, 然而) the whole tenor of the text changes from v.4, into the change Christ has made in us Christians. "But God, who is rich in mercy, out of the great love with which he loved us, even when we were dead through our trespasses, made us alive together with Christ, ...and raised us up with him and seated us with him in the heavenly places in Christ Jesus. Note the repetition in the following verses: (in English in reverse order, but in Chinese the order is the same): v. 1 "you he made alive when you were dead" (RSV), in Chinese "你们死在过犯罪

恶之中，他叫你们活过来" and v. 5 "even when we were dead through our trespasses, made us alive together with Christ," in Chinese "当我们死在过犯的时候，便叫我们与基督同活过来。"

Three important theological propositions in this passage:

1) The initiation of redemption and reconciliation comes from God himself through Christ.

2) The great theme of justification by grace through faith, not by work, is emphasized by repetition: in v.5 parenthetically, in vv. 8–9 straightforwardly.

3) The importance of the death and resurrection of Christ for our salvation. "The passion event of Jesus becomes the model or symbol for the life of the believer; each was dead and brought to life as in the crucifixion and resurrection of Jesus."[6]

*Excursus on *"by nature the children of wrath"* The term "by nature" is as ambiguous in Greek as its English translation. Barth has a long comment on this.[7] The Chinese translation "本为可怒之子" is still more ambiguous. Perhaps the translators (of the 1919 Chinese *Union Version*) intentionally refrained from using the word *nature* (*physis*) and used 本 (originally) instead, because most Chinese believe that human nature is originally good (人性本善). For elementary education in old China children were required to remorize the *Three Character Classic*《三字经》. The beginning sentences read: "人之初，性本善，性相近，习相远，苟不教，性乃迁。"[8] In China there were three schools of thought about human nature: (1) Confucian, (Mencius 孟子), that human nature is good; (2) Xunzhi (荀子), that human nature is evil; and (3) Gaozi (告子) or Gongsunzhi (公孙子) that human nature is neutral (无善无恶). The Confucian teaching of "good nature" had prevailed over the other two schools. Hence the difficulty for most Chinese in accepting the Christian doctrine of original sin or human "total depravity." However, as in Eph. 2:1–3 and 12, the description of empirical experience of human life before redemption as living "in the passions of our flesh, following the desires of flesh and senses," is more understandable and acceptable to the Chinese mind.

---

6. Thurston, 1995, p. 104.
7. Barth, 1974, p.231–232, cf. IBC 641–2
8. In the beginning human nature was good. Nature brings humans near to each other, while "learning" (习 or following the custom) alienates. Without education nature will change. – my paraphrase. There is a Chinese proverb "习非成是"(Accept what is wrong as right when one gets accustomed to it.)

(2) Verses 11-18, Reconciliation in Christ

The focus shifts to what Christ has done to reconcile communities. The estrangement of the Gentiles is now overcome, and thus Gentile Christians and Jewish Christians are being built into God's house. This section is made up of three parts:

(1) Vs. 11-12, condition of the Gentiles "without Christ," as being

    a) aliens from the commonwealth of Israel,

    b) strangers to the covenants of promise,

    c) having no hope in the world, and

    d) without God (in the world)

By most Chinese, of the four "woes" under "without Christ", the first may be considered more or less irrelevant, because we are after all "gentiles" or "pagans", and naturally do not care much for being "aliens from the commonwealth of Israel." The reference to the "commonwealth of Israel" and circumcision has meaning only to readers who know something about Judaism and take the reference in a symbolic way. But the other three strike home in depicting the miserable and hopeless life before being saved in and by Christ. Many sermons have been preached on this verses with the imperative *"remember"* (你们应当纪念!) Think how you had lived in the past!

(2) Vs. 13-18 Christ is our Peace, so that we may become One in Christ

In this passage, the "before and after" format appears again. Striking comparisons between "without Christ" and "in Christ"; "far and near," (13,17); "peace and hostility" (15, 16, 17); "broken down and built up" (14, 20-22); "aliens and citizens" (12, 19); and "strangers" and "members of God's household" (12,19) are presented in a balanced and symmetrical way, using "peace" as the center. Thurston points out that it begins and ends with references to "far and near"(13,17) and within those verses the terms "peace" and "hostility" alternate as the following scheme:

v. 13 far/near a

v. 14 peace b

hostility c

v. 15 peace b

v. 16 hostility c

v.17 peace b

far/near a

I think this is a most interesting example of literary analysis. Some have read in it a kind of ancient *chiasm* (a crossing style of rhetoric). But the message is more important. We who are once far off have been brought near in the blood of Christ. He has broken down the dividing wall of hostility (between God and us, between our divided selves, between our selves and others who are far and near), and has brought us to reconciliation and peace in Christ, "For He is our peace." The "dividing wall" refers to the fence separating the Court of the Gentiles of the inner portions of the Temple that were open only to Jews. Do we sometimes find ourselves separated or alienated from God, from our selves and from other people by a kind of wall of "self-protection" or self-righteousness? Christ in his flesh (translated by Mitton as "by what he said and did") has made "both groups" into one. In Chinese: the "both groups" in vv.14 and 16 is translated into a rather ambiguous expression in the vernacular 两下: "将两下合而为一(14)." "将两下归为一体 (16)." Many exegetes think that the "both" in these two verses refers to "Gentiles and Jews" in the Biblical context. In the Chinese context its very ambiguity makes it applicable to broader association. Who are the "both groups"? To which group do you belong? How have you been separated by the "dividing wall," and from whom? Are the hostility: distrust, malice, hatred, and all the evil-mindedness among us, or in ourselves, "put to death"? Have we, or you, been reconciled to God in one body? How? All these questions strike home to ourselves in self-examination and introspection when we read theses sentences.

V. 17 is introduced by the conjunction "so" ("and" in AV. and RSV, "并且" in Chinese). I see in it both a continuation of the previous verse as the work of Christ and also a "commission" to us who have been reconciled to God in Christ. The following passage (vv. 19–22 on the construction of the church) introduced by "So then" (这样) makes it sound like an imperative or command. I like the Chinese translation of this verse better than the NRSV. "来传和平的福音给你们远处的人，也给那近处的人。" The Chinese translation of the Greek verb *eueggelisato* as "来传(和平的) 福音". (which brings out more clearly the root meaning of "gospel," *good news*) sounds more like a bugle call than the plain English "preached" or "proclaimed" in the indicative past tense. The reference to distance (far off and near) makes me think of the words on the cover of the brochure for our present Global Mission Conference "East and West, Old and New. . .": We Chinese who are far off and you Americans who are near (near to what?) are both brought together into one in God through Christ by being reconciled to God and to each other. This is the gospel of reconciliation.

(3) Verses 19–21 The Church as the Temple of God and Dwelling Place of the Holy Spirit.

The conjunction at the beginning of v. 18 "so then" (这样) introduces a reward, a promise and a charge. "You are no longer strangers and aliens, but citizens with the saints and also members of the household of God." Many comforting and challenging books have been written on this great verse. I have in mind the one by Bishop K. H. Ting, *No Longer Strangers*.[9] There is no need to go into the contents of the book. Suffice it to say that it is a thought-provoking commentary and exposition on this verse in Ephesians based upon from the experience and theological reflections of a Christian leader in China.

Now I will turn to the last three verses of this chapter, the construction of the edifice of the church. Thurston points out that there are "no fewer than ten words that refer to building in these three verses which describe the house of God."[10] It is to be "*built upon* (建造) the *foundation* (根基上) of the apostles and prophets, with Christ Jesus himself as the *cornerstone*(房角石). In him the *whole structure* (各房) *is joined together* (联络得合适), and *grows into* (渐渐成为) a *holy temple* (圣殿) in the Lord, in whom you also are *built together* (同被建造) spiritually into a *dwelling place* (居住的所在) for God."

Now, since 1979 when the first church was reopened in China, Protestant Christianity has been growing in unprecedented speed and scale. In a period of less than two decades the number of Christians (church attendants) has grown to at least more than ten times the pre-1949 total.[11] We are in a "post-denominational stage," which means that, as a whole, there are no denominations in China. The churches or congregations are organized into "Christian Councils" on local, provincial and national levels. We are thankful to God for His blessings and guidance. Many visitors and observers have expressed, in guarded tones, their sympathy, appreciation or even admiration for the preliminary and experimental steps we are taking towards a church unity. But we are aware that this is a very precarious stage, and is far short of fulfilling the demands articulated in these last three verses of Ephesians Chapter 2. To be frank, the present CCC, China Christian Council, is not yet a Church of Christ in China, the CCC we are striving at. Because of the abandonment of denominations we now have no valid and feasible church

---

9. Ting, K. H., Orbs Books, New York, 1989.

10. Thurston, p. 110, I think she is counting in Greek.

11. See an abstract *How Many Christians Are There in China? From Amity News Service*, August 1995, in *Christian News Update*, January 1996, pp. 10–11.

policy to follow for sound and efficient administration, and to safeguard a real and stable unity. One of the important weaknesses and difficulties we are facing is the lack of a sound theology of the church, an ecclesiology grounded on Biblical teaching and experience of the traditional historical Churches. In order to become a member of the "household of God," to fulfill the mission of preaching the gospel of peace and reconciliation to those far off and those who are near, the church must be "built upon the foundation of the apostles and prophets, with Christ Jesus himself as the cornerstone." We have not learned how to "join the whole structure together," (not as apartments, so to speak), and to learn how to *grow into* a holy temple of the Lord. The word "grow" is very important, because it suggests that it has not yet become, and has to undergo a process of growing and evolving, "until all of us come to the unity of the faith and of the knowledge of the Son of God, to maturity, to the measures of the full stature of Christ," (Eph. 4:13), and become really "a dwelling place of God."

To sum up what I have seen as the message of this chapter as the mission of the church: the mission—to preach the gospel of reconciliation and peace, the church—as being built together in unity into a dwelling place of God.

I am looking forward to the expounding of the third chapter by Dr. Philip Wickeri tomorrow, on the "mystery of God's plan," and on the practical, didactical teachings in the following chapters by Dr. Man-King Tso and . . .

Intensify Theological Reconstruction in the Chinese Church
Address at the Jinan Conference
(Jinan, November 20, 1998)

Chen Zemin

I WAS VERY INSPIRED by the speeches given by Bishop Ting andRev. Su Deci. One of the main themes of this conference is strengthening theological reconstruction in the Chinese church, a theme Ifind very important and one I would like to address today.

We might consider this second session of the current NationalChristian Conference here in Jinan a "midterm exam" for this presentfive-year term of the Conference—a retrospective on achievementsand experience in our work during the two years since the presentterm began in 1997, and a look forward at the direction and tasks wemust strive for in the next three years. It is also the last meeting of the *lianghui (两会)* in the present century. Soon we will celebrate the 50th anniversary of the Three-Self Patriotic Movement of Protestant Churchesin China. And in 2000, during the third meeting of the Standing Committees, we will be standing with all the people ofChina on the threshold of the 21st century and that will be the first meeting of the newcentury. To use seminary language, this "midterm exam" is a preparation for the "final exam" and the start of the new semester (historical period). Thus alluding to the task of strengthening theological reconstruction in the church is of tremendous historical significance.

During these two days, each delegate has received, in their packet of materials at registration, a thick, hardcover copy of *Love Never Ends*. This is a gift to each member from the *lianghui (两会)*. My foreword to the book has already appeared in *TianFeng*(《天风》)and in the *Nanjing Theological Review* (《金陵神学志》), but the book itself came out only a week ago. We in Nanjing, privileged as those who live near the water are first to see the moon, already have the book. It is extremely topical and pertinent to the subject of this conference.

A year ago, Bishop Ting gathered some of his papers from over the past twenty years, over eighty pieces in all, put them in order and edited them, with a view to publishing them as a selection of his works. He asked me to read them and to write a foreword. I was both anxious and pleased. Anxious because I was afraid I did not completely understand his thinking, that I had not digested the profounder meanings of his essays, and was not up to writing a foreword, and pleased because it gave me the chance to read his selections first. After reading through them all conscientiously, I felt that they could serve as a general summing up of the several decades of experience of the Three-Self Movement of our church. They contained views that were theologically innovative and creative, worth our conscientious consideration and study. I wrote my foreword based on what I understood of my reading, my main purpose being to aid the reader (including intellectual circles outside the church) in understanding the history and present circumstances of the Chinese church, and to serve as background for reading the volume. I asked Bishop Ting to read and edit my draft and circulated it among some friends, both in and outside the church, for their comments. When I had my final *draft, at Bishop Ting's suggestion, I first published it in TianFengand the Nanjing Theological Review. When Love Never Ends was* published, I read my foreword as it appeared there and discovered that two sentences I considered important had been edited out. They should appear beginning on line 2 of page 3. I would like to read them now and ask you all to pay particular attention to them:

"Bishop Ting is a man with a strong sense of mission and a great devotion to his work. As a church leader, his whole life has been closely linked to the fate of the church in China and reflects the issues and challenges which the Chinese church has faced in different periods, as well as the church's response. On this level of meaning, *his explorations of theological issues [Before publication of Love Never Ends, Bishop Ting considered My Explorations into Theological Issues as a title], were also the church's investigation of and pondering of its times, future and destiny. The publication of Love Never Ends* has great historical and epochal significance for the Chinese church."

This passage is a good general summary, very pertinent and pre*cise*. It was not my own (I'm not that good at generalizing), but was added to my draft by Dr. Li Pingye of the Central Religious Affairs Bureau when she read it. She is an old friend of Bishop Ting, well versed in Christianity, who has a great understanding and care for the Chinese church. Her addition of these sentences to my draft is very important and apropos and functioned to "dot the eyes of the dragon." *They show that the publication of Love Never*

Ends raises a challenge to our expressed need to consider theological reconstruction seriously and point out a direction for the future. When the book was published without these two sentences, I asked Bishop Ting about it and found that he had felt the passage placed too much importance *on his own role. Out of humility, he asked that they be deleted.*

Please permit me, as the author of the foreword and with Dr. Li's permission, to beg Bishop Ting's indulgence for rereading the passage. And I would like to take this opportunity to suggest that this *book be made a required text for seminary students and a reference for theological and pastoral workers. The publication of the book can be said to be an important milestone in the history* for *Chinese* theology. Today you each have a copy, a gift from the national *lianghui*. I would like to take this opportunity to suggest that you read it care*fully and make some of the proposals and views therein topics for* your discussions. Of course, there will be differing understandings and views. Our essential Christian faith is one, with the Bible as its foundation. Theology is an understanding and elucidation of faith, it can and should develop in diverse and abundant ways according to different social backgrounds and cultural conditions. For two thousand years of theological history, it has never been unchanging or *defined by one voice. There must be differences in order for com*parison, exchange, discussion, mutual learning, supplementing to take place, in order to have development and progress. This conference encourages the idea that there cannot be one voice in theology and that space for all kinds of theological thinking, mutual respect and learning should be permitted. In this way only can our theology flourish and abound, only then will there be progress. The publication of *Love Never Ends* offers us rich topics and views for theology; there may be some which are not very similar to some old-fashioned views. I hope that careful reading and consideration of these essays will enliven our theological thinking.

Some at this conference have said that current Chinese theology is backward. How should we view such an assessment? Others say that in comparison with mainstream foreign Christian denominations' theology, we are backward. And others say that friendly evangelicals overseas, after coming into contact with us, say we (our theology) are fifty years behind them. Some people think that the theology expressed in our pulpits does not get beyond the negative world-weary theology the western missionaries preached in the late 19th century or the 30s and 40s of the 20th century. Many spread fundamentalism-premillenarianism-dispensationalism (these three were nearly identical in American usage; they belong to the same trend). At the time, China was variously caught up in the battles among warlords, the war of resistance against Japan, the war of liberation. The people were frequently subjected to the disasters of war, uprooted and suffering, pessimistic and without hope in their feelings toward their reality. This made them very receptive to this type of negative, other-worldly thinking—characterized by waiting for the end of the world, the Second Coming, the "rapture," and by pious thinking focused on personal salvation. This type of theology was mainly brought by English and American "fundamentalist" missionaries in the early part of this century, and through elaboration and agitation by some "revivalists" and "evangelists" (like John Song 宋尚节, JiZhiwen 计志文 and Zhao Shiguang 赵世光) had a broad and deep impact among Chinese clergy and believers. It came to be thought of as "orthodox" Christian theology and became the "mainstream."

There were also some "modernist" missionaries, whose theology was more open, mostly teaching at seminaries and universities, scorned as "liberals" and "social gospellers" by the fundamentalists, who thought them too concerned with reason, social responsibility and moral behavior. Their impact was limited to some intellectuals. Most of those who initiated and took part in the Three-Self Movement at the beginning were from this group. The fundamentalists thought their faith insufficiently "pure" or "spiritual." To strengthen unity, the Three-Self leaders promoted mutual respect in matters of theology, on a political basis of patriotism, unity and cooperation. In the early Liberation period (the first half of the 1950s) there was a period of "mass theological movement." Some rather obvious errorsin political thinking and speech were criticized through these discussion, but since the principle of mutual respect was maintained, the theological thinking and speech of fundamentalists and premillenarian-dispensationalists was basically unmoved. From the latter 1950s to the late 1970s, China was basically cut off from the outside world. Due to many political movements and the influence of ultra-leftism, church lifeceased and theology was stagnant. In the last twenty years, religious policy has been implemented, church life has been resumed, and the church has developed rapidly. During this time, the theology of fifty years ago, almost unchanged, began to flood the Chinese church. This could facetiously be termed "no change for fifty years."[1] But Chinese society in these fifty years has undergone reform and openness, has undergone an unprecedented transformation, entering the initial stage of socialism. There are manyconcepts and thinking in the church which are not compatible with socialism and cannot adapt to it. When theology lags behind social reality, we can say that compared with the consciousness of the Chinese people today, we are indeed backward. During this fifty years, world Christianity has undergone many changes as well. There have been

---

1. CPPCC (Chinese People's Political Consultative Conference) held in August 1997 in Xi'an.

many new and important developments in theology, among them some which deserve to be drawn on and studied. It is only in the last decade and more of reform and openness that we have learned a bit about these. In this sense, we are indeed several decades behind *compared to Christian theology beyond our borders. Furthermore,* knowledge of Christianity among Chinese intellectuals has also undergone an important change in the last twenty years. Many academics have studied Christianity and have a deep understanding of it, surpassing us in terms of theological thinking. They have written many books on Christian doctrine and theology which are much deeper and more advanced than our own. In this sense, compared with intellectuals sympathetic to Christianity, we are tremendously backward.

Whether or not we recognize our church's backwardness in theology (whether or not backward in the senses outlined above), it is an important issue for strengthening theological reconstruction in the church. In August of this year, Bishop Ting spoke on the backwardness of Chinese Christian theological thinking today at a meeting of the CPPCC in Xi'an,[2] and called for a revisioning and striving for adaptation to and compatibility with socialism. This speech's (published in the *CPPCC News* and *Religion)*appearance generated a great deal of discussion. This shows that some people are very unwilling to admit their thinking is backward and cannot tolerate different voices. The publication of Bishop Ting's book may represent another voice, a kind of challenge for some people. I hope that careful reading of this book will act as a catalyst to our theological reconstruction and enliven our theology.

We stand on the threshold of a new century. What will Chinese Christianity look like as it enters the 21st century? Will we be able to adapt to socialism? To a great extent, this will determine our theology. I believe that the publication of *Love Never Ends* can aid us in conscientiously dealing with the issue of theological reconstruction. *I would like to suggest here that careful reading and study of this* book will not be unworthy of the kind intentions of the national *lianghui* in giving each of us here this gift.

Chen Zemin is Vice-Principal of Nanjing Union Theological Seminary.
Nanjing Theological Review, No. 1 (1999), p. 5.

---

2. A play on the phrase, *wushinianbubian* (no change for fifty years), used to describe Chinese policy in maintaining the status quo in Hong Kong.

Outline of Presentation
Candler School of Theology
Emory University
November 13, 1996, Wed. 1:00–2:20 p.m.
Room 301, Bishop's Hall
On Contextual Theology in Mainland China

I. **Historical background**

Books recommended for further study:

Whyte,Bob, *Unfinished Encounter: China and Christianity*, Collins, Fount, 1988

Wickeri, Philip L., *Seeking the Common Ground: Protestant Christianity, the Three-Self Movement and China's United Front*, Orbis, Maryknoll, N. Y., 1988

1) **Some historical landmarks**

   i) Tang Dynasty (618–907), Nestorian monk Aloben first introduced Christianity in 635, lasted for about two centuries, pre-imperialist period, or rather China as an imperial power. The *Nestorian Tablet* and other documents show attempts at contextualization: translation and/or syncretism?

   ii) Yuan Dynasty (1279–1368) under the Mongols, **yelikewen** (the blessed), a mixed group of Nestorians and Roman Catholics from the west, lasted only less than a *century,* no signs of contextualization (?)
   (Marco Polo in China 1275–92)
   John Montecorvino as Archbishop in Beijing (1307)

   iii) Ming Dynasty (1368–1644) and Qing Dynasty (1644–1912)
   MatteoRici (1586–1610), encounter with Confucianism, "original Confucianism" and threefold strategy of "complying with

Confucianism," "supplementing Confucianism" and "surpassing Confucianism"

The Chinese Rites Controversy, Jesuits vs Franciscans and Dominicans, cultural conflict, Christianity banned by Emperor Kangxi (1721)

iv) Protestant Christianity introduced into China by Robert Morrison (1807)

The Opium Wars (1839-42,1856-60)

Unequal treaties and the "missionary clauses"

Missionary Cases (1956-1899)

Taiping Heavenly Kingdom Movement (1851-62), *Bai Shang Di Jiou* 拜上帝教, a radical accommodation of Christianity to Chinese traditional culture Democratic Revolution under Sun Yat-Sen (1911)

May Fourth Movement (1919), "Chinese Enlightenment"

Anti-Christian and anti-religionist Movement (1919-1927), both Confucianism and Christianity criticized and attacked

Independence Movement of the Chinese Protestant Church (1872-1933)

From 1920's onward, attempts at contextualization by some theologians like Wu Leichuan(吴雷川), Wang Zhixin (王治心),Y. T. Wu (吴耀宗), N. Z. *Zia* (谢扶雅) and T. C. Chao (赵紫辰) *(See my paper p. 71)*

People's Republic of China (1949-)

From 1807 to 1949 China was the largest mission field in the world.

Catholic Christians (Whyte): 3,274,740 members,

    194,712 catechumen

    2,698 Chinese priests

    4,441 missionary personnel

    3 universities, 189 middle schools, 216 hospitals

    Protestants 1,000,000 church members and inquirers

    2,024 Chinese clergy

    939 foreign clergy

    13 niversities, 240 middle schools, 322 hospitals

2) **Since 1950, "The End of Missionary Era" "Paradigm shift"**

Korean War (1950-53), all foreign missionaries left China

The Denunciation Movement (Whyte, pp. 223-230)

Three-Self Patriotic Movement, officially inaugurated in 1954

(The slogan of "three-self"- "self-supporting, self-governing and self-propagating," was first proposed by Rufus Anderson (American Board) and Henry Venn (British CMS) in the mid-*19 century.*)

Y. T. Woo (1893–1979) (See my paper *Y. T. Woo: A Prophetic Theologian* 吴耀宗先生——一位先知式的神学家, 1993)

Anti-rightist Campaign and Great Leap Forward Movement (1957–58)

Joint-services, denominational differences obliterated, beginning of "post-denominational stage"

"Cultural Revolution"(1966–75), all religions disappeared entirely

Return to normal order in 1979, religious activities resurfaced and rehabilitated.

3) A rapid church growth since 1980,

China Christian Council (CPC) established in 1980, churches began to reopen, non-denominational uniting church, principle of "mutual respect" in doctrine, liturgy and church polity *(Church Order for Trial Use,* 1991, revised 1995, mostly practical and expediential)

Over 10,000 churches reopened and newly opened: (three churches in every two days), plus two to three thousand "meeting points." "House churches" a misconception.

Total number of Protestant Christians estimated as about 12–15 million, (more than 12 to 15 times the pre-1949 total), with about 2500 ordained ministers, (1/8 women), many lay workers. 13 theological colleges, four Bible schools, and hundreds of "short term training classes." A majority of believers and preachers are of fundamentalist-pietistic-puritanical background, seeking other-worldly salvation of individual souls, showing little interest in social, political and economic issues, taking such as "secular" in opposition to "the spiritual." Worship services mostly non-liturgical. Over 80 percent of the hymns sung are western hymns and gospel songs translated from English. Some rural churches prefer short choruses set to indigenous Chinese tunes.

(*See* my paper *Recent Developments in Congregational Singing in Mainland China,* 1996) Being "Post-denominational," there is no set polity to follow. Congregations are organized to form local, provincial and national "Christian Councils," which serve the congregations in an advisory or consultative way and do not have administrative authority. No subordinate relation between "lower" and "higher" levels. Ordination (pastors, elders and deacons) usually done in the local churches, with assistance of provincial councils, or in the provincial level. Bishops do not have dioceses, nor diosconic authority. Generally speaking, an expedient type of polity, a compromise between Congregationalism and Presbyterianism. No strong ecclesiology to guide and undergird more efficient church polity. It is a **uniting** church of conciliar nature, not quite united. (See my paper *The Post-Denominational Unity of the Chinese Protestant Church*, 1992)

Three main splitting groups or sects of centrifugal tendency: the Seventh-day Adventists, the Christian Assembly, ("Little Flock"), and the Jesus Family. Numerous small "cults" of heterodox teachings and practices.

II. Attempts at Contextualization and Problems

For most conservative Christians (fundamentalists, and "evangelicals"), no need for contextualization. Western Christianity is the "norm," "why Chinese?"

After the May Fourth New Culture Movement (1919) and the anti-Christianity accusations (1920's) *a* few theologians, mostly of liberal theological background like, Wu Leichuan, N.Z. Zia, T.C. Chao, tried to accommodate Christian doctrines to traditional Chinese classical ideas and idioms, finding similarities or parallelisms between the two traditions. Wee-chong Tan 陈慰中 (Canadian College for Chinese Studies) *The Common God* (《共同的上帝》, 1994) follows the same line.

"Theological Mass Movement" (神学群众运动) in the early years of the Three-self Movement and the denunciation movement (1950's), (see K. H. Ting's speech, *Theological Mass Movement in China*, 1984), more critical and scattered than constructive and coherent

Real conscientious attempts began from the 80's. (See my papers *Theological Construction in the Chinese Church*, 1956, reprinted 1991, and *Christianity and Culture from a Chinese Perspective: A Sino-American Dialogue*, 1992.)

1) **Making Christians (in China) Chinese**—An imminent priority—stress on *patriotism* in the Three-self Patriotic Movement—to make the church in China *Chinese*, de-westernization-politicalnuance. Hence the slogan: "Love the country and love the church" *(*爱国爱教). Some Christians in China ask: "Why put 'love the country' first? Why not 'love the church' first?"

We begin in making a Christian (in China) Chinese, and proceed to make Christianity Chinese-to "create" a contextual Chinese theology.

2) What makes one Chinese? Cultural analysis

Clifford Geertz's semiotic analysis of culture (Schreiter, Ch. 3, pp.56–74) most helpful.

Difficulty in identifying the context

A. Some important characteristics of <u>traditional</u> Chinese culture:

i) Religion and culture closely intertwined and inseparable

The present power that be is ill-disposed to and prejudiced against religion as such, but cannot extricate it from culture. So all discussions (and policy-making) on religious matters must be put within the orbit or concept of *culture*.

ii) *Confucianism* the mainstay of Chinese culture has undergone important changes

    a) *Classical Confucianism* from Zhou Dynasty (551 BC to Han Dynasty (209 BC-9AD), enjoyed hegemony. Co-existent with Taoism and Buddhism and Taoism as three main religions after the fourth century A.D.

    b) *Neo-Confucianism*, in Song and Ming Dynasties (c. 1130–1529), keeping the tenets of Confucianism, but combined with Buddhist and Taoist elements (新儒家: 宋明理学)

    c) *Contemporary Confucianism*, from the Reform Movement in late Qing Dynasty (1898), through the anti-Confucian May Fourth Movement (1919), to the present revival of Confucianism, absorbing modem Western philosophies. After the onslaughts of many critical campaigns only a small number of scholars in China would call themselves neo-Confucians. Most Contemporary Confucians are non-Christian, anti- or neutral.

    d) Exodus and Diaspora of most neo-Confucian scholars after 1950. Most people under fifty years of age know little of the Confucian classics. But Confucianism as deep-rooted cultural element still very prevalent and influential in ways of thinking and life.

    e) Since the time of modernization (1980 and after) a marked decline of interest in Confucianism among young people, most proponents of Neo-Confucianism are outside of mainland China

Outline of Presentation

107

iii) *Tolerance toward syncretism* in religious matters. The extreme "no-other name" exclusivism of fundamentalist Christianity often met with resistance.

iv) *"Harmonizing opposites,* such as heaven and earth, heaven and humanity, *yin andyang,* etc.in a dialectical way, or keeping to the middle (持中) without going to extremes. W.C. Tan's 《中庸辩证法》 1989,《中庸系统神学》 1996, may be more appealing to the Chinese mind

v) *Absence of concepts of "original sin" and "the Fall";* the tenet of Mencius that human nature isgood generally accepted, over against "evil nature" of XunZhi (荀子)and "neutral nature" of GaoZhi (告子).

vi) *Humanistic, moralistic and practical*way of thinking, emphasizing moral education and ethical up-bringing. Retributive justice (awards or punishment) in this world or after. Not much interest in eschatology in the cosmic sense.

vii) *"Folk religions"* often mixtures of popular Buddhism and Taoism withsuperstitious beliefs and practices.

B. Social changes in the modern era

Before the twentieth century social change in China had been gradual and very slow.

"Modern China" began from the May Fourth Movement (1919), acc. to most historians

The impact of westernization: industrialization, commercialization, and reform of education

Role of Christianity in modernization not to be exaggerated- a controversial issue

After 1950, a drastic change of political and social system—forty years of isolation from the outer

world—"China watchers" of 1974 outside the "bamboo screen"

New era of "Open-up and Reform" since 1980, accelerating changes in all phases of social life still too mobile and elusive, too early to analyze and characterize

Impact of western culture, secularism and pluralism, modem technology, etc.

Further decline of Confucianism- see above Return to policy of religious freedom (1979)

"The Third Opium War"—controversy on opium as the essence of religion (1980–86)

Change of attitudes of intellectuals toward religion and religious studies
Resurgence and growth of "the five religions" and "folk religions," "religious heat"
(See above I-3)
Rise of "Culture Christians" ("Chinese Apollos" debate)
Interfaith dialogue discouraged by powers that be both within and outside the religions

3) Theological Reorientation—Towards a Chinese Christian Theology

Appropriation of Chinese traditional religious and ethical teaching

i) From redemption-centered to creation-centered perspective
God as love, creative principle, (vs. Confucian benevolence -human love 仁)
The Cosmic Christ—in creation-providence—redemption—sanctification -culmination
'anakephalaio'thesis or *recapitulation* (Eph. 4:10), "Omega point," 天下大同.
Re-interpretation of **sin, Fall, election, and eschatology**

ii) Dialectical interpretation of continuity and discontinuity, imminence and transcendence

iii) Encourage dialogue with non-believers and other religions, from extreme exclusivism to
inclusivism or pluralism,

iv) From self-soul centered to a social-ecological perspective
etc., etc.

4) Criteria for orthodoxy

The three criteria of De Mesa and Wostyn (in *Doing Theology,* p. 86) and Schreiter's five criteria
(*Constructing Local Theologies*, pp. 117–121, see Stephen B. Bevans, *Models of ContextualTheology,*p. 18–20) seem not very helpful. Perhaps it is too early for Chinese Christians to apply the criteria for identifying Christianity.

5) Modals

Schreiber's three types: translation models, adaptation models and contextual models
Bevans's five models: translation model, anthropological model, praxis model,synthetic model, and transcendental model

All are helpful. Perhaps in China we began with translation model, may move on to some other type, perhaps adaptation or anthropological. Too early to decide.

"It depends on the context." (Bevans, p. 112)

Chen Zemin
Nanjing Union Theological Seminary
Nanjing, China

Inculturation of the Gospel and Hymn Singing in China
(Oberlin College, Oberlin, Ohio, July 14–18,1996)

Chen Zemin

Hymn singing is that vital part of church life that most convincingly illustrates the possibility, necessity, desirability and multiformity of inculturation of the gospel. It is *vital* because it grips the heart and soul of the congregation. In an average worship service or "meeting" of eighty minutes in China (sometimes lengthened to two hours or more in the rural churches) at least one-third of the time is devoted to singing, in which the whole congregation participates heartily. The sermon, unfortunately, may not always be powerful and interesting. When it gets too long and boring, the listeners may become absent-minded, doze, or day-dream. The scripture lessons, read by one or two persons and often without much active congregational participation, may be "far-fetched" and perfunctory. The prayers, if voiced simultaneously and out-loud, may seem mutually distracting and confusing. But when hymn singing is announced, every one becomes alert and eager to join in, either to learn a new song or to savor some beloved familiar hymns that reverberate in the soul. Hymn singing never fails to bless a church with vibrant life, and to attract newcomers to be"touched" by the gospel. I am not belittling the importance of the sermon, the Scripture and prayer in the life of Christian communities, nor the need for inculturation in all these aspects. In fact, all these must be contextualized or inculturated in order to be effective if the *Gospel* is to change the life of a community orindividuals. In this paper I want to focus on hymn singing and try to examine how it has been (or has failed to be) inculturated in the contemporary Chinese context.

Hymn singing, understood as group vocal rendering of a text expressing praise or prayer to a deity, is as old as Chinese civilization itself, with a history of over four millennia in China. It was first closely connected with and formed an integral part of religious ceremonies. The *Book of Rites* 《礼记》 (one of the Confucian *Five Classics*) contains a good part of *YueJi* 《乐记》 (*Book of Music*) which records the theory and teachings on the importance of music in the political and social life of the nation and in personal cultural and spiritual formation. In the Zhou dynasty (c. 1027–256 BCE) music was one of the four subjects required for the education and upbringing of gentility. Although Confucianism has never existed as an established religion with a church and priesthood, the emphasis on music by Confucian scholars has left its stamp on traditional Chinese culture as a means of calming the passions and aspiring for peace and harmony, rather than as a secular pastime. When Buddhism and Taoism were established as Chinese religions in the Han dynasty (205 BCE—220), each had developed its specific traditional style of religious music, mostly in the form of chanting with instrumental accompaniment. These three main streams of Chinese religious ceremonial music, with later additions of folk singing, especially of the minority ethnic nationalities, constitute the "indigenous" background and sources of Chinese traditional "hymn singing." Of course they are not Christian, or as some may think, "pagan." It is for us Chinese Christians to imbue Chinese musical form or garb with the essence of Christian gospel in order to create and develop a truly Chinese hymnody.

Christianity was first introduced into China in the Tang dynasty in the form of Nestorianism (in Chinese, *Jingjiao*, the Luminous Religion). During the period of its dissemination over about two hundred years (c. 635—c. 840), many hymns must have been written and sung among the believers. Among the Nestorian documents unearthed at Dunhuang in Gansu 甘肃 Province in 1907, the great *Hymn to the Holy Trinity* (大秦景教三威蒙度讚, written around 800) has been treasured as one of the oldest extant Christian hymns in China. The text shows some degree of syncretism, but careful reading reveals creative use of Taoist and Buddhist terminology to convey Christian faith. Unfortunately the original musichad long been lost. A modern tune composed by Liang Jifang 梁季芳 (1934) rescued it from oblivion, but it is rarely sung by modern congregations. (No. 2 of *Hymns of Universal Praise*, 1st edition, 1936, No. 385 of *New Hymnal*, CCC, 1983).

During the Yuan dynasty (1297–1368) Christianity was again introduced into China under the Mongols. Believers in this specific form of Christian religion were called yelikewen (a transliteration from, the Mongol language, which means "the blessed"). Probably they were a mixture of descendants of the extinct Nestorians and Chinese converts to Roman Catholicism during the time of John of Montecorvino (arrived in China 1293; d. 1328) and after. The yelikewen flourished for about one century, and after the fall of the Yuan dynasty disappeared almost completely in China. In recorded history nothing is left of their hymn singing.

With Matteo Ricci (1552–1610), Roman Catholicism came to China again and this time was to remain, though with many ups and downs. Ricci's Jesuit policy of accommodation is well-known and acclaimed. Had it not been for the strong opposition of the Franciscans and Dominicans, and the ensuing "Chinese Rites Controversy" which led to the ban on Christianity by the Emperor Kangxi (1721), one would expect Roman Catholicism to have been received more enthusiastically and thus to have flourished. One famous hymn attributed to Emperor Kangxi (before the ban) *The Seven Words of the Cross* (康熙十架歌) has come down to the present, and is included in the 1936 edition *of Hymns of Universal Praise*. It is a beautiful hymn written with exceptional literary skill according to Chinese classical poetic genre and form. There is some controversy among historians about the genuineness of imperial authorship. Whoever the real author might be, it has been treasured as one of the best Chinese hymns and beautifully acculturated. Unfortunately there is no trace of the original music. Congregational singing was not the common practice at that time, and was little known beyond the liturgical chanting, reserved almost exclusively for clergy. Another beautiful hymn *Lord, Before All Time Thou Wast* 仰止歌, attributed to the Chinese Catholic painter-poet-priest Wu Yushan 吴渔山 (1631–1718), has also been preserved. Perhaps it was not originally meant for congregational singing, and the music, if there was any, has been lost. The beautiful tune included with it in our *New Hymnal* (No. 386) was arranged in 1920 by QiuChangnian裘昌年, based upon a melody used by Confucian literati for reciting classical poems. The Nanjing Seminary choir sings it in a counterpointal arrangement with Chinese instruments. I wish we had more examples like these. They may be taken as illustrations and proofs for the *possibility* and *desirability* of putting the gospel message into Chinese literary forms.

Real congregational hymn singing came with the Protestant missionaries. When the first Protestant missionaries came to China in the early nineteenth century, they brought with them two books — the Bible and a hymnal. They lost no time in learning the Chinese language, (accommodating to the Chinese indigenous culture), and undertook to translate the Bible into Chinese. Of course this was an important process of inculturation. But since the Bible has been canonized and regarded as "the Word of God" with absolute authority, it must be translated with immaculate care and linguistic scholarship to be exactly true to the original texts. There is not much freedom for accommodation. (Of course Eugene Nida and others have contributed much to the translation of the Bible into various languages through the concept of "dynamic equivalence"). But next to Scripture reading, and perhaps preaching, which was to some extent rather clumsily adapted, it was hymn singing that distinguished most effectively those early communities as *Christian*. So the next thing the early missionaries did was to translate the hymnal. Robert Morrison of the London Missionary Society came to China in 1807. He and his associate William Milne concentrated their efforts on the translation of the Bible and some hymns, and the compilation of a Chinese-English dictionary. The first Chinese hymn book (養心神詩), published in 1818, included thirty hymns selected and translated from contemporary English hymnals. Morrison's second collection of Chinese hymns which formed part of a Prayer Book (祈禱文讚神詩) was modeled after and translated from *Morning Service of the Church of England* and published in 1833. This work was done in collaboration with his first Chinese convert Liang Fa 梁发. From 1819 to 1850 several Chinese hymn books were compiled and published outside mainland China, in Malacca, Bangkok and Batavia by Western missionaries. All these were translated in the "literary language," difficult for the common people to understand and sing[1]. The first attempt to use the vernacular style for hymns was made by the Scottish Presbyterian missionary W.C. Bums, who, following the principle of Paul in 1 Cor. 9:20–22, "I have become all things to all people, that I might by all means save some," had published the first vernacular hymnal in Fuzhou dialect (榕腔神詩) in 1861. According to David Sheng, from 1851 to 1879 over fifty hymnals were published in mainland China, most of them in vernaculars, some even printed in various systems of romanization.[2] Of course this was convenient and useful in popularizing hymn singing and scripture reading in the southeastern areas, especially among uneducated or illiterate Christians. But no matter what dialect is used, in most parts of China, the written Chinese characters remain the same, whether in literary style or in the vernacular. So when the gospel reached the central and northern provinces, where most people use some kind of mandarin or Putonghua 普通话, the tendency was to use putonghua as the chief means of propagation of the gospel. After the May Fourth Movement of 1919, when baihuawen 白话文 (the written vernacular) prevailed over the old classical literary style all over China, and with the publication of the Union Version of the Bible in the mandarin vernacular (1919), the use of local dialects, let alone the romanized versions, gave place to a more or less unified style of printed hymnals.

1. David Sheng, History of Chinese Hymns. D.M.A. diss, 1964, part I. 盛宣恩《中国圣诗史》
2. Ibid. part II.

We cannot go into the details of the history of Chinese hymnals here.[3] However, the publication of the following hymnals marked important steps in the popularization and updating of contemporary Protestant hymn singing in China.

(1) 團契聖歌集 (*Fellowship Hymnal*) and 民眾聖歌集 (*A Hymn Book for the Masses*) edited by T.C. Chao and Bliss Wiant, Beijing, 1931.

(2) 普天頌讚 (*Hymns of Universal Praise*), edited by United Hymnal Committee, Christian Literature Society (CLS), Shanghai, 1936.

(3) 讚美詩新編 (*New Hymnal*), edited and published by the Hymn Committee, China Christian Council (CCC), Shanghai, 1983.

Dr. T.C. Chao's *Hymnals*, with his creative and beautiful poetic expression of Christian spirituality in a plain and easy to sing vernacular, marked an important attempt to indigenize Christian hymn writing. *Hymns of Universal Praise* was a comprehensive and well-selected collection of hymns, including many original new hymns written by Chinese Christians and set to Chinese tunes. It was universally used in the churches in China until 1966. When CLS moved to Hong Kong in 1950 it continued to publish this volume and produced several revised and enlarged editions under Dr. Heywood Wong 黃永熙. *The New Hymnal* (1983) was published to "fill the vacuum" left by the Cultural Revolution (1966–1976), and has been universally accepted and widely used in churches in mainland China. It has gone through six printings (over four million copies). In the last five years four hymnals for various ethnic groups and a new collection of 640 short songs (20,000 copies) have been compiled and published by the CCC. *The Short Songs of Praise* (讚美短歌) includes 300 "Scripture hymns" and 340 original texts set to simple tunes of traditional origin or newly composed by Chinese Christians. All these consist of a single stanza, and are intended to be sung in unison repeatedly. The music is more or less a combination of Western gospel songs with Chinese pentatonic melodies. The book is printed in numerical notation, without accompaniment, and the melodies can be easily picked up by congregations. It has become very popular in rural churches, including the so-called "house churches," where the longer and more traditional hymns of the *New Hymnal* (1983) are felt to be too difficult to follow.

This brings us to the contemporary period — the post-Cultural-Revolution era since 1979. In what follows, I will discuss aspects of the current situation which show the possibility, necessity, desirability and multiformity of inculturation of the gospel in congregational hymn singing in China.

---

3. To the best of my knowledge, David Sheng's History remains the best account on this topic; but it is still far from complete or exhaustive.

A SINGING CHURCH

There has been rapid church growth since its revival in 1979. The total number of worshipers is conservatively estimated to be over fifteen million.[4] The number of "churches" has increased at an average rate of three churches in every two days since 1980, with a current total of over ten thousand, plus over twenty thousand "meeting points" (congregations without permanent church buildings which depend mostly on lay leadership). Many churches are large enough to hold over one thousand worshipers, and many have to hold two or three services on Sunday (or Saturday). Most congregations spend about half an hour in hymn singing before and during services. Over half of the churches have choirs (some have two or more choirs) to help congregational singing and for special "sung offerings" (獻詩). Many newcomers are attracted to the church by hymn singing.

WESTERN OR CHINESE?

Most Christians are accustomed to and prefer Western hymns and gospel songs. Over 90 per cent of hymns sung by congregations (and choirs) are Western. Many foreign visitors have observed that almost all the hymns sung in the services are those that are quite well known in the West. There is no reason not to treasure the great traditional hymns like *Holy, Holy, Holy, O God, Our Help in Ages Past, O Master Let Me Walk with Thee, Rock of Ages, Jesus Loves Me*, etc. Three-fourths of the 400 hymns in the *New Hymnal* are Western in origin, and over half of these are "gospel songs."[5] Some hymn leaders and choir directors, especially in the city churches, have shown a tendency to regard the few Chinese hymn tunes as "secular," "pagan," or even "vulgar" and not "Christian" enough; therefore not suitable for a worship service. Even the use of Chinese instruments as accompaniment or solo during worship services is thought too secular. They tend to think that Western music is "superior" to Chinese. It is very difficult to change this

---

4. This is a controversial issue. The total number of Protestant Christians has been variously estimated as 10 million, 12 to 15 or even 50 million. If we accept the lowest, it is at least more than ten times the pre-1949 total. See "How Many Christians Are There in China?" Amity News Service, Hong Kong: August 1995.

For the so-called "House Church Movement" or "home meetings," see Bob Whyte, *Unfinished Encounter: China and Christianity* (Collins Fount, 1988), pp. 317–9; 400–4.

5. It is difficult to distinguish between traditional "hymns" and "gospel songs." By the latter I refer roughly to songs composed and usually used during evangelical and revival meetings in late 19th- and 20th-century America. These were introduced into China in the thirties and forties, with *In the Garden* and *Amazing Grace* being favorites of young people.

pro-Western mentality. Some have asked "Why Chinese? Is it not sufficient to be just Christian?" According to these people to be Christian means Western. But rural areas where most worshipers have not cultivated this kind of pro-Western "mind-set" often show a special liking for Chinese hymns and enjoy singing them. They find it difficult to sing the half-tones (4th and 7th in the Western hepatonic scale), and delight in singing simple pentatonic melodies. I have seen whole congregations in many rural churches spiritedly singingindigenous Chinese hymns accompanied by the *er-hu* 二胡, *pipa*琵琶, bamboo flutes and other instruments. I think they are more worshipful in this way than they would be listening to Bach's B-minor Mass.

In compiling the *New Hymnal* in 1981–82, the Hymnal Committee made special efforts to encourage the writing of original Chinese hymns with Chinese tunes, and after screening hundreds of "contributions," finally decided to include about fifty "new" hymns in the *Hymnal*, (the other fifty Chinese hymns were considered "old" as they were written before 1949). I have heard many Western visitors who, after hearing these hymns sung in the churches or from cassette tapes, comment that they sound "very Western" to them. Now, what is it that makes a hymn Chinese? What are the valid criteria by which one can judge whether a hymn is really Chinese or not? These are very difficult questions to answer. Some hold that it is the nationality of the composer that determines the Chineseness. Others believe that it is the subjective feeling or reaction on hearing the hymn. Perhaps different people give different answers. This is not a question of better, less good or bad hymns. The issue is that as the Chinese Church is trying to change the former infamous and unwelcome image of Christianity as an "imported foreign religion" into one that is really *Chinese*, whether it is necessary, possible and desirable to change its hymnody to make *it* more *Chinese*. The purpose of the Hymnal Committee is to try to encourage production of more hymns that will appeal more to the sensitivity of Chinese Christians at large, to their minds and hearts in public worship and private devotion. Personal taste and liking may have a part to play in making judgments. I believe majority opinion and time will be the court of final appeal.

Assimilation with Traditional Classical or Folk Music

China has a rich historical cultural legacy in music. The repertory of *guqin* 古琴 (a long lute or zither with seven strings) and of other classical instruments is an abundant wealth and resource to be tapped and appropriated for religious uses through reproduction and arrangement. The late great hymn writer and hymnologist Prof. Ernest Y.L. Yang 杨荫浏 must be taken as our exemplary mentor.[6] Forty years ago when I tried to dabble

---

6. Several of his arrangements from ancient *guqin* tunes are included in *Hymns of*

Inculturation of the Gospel and Hymn Singing in China 117

in the art of *guqin*, it suddenly dawned upon me that some of the tunes could be used with the words of the Psalms for congregational singing. That was how I came to experiment with Ps.100 and 103 (Nos. 380 and 381 of the *New Hymnal*). Sometimes it is the motif or idiom of a piece of music that ignites one's imagination, and there is more freedom for creative accommodation. No. 178, *The Miraculous Pen of Divine Work*, 神工妙筆歌 developed from the motif of a well-known lute tune 平沙落雁 (*Descending swans over the beach*, attributed to Zhang Quan 张权 of the Ming dynasty) is an illustration or this. These arrangements seem to be well accepted by congregations in China.

Folk music, both vocal and instrumental, also provides a wealth of resources for assimilation. The following are some illustrations from the *New Hymnal*:

No. 30 天恩歌 *Great Are Thy Mercies, Heavenly Father*, words by T.C. Chao, tune 鋤頭歌 (Song of the Hoe), a popular folk song in north China.

No. 43 尊主歌 *Gracious and Loving is our Lord*, words by T.C. Chao, folk song tune from north China.

No. 51 耶穌美名歌 *Sweet and Holy Jesus' Name*, words by C. Goodrich (1836–1925), who used a Chinese folk-song tune *Molihua* (茉莉花) for his famous hymn found in 頌主聖詩 (1911).

No. 59 聖靈歌 *May the Holy Spirit's Sword*, words by T.C. Chao, the music I derived from 如夢令 (As If Dreaming) a tune for chanting *ci* poetry.

No. 83 歡樂佳音歌 *Shout the Glad Tidings*, using the melody of the folk instrumental *ensemble*, (歡樂歌) included in 頌主聖詩 (1921, 1934, 1939, 1940), a Christmas hymn very popular throughout China.

Nos. 379, 382, 383, 384: Psalms 23, 121, 133, 150. The tunes for these Psalms are taken from traditional folk music of unknown origin. They are all well-loved and sung by almost all congregations all over China.

A special project to collect and publish hymns written and composed by Chinese Christians in mainland China, Taiwan and overseas in Southeast Asia was launched in Singapore under the sponsorship of Trinity Theological College, with Mr. David Yap (业志明) as chief-editor. As a result, three issues of *HuaxiaShengshi* 華夏聖詩 have been printed in Nanjing and the fourth in Singapore. Each issue contains twenty to twenty-five hymns and short anthems composed by Chinese musicians or arrangements from traditional folk tunes. A new *Popular Edition* in numerical notation was just published in 1996 (Singapore: Trinity) for distribution among Chinese speaking churches in Asia. All theseappear to have been warmly welcomed by congregations both in the cities and rural areas in China.

Universal Praise and the *New Hymnal* (Nos. 13, 195).

MUSIC OF THE MINORITY ETHNIC NATIONALITIES

Of the fifty-three ethnic nationalities in China, many are well-known for their talents in dancing and singing. Korean and Miao (苗)Christians are exceptional in the use of harmony in their choral singing. The tune to 耶穌升天歌 *Behold, There Came a Cloud So Bright* (No. 115), composed by the Chinese-Korean Minister Rev. Wu Ai' en (吴爱恩) of the Xita (西塔) Korean Church in Shenyang (沈阳), is one of the most popular hymns for Ascension. I have heard a recording of a Miao nationality choir in Yunnan (云南) singing my anthem *The Easter Morn* (復活的清晨) in four-part harmony beautifully without instrumental accompaniment. The Miao have compiled a hymnal with four-part staff notation, but they are accustomed to sing in harmony spontaneously (faking) by ear, usually a *cappella*. I think the Chinese ethnic nationalities are a rich mine of talent which we should make special endeavors to tap and excavate for the development of church music in China.

IS THERE A ROLE FOR BUDDHIST AND TAOIST MUSIC?

One of the earliest Chinese hymns to be included inmany Western hymnals is *God, We Praise You for This Lord's Day* (words later revised by T.C. Chao). The tune name is *Pu-to* (普陀), the name of an island off the coast of Zhejiang (浙江) province, known for the famous Buddhist monastery situated there. The tune was originally the melody of the chanting of the monks in the temple. As a Christian hymn, it was sung in many churches in southern China in different local dialects. Perhaps it was the very first Chinese hymn tune to be included in many Western hymnals. Recently I learned that it had been used toset a poem written by Dietriech Bonhoeffer to music. Most congregations in China did not know it had originated in Buddhist tradition, and found it quite congenial to their faith. But when its Buddhist origins became known to the learned hymnal editors, it was discarded because of its "syncretistic nuances." Over eighty per cent of Chinese Christians are fundamentalists, and any suggestion of assimilating Buddhist or Taoist elements in hymn singing (or in translating) would be immediately met with opposition and protest. (There was a heated argument over the translation of the word *mystery* in the great hymn *Holy HolyHoly* as 妙身 because the expression was thought to be Buddhist usage!) When I tried to arrange the beautiful ancient lute tune 普庵咒 (all monastery chanting) for Ps. 103, I changed the tune-name to普安頌 (*Hymn for Universal Peace*). The first two characters in both names sound exactly alike, and the tune was accepted without ado.

Now Buddhists and Taoists in China have developed their temple music to an amazing degree, and have produced many high quality recordings for propagation and distribution. Most are traditional in style and very beautifully performed. But occasionally I seem to detect in their temple ensembles some resemblance to Western melodies and even phrases or lines of Christian hymn tunes wrapped up in traditional instrumental accompaniments plus modem electronic sound mixer. Perhaps Buddhist and Taoist believers are less afraid of being "contaminated" by the Christian religion. It may take some time before we can have interfaith theological dialogues in China, but would it be possible and profitable to begin right now to try to have some interfaith musical dialogue? I like to quote Paul's admonition in Phil. 4:8 for our Chinese Christian friends who are afraid of being syncretistic in hymn singing, as well as in other areas of Christian expression:

Finally, beloved, whatever is true, whatever is honorable, whatever is just, whatever is pure, whatever is pleasing, whatever is commendable, if there is any excellence and if there is anything worthy, of praise, **think about these things.**

In the course of writing this paper, two things came to my mind.

First, I was recently given a small book entitled *I don't like That Music*, by the author.[7] He has taught church music for over forty years in many countries and areas, and is a hymnologist well-known for having a personal collection of over 7,500 volumes of hymnal material, with an emphasis on non-Westem hymnody. The analyses and advice in this book can be taken as guidelines for contextualization of hymns in the non-Western world. "Why don't we sing new songs to the Lord?"[8]

Secondly, a consultation was recently convened by the Hong Kong Chinese Christian Churches Union in Hong Kong, September 6–8, 1996, on the theme "Whither Chinese Church Music in the Future?" Invited to this consultation were church musicians from mainland China, Hong Kong and Taiwan, among them the editors of the CCC *New Hymnal* (1983), Dr. Heywood Wong, editor of *Hymns of Universal Praise* (Editions 2 to 6), and Dr.I-To Loh (骆维道), editor of *Bamboo* (The Christian Conference of Asia). The theme of this consultation indicates that the necessity, possibility, desirability and multiformity of indigenization of hymn singing, as one important dimension of inculturation of the gospel, is now being made a priority.

---

7. Robert H. Mitchell, *I don't like That Music* (Hope Publishing, 1993).
8. Ibid. Chapter 6.

In conclusion, I want to turn to the illuminating paper by Prof. Justo L. Gonzales which is included in the present collection. In his conclusion, he makes reference to two passages in the book of Revelation. Both passages make direct reference to hymn singing:

They **sing a new song**: you are worthy to take the scroll and to open its seals, for you were slaughtered and by your blood you ransomed for God, **saints from every tribe and language and people and nation**; you have made them to be a kingdom and priests serving our God, and they will reign on earth (Rev. 5:9–10).

After this I looked, and there was a great multitude that no one could count, **from every nation, from all tribes and peoples and languages**, standing before the throne and before the Lamb, **robed in white, with palm branches in their hands. (Rev. 7:9).**

This paper is based in part on my presentation Recent Developments in Congregational Singing in Mainland China, made at the 1996 Annual Conference of the Hymn Society in the United States and Canada, July 14–18, Oberlin College, Oberlin, Ohio.

Chen Zemin is Vice-Principal of Nanjing Union Theological Seminary where he is also Professor of Systematic Theology. He is a past Vice-President of the China Christian Council and a respected authority on church music.

Reconciliation with the People
(Montréal, 1981)

Chen Zemin

PRIOR TO 1950 THERE was hardly any theology that the Protestant Church in China could claim to be characteristically her own. For almost a century and a half, the "Chinese Churches" were never anything other than outposts of Western missionary societies. They were just dots on the maps of missionary activities. Although sincere and arduous attempts had been made by some Christian leaders to plant the Gospel on Chinese soil, because of historical circumstances they could hardly go any further than just vending fragments or parcels of Western traditional or current theologies, dabbed with some sprinklings of Chinese phraseology. Theologies of this sort could never take root, and meant very little to the grassroots Chinese Christians, because they did not grow out of the real experience of the Chinese Christians.

Now, thanks to the Three-Self Movement, a truly Chinese Church, having rid herself of Western domination and tutelage, increasing identified with and accepted by the Chinese people, is emerging. The historico-social setting is entirely new. One fourth of the world's population has embarked on building an independent socialist country. Chinese Christians, while working shoulder to shoulder with our compatriots in this common task, are sincerely trying to relate the Christian faith and commitment to the great experience the Chinese people are going through. Our church is as yet small and young, and we have many problems and difficulties, but we can say now that there is a Chinese church, a "church" coming of age, not quite in the ecclesiological sense, but a viable community committed to the Christian faith. During the three decades of struggle and experimentation, we have gained some theological insights that we would like to share with our fellow Christians abroad.

Our point of departure is to opt for the people, to opt for the welfare of our country, and to opt for a social system that is more just and humane than anything the Chinese people have seen in our history of our four thousand years. The People's Republic is by no means perfect. There is much to improve. There are defects and mistakes and, consequently, tragedies. After all, to err is human. But to more than ninety per cent of the population it is in a realistic and historical sense "the best of all possible worlds"— to use the Leibnitzian phrase. And to follow his theory of theodicy further, as the God we Christians believe in is omnipotent, omnipresent, omniscient, at once just and loving, we are convinced that there is God's salvific purpose in the historical event of the liberation of the Chinese people, under the "mask" of God, as it were. God does not take a neutral stand. He sides and struggles with the people. In a class society, He sides with the oppressed, the poor, the sinned-against, as Jesus Christ has manifested, according to the Gospels. So all who choose to side with the people are actually on God's side. This opens up an extensive vista to our theological thinking.

Take, for instance, the problem of nature and grace, and some of the important theological issues connected with it. The dichotomies we find in traditional or classical theology seem to be dissolving in a monistic synthesis. To retain the classical terminology I endorse the Thomist declaration that "grace does not remove nature, but fulfills it." But to think of grace as a *donumsuperadditum* and to accept the two-storeyed structure of a natural-supernatural universe seem somewhat stigmatic of a medieval world view. Would it not be simpler and more comprehensible to conceive the cosmos as an evolving continuum of creation-evolution-salvation-consummation process? In the Chinese language cosmos is properly conveyed by the expression 宇宙. The first character literally means infinite space and the second means time from and to eternity. If we add the Greek idea of order and harmony in all its complexities, and infuse it with the Christian faith in a God as the sovereign Lord of universe and history, I think such a view will not prove too unacceptable to the Chinese mind. As to the trinitarian concept of God, if we forgo such archaic expressions as *homoousios, filioque-* and the like, however important they were to the Greek and Latin Fathers, the social implication of Trinity could be made appreciable to the Chinese people who have been culturally and traditionally more communal than individualistic. I might add that contemporary existential thinking finds little resonance in China. Generally speaking, the Chinese mind is more ethical than metaphysical, more practical than theoretical or mystical, more this-worldly than other-worldly. There is a strong and far-reaching tradition of humanism and humanitarianism. Here we find the concept of community an essential point of contact. Man's being is realized only in community, in the relationship of man with man. It is in human community that God is known and realized, that the divine activity in the world is manifest.

Therefore, if we understand Incarnation as the Son of God, the Word, or the Cosmic Christ made flesh, that He came to dwell among us (Jn. 1:14), taking humanity as the temple of God, realizing God's creative and salvific power and purpose in human history, I think the doctrine should not be too much of a stumbling block to us. We see history as one, and the partition of a secular or profane history and a history of salvation seems rather arbitrary and not so convincing. There is no absolute distinction between sacred and profane. Every event of life is a sacrament. In the same vein the separation and antithesis between general and specific revelations, reason and faith, law and gospel, progress and the kingdom of God, and so on, can be bridged over and seen in a holistic way. The two foci in theology, God and Man, may be so co-ordinated that the *loci theologici* which form an ellipse, may be seen gradually becoming a circle of which the cosmic and incarnate Christ is the center and human community the circumference.

The idea of sin is not at all discarded or dimmed. Rather, it takes on a more realistic significance. To think of sin as essentially human self-assertion against the sovereign God does not appeal so much to the Chinese mind as failure to obey the two great commandments or violation of God's will in human relationships. The traditional belief-unbelief antagonism is gradually giving way to taking social justice and attainment of *summum-bonum* of the community as the ideal of Christian life. But man is always falling short of the highest good after which he is forever aspiring. Here the Pauline expression of struggle between flesh and spirit epitomizes the whole history of human dilemma in his striving to reach the Omega Point, to borrow Teilhard's obscure terminology. The redemptive function of Christ lies in the enhancement of the capacity of whosoever accepts Him and lives in Him and is freed from the bondage of sin. "Thanks be to God, who does this through our Lord Jesus Christ" (Rom. 7:25).

We are thankful that we did not have the historical burden of a Christendom mentality. There has never been a Christendom in China and we do not strive to have one. The church is primarily a *koinonia*, a sharing fellowship, and secondarily an *ecclesia*, the called out, and certainly not an institution or a hierarchy or a ruling body. It is a community in which the presence of Christ is taken as a dimension of human potentiality revealing higher levels of mutual self-realization, a community for the development of personal relationships of depth. The church is commissioned not to rule the world but to bear witness to the Kingdom of God, working as leaven or yeast (Matt. 13:33). The post-denominational nature of the Chinese Church is closer to the New Testament pattern. The Cyprianic formula of "outside the church no salvation" is giving way to the ideal of universal brotherhood. Traditional emphasis of evangelism on making converts and increasing the quantity of church membership is shifting to improving the quality of the church's relations with the people. Compassion and service take the place of a self-righteous Jonah mentality. Mutual respect and a healthy spirit of latitudinarianism have submerged and allayed age-long denominational disputes. As to church policy and matters of ministry and liturgy, we are moving rather slowly, making experiments under the guiding principles of indigeneity and unity in diversity instead of uniformity.

More and more Chinese Christians have come to question the validity of traditional eschatology. I myself *agree* with Moltmann's etymological analysis and criticism that the term *eschato-logy (eschatos* and *logia)* is wrong, and appreciate his theme of hope. Why speculate on the last things when history is just beginning? We can only think of the future, have faith in the future, hope for the future and struggle for the future. Why posit a catastrophic destructive end to a world that God was pleased with in His creation? To pronounce a Final Judgement before which all human achievements will *come* to naught does not sound like a Gospel, and certainly runs counter to the purpose and promise in God's creative activity, with men as His co-workers. One senior teacher in our Seminary shifted his chiliastic view from premillenarianism to postmillenarianism because he saw new China as too good for him to wish it to be destroyed, and he would like to see it develop and grow and progress for at least another thousand years before the final judgement. This change within the limit of a set theological framework is prompted by his option for the people and for the new socialist system. Others would rather remain open for some new light on the subject, because they now feel it not edifying to "prophesy" against humanity.

These are just some salient points of our theological reflection, which is still in a nascent state. Every topic may become a growing edge and we should like to keep it this way. To systematize prematurely may jeopardize the viability and creativity of our young church. We are thinking in the spirit of "letting a hundred flowers bloom." Not long ago a group of Christian thinkers of different backgrounds got together to share and discuss their theological insights. From the diversified expressions and expositions one senses a common point of departure and a common trend. Paul Tillich suggested that theology must *be* done again in every age. If I am to give a general description of what we are doing in our age, based on our experience and understanding, I would venture to say that it is a theology rediscovering God's greatness, goodness, and gracefulness to our people and to humanity as a whole, a theology full of hope, a theology full of struggle to live a communal life more bountifully and harmoniously, guided by a "faith which is the assurance of things hoped for and the conviction of things not seen" (Heb. 11:1).

Aside from historical praxis, we are drawing as sources of theological thinking from what I may call Chinese contemporary secular thinking among academic circles as reflected in the mass media. Discussions on the value of philosophical idealism, on the meaning of life, stress on the "beauty of mind and spirit," controversy on the nature and social functions of religion, and many others, have been very thought-provoking. Contacts with contemporary Western theologies also prove illuminating. You may have noticed that what I have said above seems to bear some similarity to Liberation Theology. I want to point out that Christian thinkers in Latin America and China have both started with a social background of colonial or semi-colonial nature, and our points of departure are comparable in our historical praxis and option for the people. These account for the parallelism of theological thoughts. But while we are comrades-in-arms on different frontiers, our Latin American friends are using theology as a social and political weapon for the cause of liberation. Chinese people, Christians included, have been liberated thirty years since, in the sense that political power and ownership of means of production have been transferred from the hands of a minority of oppressors to the people. Our theological task is not liberation as such, in the Latin American sense, but reconciliation-to be reconciled to and identified with the Chinese people as a whole, from whom we had been alienated, for the carrying on of our task of liberation for the further betterment of our society; and at the same time, to be reconciled to God, from whom the human race has been alienated and with whom we all yearn to be united through the mediating mystery of the incarnate Christ in the endless course of human history.

The teachings of some Western theologians, particularly those who give importance to history, have been very stimulating. But I must add that we have come to know them rather recently. Therefore, while I am audacious enough to share some insights with you, in a simplistic manner, I must say there is much that we can and hope to learn from you, especially from those who are standing on the people's side. I say the people, which carries a concrete, historical and social connotation in contrast with the abstract philosophical concept of humanity.

RESPONSE:

DAVID PATON: What Dean Chen has just said makes me aware that somehow in the various Christian attempts *to* get into China, we have failed to present the Eastern Orthodox tradition, which is barely known in China. If you wanted to push, expand, and explore what Dean Chen was saying, you'd get much more help out of the Greek Eastern fathers than from us Latins, whether we are Protestant or Catholic. He is not the only person who is feeling after the insights of the church *before* the division between East and West. One of our sins, I think, was that we failed to bring Eastern Christianity with us when we went to China one hundred and fifty years ago.

MASAO TAKENAKA: I find the theological formulations presented today full of new insight, coming out of new socio-political situations, in the process of people's struggles. And I think we acknowledge the reality of social and political suppression and domination very much. At the same time when we say we take sides with the people, that means people not only as they are in the modem period of oppression, but also in the long life of the community with all its historical background. How does the relatively recent status of political and social domination and of struggle for liberation relate to a long cultural tradition such as in China? I am thinking of the long, accumulated Confucian teaching. In this new theological formulation, how does one relate to the traditional thinking such as Confucianism? Could you illuminate this point a little?

CHEN ZEMIN: I shall make a very brief comment on the Chinese traditional culture. We have had a very far-reaching and long tradition of humanism and humanitarianism. By saying so I think Confucianism is included. We have been trying to indigenize Christianity, but at present I think the idea of contextualization is much better and more extensive than just trying to indigenize, which carries more or less a sense of looking backward through history. But to think of theology in context includes, I think, the taking over of the positive elements of Chinese historical cultural tradition, although the most important thing for us remains to emphasize the present historical and social context.

JEAN CHARBONNIER: I just wish to say that I feel very happy with the clarification which has been made by Chen Zemin on the theology of liberation and how it is viewed from China. You made the point very clearly. Also, because *there is* a long Chinese tradition on the centrality of the people from Mengzi (Mencius) to Sun Yat-sen, it would be a great contribution to the whole of theology if there were a Christian interpretation of this same notion.

Theological Construction in the Chinese Church[1]

(Nanjing, 1956)

Chen Zemin

THE CHURCH AT REFLECTION

THEOLOGY IS THE THEORY of the spiritual experience of the church; it is a summation of the religious experience of the church in a given historical period. As a system of thought, it begins with traditional doctrines and beliefs, but then takes fresh and distinctive spiritual experiences, systematizes them and elevates them to the level of theory which is then used to guide the work of the church and to indicate the direction in which it should move. The truth of the Bible and the gospel of the Christ are not limited by time and space. Theology, however, is limited by specific historical conditions, the particular era, people, nation, and church experiences vary with time and place. Certain individuals may, due to their religious endowments and experiences, have unusually outstanding theological insights and make special contributions. But if spiritual experiences which serve as basis of theology, are to have any influence on the broad masses of the church, they must achieve a certain level of popular acceptance and have the ability to call forth a response from their believers. We speak of the theologies of certain theologians (such as those of Augustine, Luther, Schleiermacher, or Ritschl), but these theologies represent only the experience and insight of a few individuals. It is only when these experiences and insights are broadly representative and reflective of the communities from which they spring

---

[1] This essay was written in 1956 and originally appeared in the Nanjing Theological Review, Nos. 5 and 6, 1957.

Chen Zemin (Rev.) is vice-principal of Nanjing Theological Seminary where he is also professor of systematic theology.

that these theologies will attract noticed and be accepted. Theology is created by the church, not by individuals.

The church has historically been subject to the economic, political, cultural and social influences of its era, people and nation; therefore, there are theologies of different eras and regions, of peoples and of countries, such as the theology of the Greek Church Fathers, of the ancient North African church, Reformation theology, Germanic theology, etc. All these were responses to the different needs and special experiences of their times. Even though these theologies were all based on the revelation of the Bible and Christian faith, and preserve to a certain extent the historical traditions of Christianity, they all reflect different Christian experiences and understandings as people sought to live put the gospel, as inspired by the Holy Spirit, in their own times. Because theology encompasses life experience, it is intrinsically alive and dynamic, and it grows and develops with the life of the church. It contains faith, but is not equivalent to faith; it contains the truth of the gospel, but is not the whole truth of the gospel. It is a commentary on the faith and truth of the gospel, an expression of the life of the church; it is the church at reflection. The content of the reflection is the faith and experience of the church. Reflection without content is mere formalism or dead dogma—it is not theology. Unexamined experience is simply immature feeling; it is puerile and may well be misguide and misleading. So religious experience precedes theology, and is the foundation of theology. And mature church must have its theology, just as a mature person must be capable of conscious, coherent thought.

The church of new China is growing, and with the development of the Three-Self Patriotic Movement (TSPM) it is now embarking on a new chapter in its life. In the five or six years since 1949, it has accumulated much precious and significant new spiritual experience. The process of growth and maturation which the church is undergoing demands that the church sort out and make sense of these experiences. In order that the church be better able to reflect, and become a self-aware and united church, it must have its own theology. This timely demand has been raised, and now a task lies before the church which has never and never could have arisen before. The young Chinese church stands now in the forefront of process, and faces a new historical era unlike any in the two thousand year history of the Christian Church. If the church wishes to continue to exist in the midst of a new society, it must recognize its duty and complete its mission. It is now bearing witness both to itself and to its lord Jesus Christ. It already has sufficient experience and material upon which to reflect, and can review the road along which it has come. The church must tell the many Christians who live beyond the environs of this social system how the church has chosen its path and how it has moved forward. It must use the language of theology, a language easily understood by Christians and theologians, and through faith and in the context of the history of Christianity, it must tell the story of its spiritual experience to prove that it has chosen the right path. The church should also make use of this same mode of thinking to determine and indicate its future direction. This task is unprecedented in the experience of the Chinese church.

THE THEOLOGICAL POVERTY OF THE PRE-1949 CHURCH

It has already been one hundred years since Protestant Christianity entered China, and many Chinese have accepted the Christian faith and joined the church. But until the unfolding of the TSPM, a truly "Chinese" church had never been established. The word "Chinese" had been appended to the names of many churches, but this was not enough to show that these were really churches belonging to Chinese believers. This obviously applies to those churches with a western mission agency background. As for the churches that called themselves "self-established" such as the "Chinese Independent Church of Jesus" and the "True Jesus Church," though they had no economic or administrative links with western mission agencies, their thinking was dominated by western theology. The point is that not the Chinese churches must be completely different from western churches in administrative forms and theologies. Since we are Christians, we necessarily have many things in common with western Christianity, we cannot possibly cut ourselves off completely from the historical traditions of western Christianity, nor do we desire to do so. If that were to happen, we would cease being a Christian church. The main problem is this: Before 1949, the introduction of Christianity to China was closely bound up with the process of colonialism, so it was impossible for the Chinese church to develop any independent theological thought that could be termed Chinese. Some western missionaries, internationally or unintentionally, used their mission work as a method and means of aggression. For some, their original intent was not the spread of the gospel. As E.C. Bridgman intimated, their purpose in China was not so much religious as it was political. Of course, such people could not possibly help us gain true spiritual experience of the kind that could serve as the basis for a theology of the Chinese church. When such people did discuss theology in China, as happened when missionaries established seminaries here, they only bandied about worn-out theological clichés and could not do very much to cultivate real theological interest.

There were missionaries who may not have consciously and actively used religion as a means of aggression, or who really believed that their purpose in China was to spread the gospel. However, guided by the erroneous policies of western mission agencies, in an environment of culture imperialism, and in a period in which China was not a truly independent nation, the spread of gospel and the spread of western culture and lifestyles became inextricably intertwined to the point that speaking English and eating western food virtually became necessary conditions for discussing Christian theology. A Chinese person who accepted this kind of Christianity was to a certain extent also accepting the influence of western thought and lifestyles, and therefore to some extent abandoning the thought patterns and feelings of a true Chinese and becoming alienated from the masses of the Chinese people. In this way the Chinese Christian church actually became a parasitic "daughter church" of western mission agencies. Because it was not a true Chinese church, how could it theologize in a genuinely Chinese way?

In the past, western missionaries opened seminaries in China and taught "Christian theology." Western missionaries brought the Bible to China, and through the guidance of the Holy Spirit we found the gospel in God's word and revelation. We gained some knowledge of the Bible and the Christian religion from the west. We do not deny that such knowledge was of some help in our study of the Bible, in our search for truth, and in our acceptance of the gospel. But with regard to theology which must be based on the spiritual experience of believers, we must plainly state that we cannot simply copy the theology of the west. If we were to swallow western theology whole without critical examination, it would choke the Chinese church's own theology and stifle the newly-born spiritual experience of Chinese believers. Here we must make a distinction between the age-old Christian theological heritage and harmful modern western ideas. The Christian heritage is of the value to us as long as we can accurately understand, absorb and use it, because it is the distillation of many generations of accumulated rich Christian spiritual experience and achievements in the search for truth. Harmful western ideas will only be an obstacle and a hinderance in our spiritual experience and search for truth. Yet it is frequently only through the latter that western theologians introduce and explain the former. This serves to explain the pathetic state of theology in the pre-1949 Chinese church.

It may be helpful to mention a few examples to illustrate this situation. In the first decade of this century, American theologians wrangled endlessly over the issue of fundamentalism vs. modernism, and the fray was soon introduced into the Chinese church. Before most Chinese Christian had even figured out what fundamentalism and modernism were, and what these arguments represented in America, they had already fallen into blind, narrow denominational disputes, fighting vigorously and loyally for their western teachers, and causing divisions in the young Chinese church. After the First World War, when western nations sank into poverty, bitterness and despair, the western church turned from blind optimism to pessimism and bewilderment. The "theology crisis" was immediately exported in China, and China's theologians took pride in quibbling over Kiekegaard's "sickness onto death," and the paradoxes of "dialectical theology." When Catholic theologians tried to disguise medieval obscurantism under the high-sounding name "New scholasticism," Chinese theologians lost no time in discussing Jacques Maritain and Etienne Gilson. When western psychology and psychiatry began to make inroads into pastoral theology, many ministers tried to lecture on Freud and Jung's "depth phycology" from the pulpit, rather than preaching the gospel. Stanley Jones' *Victorious Living* became a bargain-basement gem in China and was passed around as best-selling spiritual nourishment. When western rostrums blared opposition to the Communist Party and the Soviet Union, many theologians in China abandoned the slogan of staying above politics and preached about the fundamental antagonism between Christ and Communism. Even the crudest distortions of the Bible (such as allusions to the red horse in Revelation and Rosh in Ezekiel) were all treated as reliable exegesis of prophecy. In reality, this so-called "latest western theology" reflected the spiritual deterioration of the western church, but because of the Chinese church was the "daughter church" of western church, such rubbish was introduced into China as if it was treasure.

If we examine theological publishing in the pre-1949 Chinese church, we find little to recommend it. Most of the publications were translations, and most selections were made by western missionaries. Most theological books edited or written by Chinese authors were compilations rather than original works, or were general reviews. Genuinely creative works were rare. At such a time there could be no genuinely Chinese church, the Chinese church could not govern or support itself, and we had little authentic spiritual experience of our own upon which to draw for self- propagation. In such a situation, poverty of theological thought was only natural, and a theology able to transcend its time was an impossibility.

This explains the dispirited theological ambience of the pre-1949 Chinese church, and the meagerness of contemporary theological thought. It was not until the birth of new China that Christians were roused from their benighted and half-starved condition.

THE AWAKENING OF THEOLOGY IN A NEW ERA

Spiritual experience is the foundation of theology. In 1949, Chinese believers awoke to the clarion call of the Three-Self Patriotic Movement. In the beginning, many people looked on the TSPM as primarily a patriotic movement. Through this movement, they came to see the true face of imperialism and realize that Christianity had been used as a tool of imperialist aggression in China; they learned how to stand on the side of the people in making distinctions between friend and foe, and how to enthusiastically love new China; and they criticized some of the poisons of imperialism. However, until recently, many believers had not realized the religious and spiritual significance of the movement, and therefore had not taken the trouble to sum up its spiritual value and meaning. In fact, from the very beginning, this awakening from stupor, this move from darkness and ignorance into light, and this intense struggle against the forces of evil have all been precious spiritual experiences for Christians. In the last few years, both individuals and the church have been through a baptism of fire and have seen such new light. It is when we realize that it is the Spirit of Christ which has led us along this bright new road, when we suddenly realize the spiritual significance of this experience, that we naturally express a desire for theology. Through theology we hope to sum up the experience of these few years, through faith we desire to consolidate our gains, and we hope to point out the path we should travel in the future. Even though we firmly believe that it is Christ himself who has opened the way for us, these experiences are too fresh—we have never been through such experiences before—and they require us to reinterpret some traditional views to which we have long been accustomed. In the process of reinterpretation, we may experience doubt and pain. We need to pray and reflect much before we can have the confidence to lift our feet and stride forward. Under these circumstances we may feel spiritually starved and intellectually weak. Like someone just recovered from an illness, we may have a convalescent hunger—a craving for spiritual satisfaction. This is a healthy sign. The scraps that we ate in the past now disgust us; we demand more nourishing food.

Several factors have caused our theological awakening, and that made this work of theological reconstruction possible:

1) The western mission boards and missionaries who controlled us for more than a century can no longer bind and direct us. Now we can completely throw off their restraints and manager our own church; relying on our own strength and piety, we can search for the light of Scripture. We have begun to think for ourselves and no longer need to

rely mentally on others. No matter how fragmentary and incompletely, this preliminary experience of self-government and self-support—this road of our spiritual Exodus—is a most precious experience for the church and is the foundation for our self-propagation. It would have been unimaginable for the pre-1949 Chinese church, dependent on the west for finances, administration and personnel, to think independently or to have had any message of self-propagation. Today the church of China has begun to breathe the fresh air of freedom and independence, and in this new ear of history it will continue to survive and be a vital witness.

2) Because the church has begun a free, independent existence, it has gradually come to realize that the western "mother" did not do a good job of supporting and helping. Instead, in many ways this mother restrained, obstructed, even poisoned. We no longer accept things as blindly as we once did, and have started to view western theology with a critical eye. We must search for new light and revelation in the Bible to explain and guide our spiritual life. Whoever seeks will find, and we have indeed found. We have also made quite a few new discoveries. Our spiritual knowledge is gradually increasing, and God's grace is being showered on us ever more richly each day.

3) In this new era, Chinese Christians and the broad masses are together actively building our great socialist motherland. In our social, economic, political and cultural life, we have become a part of the new Chinese nation. In our thoughts and emotions we are becoming true Chinese. This important turnaround has been acknowledged, accepted and welcomed by the Chinese people. In the midst of daily life, the church has begun to shine its light, and we have come to realize even more that the life of church in society cannot be separated from the church's spiritual life. The experience of our church is becoming richer, and this is providing us with an inexhaustible supply of theological source material.

4) In the church's life in society, through shared work and experience we have discovered much shared light. The separation and disunity created by the denominationalism of the western missionaries is gradually vanishing. We have learned how to consider ourselves parts of the same body and how to build up the church; we have begun to see our own shortcomings as well as other people's strengths. We have truly experienced the daily richness of God's grace in the increase of our numbers. Different experiences and views need not create division. In fact, they enrich our religious life and thought. Mutual respect has

already gained increased significance and has brought our church both richness and a lively atmosphere.

5) The church is living in the modern age, and is in the process of exploring new paths. It is situated in an environment in which new China's academic and intellectual circles are broadly investigating materialism and freely discussing issues in accordance with the policy of "letting a hundred schools of thought contend." This forces Christians to re-examine the basis of their faith. Accepting religious faith is no longer a natural or casual matter, and theologians and ministers must convince people of significance of Christianity. People with questionable motives no longer surge into churches as they once did. Religion cannot be made use of for mom-religious goals any longer. Judging from the demands of this situation, evangelism naturally seems somewhat more difficult than it once was, but this is now real evangelism. Difficulties only serve to purify the work of evangelism and clarify its goals and significance, thus making it more noble and precious. Because of this, theology is spurred on to further development.

6) In the course of social revolution, our whole lives—including our economics, politics, culture, customs, and even our thoughts and emotions—are changing according to a new model of socialist life. This thoroughgoing change must necessarily influence the life of our church and our social experience, and requires new adjustment and adaptation. Now we are still caught up in these changes, but we firmly believe that these changes and adaptation will bring richness and glory to the life of our church. In our theology we must face such changes candidly and without reservation, we must not flinch, but believe that the socialist revolution will bring us good things. This obviously presents a new and stimulating task for theologians.

7) For the reasons mentioned above, we now have a new historical vantage point from which to view some western "theologians" as they struggle in the adverse currents of their culture. In the long march of human history, we are moving ahead. When we look at western theology, we no longer admire it blindly as we once did; we can see that many in the west are groping their way into blind alleys, having strayed from the true gospel of the church, and much that is precious in the historical tradition of the church has been lost. They are now gathering out-dated, useless things left behind by earlier generations of theologians and using obscure ancient terms to cover their spiritual poverty and ignorance of the truth. No one with any common sense would be in the market for such things, so they are compelled to borrow dead

Greek and Latin phrases praising the God of irrationality (*Deus irrationalis*), proclaiming the faith of absurdity (*Credo quiaansurdum*), and extolling ignorance (*Ignoramus et ifnoramibus*). They feel that the gospel can only be established on people's sense of hopelessness; they feel that if the church is to have a future, then the human race must have none. Observing some of the developments in western theology from our vantage point, we see that they are regressing in a direction exactly opposite of our progress; ahead of us, in contrast, there is endless light. Even though at present we have only limited material for theological construction, and some precious experience, we can confidently advance in the direction we have chosen. We know that we have the heavy responsibility and mission to lead people to God and to seek truth. We can proudly—bur not arrogantly—carry out our theological task. As we realize the nature of the mission that faces us today and accept this heavy responsibility, we do not feel arrogant, nor are we unwilling to humbly assimilate the precious historical heritage of Christianity from the west. We are fully aware that in the past our theological foundation was relativelyweak, and that in many areas we must painstakingly research and humbly learn. But God has already called us and placed us in this important position in history, so we cannot refuse this grace or responsibility.

Looking back at the history of Christianity, we see that Christian theology has advanced with the times and has already undergone many adaptations and transformations. The Church Fathers of ancient Greece expounded the Christian gospel to the believers of that day through Greek patterns of thought and language. The theological doctors of the Middle Ages attempted to use scholasticism in the interpretation of the gospel. The reformers of the sixteenth and seventeenth centuries found that the gospel could help them throw off the shackles of feudalism, resulting in great developments in theology during the Reformation. Following the new view of the universe ushered in by the development of the natural sciences, theologians of the eighteenth and nineteenth centuries expanded and deepened our faith in and understanding of the gospel. If the past two thousand years of theological work has indeed enriched our theological knowledge and expanded the domain of theology, it is only because theologians did not fail to promptly sum up those spiritual experiences characteristic of and significant for their times, organize them and elevate them to the level of theory, and add their achievements to the river of theological knowledge. Today we stand at an extremely important point in the history of human society, and the church is thus also brought to this critical stage in history. The church must bravely face this era, and explain the changes which it has brought from a spiritual viewpoint. This is the theological task of our church today.

LOCI AND FOCI

Although minute, fragmentary and incomplete, our experience, understanding and knowledge are not haphazard, chaotic and unrelated to each other. In this age of change, in this society brimming with creative energy, in this exceptional era in history, many things are advancing by leaps and bounds. Because of the dullness of our faith and our clouded spiritual eyes, our views and understanding often lag behind events. God's revelation appears in the earthquake and fire, yet our weakness causes us to cover our ears and eyes, afraid to face it. But we must never flee from the surging current of progress. Our faith is sluggish but not dead; our eyes are clouded but not totally blind. In the flood of history, we are still washed forward by an overpowering force. From amidst the scattered small whirlpools and the spray of the waves, we can still make out the main current. If we carefully pick up the crumbs scattered on the ground, when we have collected twelve full baskets, we will see the goodness of the one who gives us the broad of life. Spiritual hunger compels us to grope our way forward. The road which we have travelled has been marked for us by God.

Our theological pilgrimage is much like the geometric process of connecting many points into a locus chart, seeing its significance and then systematizing and drawing deductions and inferences from it. The first Protestant systematic theologian, Philip Melanchthon, called his systematic theological work *Loci Commenesreum Theologicarum*. The marvelous works of God are something that our limited human intelligence cannot fully grasp and comprehend, but he has given us revelation for the salvation of the human race. In history the dim pattern of his truth, of his loving, holy and just nature, and of his holy will can be traced in outline.

Let us continue to use this geometric concept for a moment. We find that the locus we explore shows a certain pattern; an unlimited wisdom and unfathomable love are guiding us. His will is the pattern of the locus, and this locus appears to be an ellipse. The moving point endlessly orbits around two foci—God and humanity—the focal points of theological thought over thousands of years. As history progresses, the moving point of the ellipse sometimes moves closer to God, taking him as the center, and is relatively distant from humanity; but sometimes it moves closer to humanity and further from God. Between God and humanity, a certain relation or connection is always preserved, but there is also distance between them. If the distance between these two foci were to be reduced to nil, God and humankind would become one. God might be absorbed by humankind, and the resulting extreme humanism would end in a denial of creation, the atonement and the gospel; the ellipse would vanish and become a circle. But if the distance between these foci were to increase infinitely, there would be absolute distance and opposition between God and humankind. The two end points would be pulling in opposite directions, resulting in the perishing of religious life. But history and experience tell us that the relationship between God and humanity involves both repulsion and attraction. God's love of the world and human dependence on God draw the two foci toward each other, but God's holiness and human sin prevent them from uniting and becoming one. This causes religion to become a necessary part of real life, and makes theology possible.

However, this ellipse is not stationary. As the moving point orbits around the two foci, history progresses and the relationship between God and humanity also progresses in time. Our elementary geometric metaphor fails at this point. This locus actually becomes an oscillating line formed by the moving points as it moves along the circumference of an ellipse which is advancing in a certain direction; this is a very complicated and advanced oscillating line. At this point, this geometric maze no longer benefits our theological thought, and instead becomes a hindrance. Here we have to give up this Cartesian theological approach. Before putting aside this advanced locus model, we must point out that the ellipse analogy contains another serious flaw: these two foci are not equal and symmetrical. God is always active, and humankind is always passive, though only relatively so.[2]

With the assistance of the locus model and the simple discussion above, we can easily grasp many of the central theological propositions debated in Judaism and Christianity over thousands of years. Many doctrines are actually explanations of this model; they explain the relationship between God and humankind are reflected in human religious life. On the one hand, God is actively seeking humankind through his creative and saving love; on the other hand humanity is in the midst of sin and weakness, accepting God's grace, responding to his gift of salvation and seeking a life directed toward him. In this meeting between humanity and God, humankind has ever-changing religious experiences and produces many doctrines and theological theories. The final end of these is nothing other than to explain what kind of relationship should exist between God and humankind. And to solve the conflicts which exist between God and humanity.

2 I was delighted to read of Karl Barth's *The Humanity of God* in 1983 in which he used the idea of an ellipse with God and humanity as the foci. –author's addendum, 1992.

This contradictory relationship appears not only in human religious life, but everywhere in the relationship between people and society. Thus, our theological duty is not only a metaphysical theory; it also touches on a human existence which includes all of the life of society, and theology thus becomes a produce of history and society, closely related to philosophy, anthropology and sociology.

Let us consider a few more examples to explain the relationship between the ellipse and its foci. A basis problem in Christian theology is the relationship between revelation and human reason. Are God's revelation and natural human reason in opposition to each other, or are they complementary? Is revelation opposed to reason, above reason or completely within the bounds of reason? Does so-called natural revelation really exist? Outside the special revelation of the Bible, can we see the movement of the will of God in the progress of history? Circling the two foci of a God who has revealed himself and a human race which has responded to God's revelation, there are different experiences and theories. There are extreme supernaturalists who totally reject natural revelation and repudiate the use of reason; there are also extreme rationalists and naturalists who take reason as the absolute criterion for judging revelation, who consider natural revelation to be the only kind of revelation, and who reject any supernatural revelation. Between these two extremes there are a variety of compromising and conciliatory viewpoints which form a curve.

Let us also look at the doctrines of the Trinity and Christology. Historically, theologians have wavered in their emphasis between Christ's divine and human natures. Though orthodox doctrine holds that Christ was fully divine and fully human, it is not easy to maintain this delicate balance perpetually. So, in ancient times there was Modalistic Monarchainism, which emphasized Christ's divine nature while neglecting his humanity, and Dynamic Monarchianism and Arianism, which stressed Christ's subordinate status. In the Reformation period, many of the theological disputes between Luther and Calvin revolved around this question of Christ's dual nature. With regard to the theories of the atonement there are extreme "objective" theories which place God at the center (like Anselm's substitution-satisfaction theory), and there are also extreme "subjective" theories, which place humanity at the center (Abelard), and a variety of schools of ethics. Other issues closely related to this problem have to do with theories of human nature and of sin. Advocates of "objective" atonement without exception stress original sin, total depravity and the absence of freedom. Those who hold to "subjective" atonement tend toward a variety of humanistic Socinian and Arminian positions. In between these extremes there are many compromise theories. Another example is the problem of the attitude of Christians toward the world, and of their relationship to the world. There are "otherworldly" and " apocalyptic" schools which totally reject this world and place their hope in the life to come; there are also the "social gospellers" who stress the present life and take the afterlife only as a theoretical possibility or a symbol.

These problems have been interminably debated by theologians over the ages. According to the spirit of the age, the social system and the experience of believers, the curving arc of the ellipse oscillates right and left, up and down as it circles the foci. Having stepped into this new era, we have the opportunity and the right to look back and study how this curve has changed in the past. Even more, we have the responsibility to explore the ways in which it will continue to develop in the future. We have seen many extremists and their fates; we also know that superficial compromise cannot last. In what direction is the experience of this new age pointing us? What problems will it solve? What unresolved problems lie before us, waiting for us to come to grips with them?

CONTINUITY OR DISCONTINUITY

Before we examine the ways in which theology can sum up the religious experiences of the Chinese church, we must raise a question which has faced theologians for centuries. Actually, it is the question of the relationship between the two foci mentioned above, but stated as a question of principles. We must decide: between God and humankind, between revelation and natural reason, between the gospel and ordinary ethics or cultural values, between Christianity and other religions, between faith and the absence of faith, between the church and society, between the kingdom of God and that of the world, between eternity and history—is there continuity or discontinuity? Over the ages, and with regard to many important theological questions, theologians have chosen their viewpoints and the foundation or standard of their faith from between this two contrasting principles. For example, with regard to the question of the relationship between God and humankind, those who hold to a discontinuity position naturally emphasize God's transcendence and distance from humankind. Those who hold to continuity stress God's immanence and closeness to humanity. The former treat God as "wholly other;" unreachably high, inaccessible to reason, and infinitely exalted; because of this, humankind's finitude and limitations are also seen as absolute, and humans are viewed as totally depraved, hopeless, and evil—as mere objects of God's wrath. The latter emphasize a God who lives among us, an affectionate, loving, forgiving father. Though humanity is fallen and evil, it is not to the point of hopelessness and death. Humanity is created in the image of God, we have freedom and moral obligations, we are objects of God's love and grace of salvation. The former stress God's act of salvation as the purpose of creation; the latter stress God's work of creation, with salvation as its fulfillment and completion. The former believe that God's revelation is absolute and special, they do not acknowledge natural revelation or natural theology, and they see human reason and knowledge as standing in opposition to God's revelation. While the latter admit that God's revelation is absolute and special, they do not deny that revelation can also be found in nature and history, and they see reason as the basis for accepting God's revelation. The former emphasize an absolute "quantitative difference" between eternity and time, so they view all movements in history through the eyes of eschatology and deny the possibility of any real progress within the realm of history. The latter see eternity as an endless extension of history, affirming that God's kingdom is both eternal and historical, and affirm that progress in history is under God's guidance and control. The former set the gospel and religion in opposition, seeing morality and salvation as in opposition, and feel that anything which is human—be it religion, morality, culture of arts—is of no value in God's eyes; it may even be evil, of the devil. The latter fell that all good things come from God, though human morality and culture are not sufficient for salvation. The former consider human pride and self-satisfaction the greatest of sins; the latter have hope for and confidence in humankind. The former criticize the latter for being naive, shallow and presumptuous; the latter see the former as being too one-sided, arbitrary and negative.

There is no need to continue with an endless list of comparisons. However, it should be noted that it superficially appears that those who stress discontinuity are emphasizing God as the center, while those who accentuate continuity are humanists. In reality, this is not the case. The former have definitely always considered themselves as orthodox theists, and have criticized the latter for humanistic heterodoxy. The latter certainly do value human nature and reality as a special characteristic of their thought. However, the key issue is not which of the two above-mentioned foci they weight more heavily, but lies in how they explain the relationship between the two. It is necessary to concede that both of the foci have unmistakable importance before there can be any discussion of the question of the relationship between them. For example, proponents of the discontinuity view do not deny that the problems of humanity, society and evil are important religious questions. So the "humankind" focal point is one of the central points of theology. But in the solution of these problems, they suggest that the absolute separation between God and humankind must be recognized before a way can be found to deal with this separation. Likewise, those who hold a continuity view do not deny God's transcendence, ignore human sin and fallen-ness, and do not oppose all supernaturalism. They are decidedly not simply extreme humanists. But they do feel that while God and humankind are distinct, they are not cut off from each other. Through a thousand ties and connections there is to a certain degree some kind of continuity, and this continuity makes atonement both necessary and possible. Since there is continuity, there must also be distance. If two points coincide and become one, there is no continuity.

We must also point out that although in theory the discontinuity and continuity viewpoints appear to be diametrically opposed, isolated systems which cannot be reconciled, in reality a theologian may belong to both camps to differing degrees with regard to different questions. That is to say, with regard to one question he may hold to some kind of discontinuity position, while on another issue he may take some kind of continuity position. It is not only a few individuals or a minority of theologians who hold such dual positions. On the contrary; it is those who hold absolute continuity or discontinuity positions who are extreme cases. Our locus thus becomes an ellipse which is smaller at the two ends and broad in the middle. The real world is complex and changing, and pure theory easily leads people to forget reality.

Analysis of this kind of comparison may be helpful to our inquiry. It helps us to see more clearly the paths we had chosen and how theological studies developed in the past. It shows us that the church had often used the discontinuity view as the criterion of "orthodoxy," and it shows us that the courageous spirit of the reformers who advocated the continuity view. It is only through the complementarity of these two views together that theology can progress with the times. They represent two kinds of attitudes, two tendencies, and over the ages theologians representing a diversity of leanings have appeared. If Irenaeus is a "father of orthodox theology" who was relatively close to the discontinuity view, then Justin Martyr clearly represents the continuity view (although he has never been criticized as heretic). In the disputes after the fourth century, many extremely far-sighted and wise theologians balanced orthodox doctrine between two contradictory principles. In the debate over human nature and atonement, Augustine gradually moved toward a discontinuity position, even to the point that he eventually became the predecessor and symbol for all those in later generations who held discontinuity views. The unfortunate Pelagius and the semi-Pelagians became scapegoats for the continuity position, but within that position there existed a certain inextinguishable truth and power, which even Augustine could not kill, and in succeeding ages many spokesmen for that position continued to appear.

Although medieval scholasticism produced proponents of the discontinuity position such as Anselm and the outstanding continuity advocated Abelard, the "school men" of the twelfth and thirteenth centuries wisely maintained a flexible compromise position. In reality they were using limited compromises to uphold the intellectual control which feudal papal authority had over people. By the fourteenth and fifteenth centuries, philosophy had been freed from the bounds of theology, like a maid servant escaping the control of the queen. This signified human intellectual liberation. The rise of continuity principles caused a crisis in scholasticism and medieval orthodox. During the Reformation, Luther and Calvin were forceful representatives of the discontinuity position, saving theological orthodox from decadent Catholicism, but at the same time Zwingli and Melanchthon showed streaks of the spirit of the continuity view. Seventeenth century Arminianism, German Pietism and the spiritualist movements—as represented by Franck and Schwenkfeld—showed a tendency to move from supernaturalism to naturalism.

The Enlightenment of the eighteenth century was the high tide for the continuity position, creating a serious crisis for traditional theology. The nineteenth century was an extremely chaotic period in theology. Western theologians tried to build theologically on the ruins left by the "New Though" of the eighteenth century, but we do not see that they established anything stable. They soon encountered a series of unavoidable crises. Even in the nineteenth century, while most western theologians still naively indulged in complacent dreams, the sensitive Danish theologian Kierkegaard was already sending out a discontinuity position alarm. He said that the basic principle of religion and human life was not "both/ and" but "either/ or." He stressed that God was "wholly other," that eternity was outside the realm of time, and that humanity was "sick unto death." He foresaw the collapse of western culture, but this melancholic prophecy was too much ahead of its time. It was only when Europe was awakened by warfare in the twentieth century that his pessimistic views found an audience. Today's west has rapidly and broadly accepted the principles of the discontinuity view because from within their own "lost-ness" they could not see hope for the human race; they were hostile to all progress and insisted on taking historical progress as an illusion, as a plot of the devil. They cheerfully hailed the bankruptcy of nineteenth century liberal theology, the abandonment of the continuity position, and the trampling of the banner of freedom and democracy. They lauded the final victory which the discontinuity view has achieved. But in the midst of this tragic victory they united to sing the swan song of humanity. Like many theologians before them, they raised the banner of orthodoxy—"Neo-Orthodoxy."

This was when the church of new China came on the scene. We have spent a little time above, using the principles of discontinuity and continuity, to briefly examine the path of the historical development of theology. Because we are in the midst of history, we cannot break its flow, but must instead inherit and develop it. Equipped with this preliminary historical perspective, we can even better understand our position and conditions, and clearly see our mission and the task before us.

OUR PROBLEM AND PATH

Upon first entering this new era, we did not immediately see the full nature of our problem—nobody presented us with a ready list of the issues. At first we felt insecure and apprehensive about our future; we hardly dared open our eyes. Like someone who has long lived in darkness, our eyes could not bear the sudden light, and we were forced to squint. We were much like the blind man in the Bible who, after being cured by Jesus, could only dimly see figures that looked like trees walking about (Mk 8:24). Naturally, he first asked: Are those people or trees? How is it that they can walk? How are they going to treat me? In the past seven years, we have gradually come to realize what our problems are, have solved some, and have discovered others. As our field of vision expands, we see a little more, a little farther, and a little more clearly, but we also encounter increasing problems. From the beginnings of human intellectual development down to the present, knowledge has always increased in this way, and human character has also developed in this way. This is a process of spiritual exploration, and also a process of growth in spiritual life. The heritage of western Christianity is rich, but to us it is the same as the entire historical and cultural heritage of the human race is to a new-born infant; he must learn and come to understand it gradually. It is only through the process of growth and his life experience that he understands that a part of this heritage does have significance for his life, because it is only as this heritage is gradually absorbed and assimilated that he can take it as his own knowledge, as a source of assistance in considering and solving problems. There is much other material stored in history which is precious but has no significance for him. Many problems and methods for solving them found in history can be of indirect assistance to us, but only as reference material; we cannot directly apply them to our own task of construction.

Here, let us simply list the problems we have encountered. All theological problems are very practical. First we encounter the two problems of understanding our environment and understanding ourselves. There two problems are mutually related because it is only when we understand our environment that we can really understand ourselves, and it is only when we clearly realize our position and standpoint that we can clearly view our environment. As we come to understand our environment, we must first comprehend what is happening around us through direct observation and contact, which leads to some rational understanding. Finally we must weigh and judge it on the basis of standards we consider reliable, using common sense from daily life and reasoning derived from practice. We must also use our moral principles and spiritual criteria of our faith to weigh everything in new China. But it is precisely in this last task of weighing and evaluating that we most profoundly discern that we must first accurately understand ourselves, that we begin to doubt the validity of the criteria which we use for evaluating our surroundings, and that we begin to question the accuracy of our judgments. We must seek the cause in ourselves.

This process of looking into ourselves provides a most important experience, an experience of objectively and boldly examining ourselves in the face of historical fact. Letting God's just and holy light illuminate the dark corners of our hearts is a spiritual experience of true repentance. It requires each person to be fully honest toward self, toward the world's affairs, and toward others, with not the slightest hypocrisy or concealment. It requires of us the ultimate humility and sincerity, admission of our frailty, sins and errors. It is only when we have fully repented of our sins that we can experience the shared love of our brothers and sisters. These experiences have been the most precious experiences of these first few years since Liberation. It is only on such a foundation that we can understand God's love, justice and forgiveness, and know what kind of standard to use in judging the people and affairs around us.

It was only in this way, through an experience of spiritual hardship, that we came to affirm the present situation and accept new China. In new China there are still weaknesses, errors and imperfections, but in view of these massive social reforms, of our sense of respect and concern for people, and of our hatred and disgust for the greatest sins of human history—war and exploitation—we confess from our hearts that our faith can only lead us to conclude that "all these proceed from God's justice and goodness." We see God's activity in the movement of history, and see reflections of God's image in the natural reason of humanity.

In the last two of three years we have heard Christians in many places discussing questions like the following: Does Christian faith require us to withdraw from the world? Can we love this world (including the society of new China)? Should we love it? Is the world completely under the power of the Evil One? What should the relationship be between those who believe in Christ and those who don't? Is God pleased with the good works done by non-believers; are they also from God? Is God carrying out his acts of justice and love by means of self-proclaimed non-believers? What should the relationship be between the church and the social system? Is there really a conflict between loving our country and loving church (loving God); is there an irreconcilable conflict? Do we now have religious freedom? In accepting and affirming new China and the leadership of the Chinese Communist Party, do we submit ourselves to some kinds of restrictions in our faith? We have already had clear answers to many of these questions, and there is no need to repeat them here, but we should point out that these answers point in a common direction: they point from western twentieth century discontinuity principles back toward a continuity view, from a view of an utterly transcendent God back toward immanence, from one end of the ellipse back toward the other.

People can't help but ask: Is history only moving in a cycle? Will humanity endlessly spin in circles? Is this real progress or an illusion? Western theologians suspiciously ask: Are you retuning to the path of nineteenth century American liberal theology? We firmly and confidently answer: "No."

We must simply and frankly point out the liberal theology is built on capitalist *laissez-faire* and the profit motive, and its slogan of freedom and democracy is only for the purpose of achieving free competition so that dog may eat dog. Theologically it distorts the teachings of the Bible and reduces religion to social morality, so it has very accurately been criticized by neo-orthodoxy as shallow, naive, hypocritical and failing to understand the basic nature of sin. We agree with these criticisms, but do not accept their inferences. Liberal theology was established on the basis of a collapsing social system; we are bearing witness to a society which is built on sincere mutual concern and an equal, reasonable relationship. It is only where the greatest majority of the people have happiness and freedom that each individual can enjoy true advancement and freedom; it is only where society has salvation that there can be individual salvation. But the social significance of the gospel does not submerge the spiritual freedom and the vibrant experiences of the individual. So we firmly state: History does not repeat itself. We see the erroneous paths of those who have gone before us; now we are avoiding those traps and following a newly opened road.

Thus, we must rely on our own exploration and experience to solve some other problems which lie before us. We must ask: What is our view of the problem of sin? Is it possible that with a general improvement in "social moral order" sin will automatically "decrease" in society or in the individual? On the one hand, we must profoundly and frankly consider the problem of sin. We cannot take the approach of evading the problem or burying our heads in the sand like an ostrich. On the other hand, we should not exaggerate the problem or absolutize it, thereby frightening or benumbing ourselves. Admittedly, the origin of sin includes social factors, but spiritually sin also represents humanity's imperfection and pride before God. Therefore, spiritual problems will not be solved just by changes in the social system, and sin will not vanish with the advance to social moral consciousness. Sin represents the ugly face of human nature, and it forces humanity to eternally look to God and seek salvation.

With regard to the question of salvation, we oppose taking sin as the foundation of the gospel and making human despair the basis for the future of the church. Instead, within God's just and loving nature we find the source of salvation. The reason the gospel is necessary, and the reason that the church has a future, is not that humanity has no future or that the world is without hope. Instead, the reason is that salvation is an act of God in his plan of creation. It is not because of our complete depravity that God seeks humankind. Humankind is the crown of God's creation, created in his image to tend this world for and with him, and it is for this reason that it is worthwhile for God to save humankind.

How then should the gospel be preached? When everyone is yearning for socialist construction, when everyone feels that the world can be transformed for the better, does not the gospel become foolishness? This is the most important question now facing us, and it forces us to go a step further and ask: What is the gospel after all? Do the answers found in history satisfy us? We must return to the Bible, and in the experience of the believers of the early church find the causes which led them to seek the good news. We must also look for the answer to this question in our religious experience. Finally, we must admit that although this question has been raised, we still do not have a wealth of experience and understanding to help us answer it. Now this is a key issue in our theological construction.

In the future we will encounter many more new problems, problems more difficult to solve. For example, how to justify on theological grounds our opting for socialism and socialist construction? How shall we deal with the relationship between church and state? In this divided world, how shall we deal with the problem of worldwide church fellowship? There is also the problem of history and eschatology... But the duty of theology is not to create problems; it is rather to help us find good answers when we discover problems in our religious life. Our responsibility is to seek the "points" which are raised by our spiritual experience, to link these points into a curve, and then see where the curve leads us.

Finally, let us return once more to the problem of discontinuity and continuity. We have already pointed out that two views are not entirely mutually exclusive, so after we turn back from an extreme discontinuity view, where shall we go? Since we are neither able nor willing to return to the old path, what should our direction be? In our experience we lack maturity, our vision is narrow and shallow, and we do not dare pretend that our ignorance is wisdom, but we firmly believe that a road leading to higher truth lies before us. It will break through the impasse of western theology, cause people in the midst of new kinds of social relationships to better understand God's creative wisdom and saving love, and cause the gospel to truly become the good news for all humankind, just as the prophet announcing the coming of Christ proclaimed the good news that the human race would exist in harmony and peace, making God's glory shine over the whole earth.

This is the theological task given to us by God. With a pious and humble attitude, without flinching or boasting, relying on the guidance of God's loving wisdom, and with hearts full of confidence, we should run the race set before us.

Author's Comments, 1991

Thirty turbulent years have passed since I wrote this essay, and even I had forgotten it. A few years ago I happened to come across it in some old theological journals kept by an alumnus, and some friends suggested that it should be republished. It is already covered with the dust of history, but I feel that its topic, the task of theological construction in the Chinese church, will never be out of date, and that some of the issues raised therein are worth exploring in today's new situation. I therefore decided to "cast a brick to attract jade," and hope for critiques, discussion and correction from co-workers who are interested in these questions. In order to preserve the original historical form of the article, it has not been revised, with the exception of a few words and phrases.

In the past thirty-five years there have been great changes in the world and in the national situation, and under the guidance of God the Chinese church has travelled along a rugged and tortuous road. It finally emerged from the valley of death and is now growing vigorously. There are many new spiritual experiences worthy of our serious attention, and deserving of theological reflection and interpretation. There are now many things to be heard, seen and done which had never been thought of and could not have been imagined thirty-five years ago. The essay now seems one-sided, shallow and naive in many places. There are several areas which I think should be considered in present discussion of the theological construction of the Chinese church.

Thirty years ago China was in a state of isolation imposed from both the outside and from within. Hoisting the Three-Self banner, stressing an independent self-governing church, and casting off the control and restraints of foreign mission agencies were basic conditions for changing the countenance of the Chinese church and establishing a sense of self-identity. Theological thought necessarily reflected this spirit. But this does not imply that we would always be isolated from the world church. The independent, self-governing Chinese church has already won the approval and respect of world Christianity. Our witness has had a positive impact all over the world. In order to enrich ourselves, we should draw beneficial experience from world Christianity. Among the most important changes in world Christianity over the last thirty years are the awakening of the Third World churches and the consequent indigenization and contextualization movements, the secularism and pluralism of the "old Christian nations" after the "turbulent sixties," the major reforms in Catholicism after Vatican II, and the development of the ecumenical movement over the last two decades. Under the open door and reform policies, the Chinese church has taken on a new stature as a part of the church universal, and as an active member of the world Christian family. This does not weaken our Three-Self consciousness, for it can even deepen and develop our Three-Self spirit. We should try to enrich ourselves by selectively absorbing some of the factors of the various theological currents and views which have emerged around the world over the last few decades, so that these may be reflected in our own theological construction.

In China, we have undergone both positive and negative experiences, and have discovered much new light on the path of the church's progress. A question especially worthy of mention is that of how to sift through China's rich historical and cultural heritage, appropriating that which is beneficial and incorporating it into Christian doctrine in order to give our propagation work more distinctively Chinese cultural characteristics and make the gospel message easier for the Chinese masses to understand and accept. In every area there are many tasks awaiting our diligent and careful effort. I believe we will certainly reap a rich harvest.

The road of theological construction has no end. Before us lies a lofty peak which calls us to unite our hearts and efforts as we struggle to climb it.

Republished Nanjing Theological Review, Nos. 14/15 (1–2, 1991), p.7ff.
Translated by Don Snow.

Christ And Culture in China
A Sino-American Dialogue
(Columbia Theological Seminary, October, 1992)

CHEN ZEMIN[1]

As part of a more general discussion of the relationship between Christ and culture, Prof. Chen focuses on the Chinese experience, discussing the attempts at contextualization and inculturation which have been made since Christianity first came to China. He points out the difficulties which resulted from the historical identification of evangelization with cultural invasion, a history which continues to complicate the long process of transforming Christianity from a foreign religion into one which is essentially Chinese.

I. THE PERENNIAL PROBLEM

The problem of how Christianity is related to culture has nowadays become a hotly debated issue on a worldwide scale. In China, especially during the last decade, it has attracted the attention and interest of many scholars, historians, sociologists, philosophers, political theoreticians and theologians, and is being pushed to the forefront of academic debates, overshadowing the once dominant religion as opium question. However, most Christians, who are deeply engrossed in the urgent and heavy task of building the church anew and trying to implement the newly regained freedom of religion in the best possible way, have only recently come to realize the significance of this "theoretical issue."

In fact, the problem is as old as Christianity. Jesus himself tackled it in the context of Jewish culture and Judaism. Paul and the early church fathers

---

1. Chen Zemin (Rev.) is vice-principal of Nanjing Union Theological Seminary where he is also professor of systematic theology.
This paper was delivered at the conference "Christianity and Culture: A Sino-American Dialogue," Columbia Theological Seminary, Oct., 1992.

wrestled with this problem amid the dominant Greco Roman secular or pagan cultural environment. Up till then Christianity had been a minority religion suppressed and persecuted, and swamped by an overwhelmingly "pagan" cultural ocean. In order to survive and develop it had to take this problem seriously and find some kind of solution. From the fourth century onward, Christianity, on becoming a state religion, with all the political, military and material support of the Roman Empire, itself became an encroaching and aggressive cultural force. The problem gradually became less acute. By the tenth century all "civilized" Europe had been Christianized. To be Christian and to be civilized had become synonymous. Cultural assimilation seemed to be the natural outcome of Christianization. But even at the height of Christian hegemony in the twelfth century, with the challenges of encroaching Islam and Arabic civilization, the Schoolmen had to struggle with this problem again. Thomas Aquinas took up the challenge, and successfully worked out the Great Synthesis which laid the foundation for another long period of ecclesial and theological development. In the East Christianity had engaged in an encounter with Byzantine culture, and through a certain amount of accommodation had grown into several powerful Eastern Orthodox Churches, which culturally dominated Eastern Europe and the Russian part of Asia for almost a millennium.

In Western Europe, during the periods of the Renaissance, the Reformation and the Enlightenment, Christianity had to grapple with this problem in a new cultural milieu amid the rising tides of secular humanism, nationalism, rationalism and natural sciences. Generally speaking, however, Christianity remained the dominant cultural power while also undergoing significant changes and developments itself. Christianity has always been a missionary religion. Committed to the Great Commission (Mt. 28:19-20), and firmly affirming that Christ is the only Saviour of humanity (Acts 4:12; Jn. 14:6), from the Apostolic Age on through all the centuries Christians have made it their first priority to make Christian converts of people of all nations. In so doing they came to encounter peoples and nations of many different religious and cultural traditions. Such encounters became sharper and on ever larger scales when missionary activities were carried on with evangelical zeal beyond Europe and America, often accompanied and backed up by colonial expansion. This reached its height in the nineteenth century, when Christianity reached practically all corners of the earth. In most of the "mission fields," Christian missionaries found themselves in the minority amidst great oceans of "heathen" or "pagan" religions and cultures, some of which had much longer histories of development than Christianity. Most of these "missionary target" peoples had been quite happy with and proud of their own cultural heritages, and did not welcome interference from the new religion. This was especially obvious in Asia, such as in the Arabic countries in the Near East (Islamic), the subcontinent (Hindu), Southeast Asian countries (Buddhist or Islamic), Japan (Shinto), and China. The not-so-successful missionary enterprises in such countries have set the sending countries and churches to "rethinking mission," leading to revolutionary mission reforms in the last half century.

II. SOME SOLUTIONS

All this may seem too simplistic. But it brings us back to the enduring problem of Christ (or Christianity) in relation to the multifarious non-Christian cultures. An avalanche of books and monographs have been poured out on the subject and many answers put forward. Here I can only select a few examples for comparison and as a foil for my presentation. Let me begin with H. Richard Niebuhr, whose classic work *Christ and Culture*[2], (the fortieth anniversary of whose publication we now have the happy occasion to commemorate) gives a splendid summary and classification of responses. They are:

1. Christ against culture, exclusivism (Tertullian, Tolstoy).
2. Christ of (or in) culture, accommodation and inclusivism (Gnosticism, Abelard and A. Ritschl).
3. Christ above culture, synthesis, (Thomas Aquinas).
4. Christ and culture in paradox, dualism (Luther).
5. Christ the transformer of culture, conversion, (Augustine and F. D. Maurice).

But almost all the illustrations in this book are taken from the West, and Niebuhr does not seem to have the encounters of Christ with great cultures in the East much in mind. In his last chapter "A Concluding Unscientific Postscript" (a phrase borrowed from Kierkegaard) he gives a long list of books and essays on the topic but leaves us in a state of bewilderment, although he himself seems to lean towards a not very well-defined "social existentialism," a specified model of Christ as the transformer of culture.

A more recent scholar of the evangelical wing, Charles H. Kraft of Fuller Seminary, follows Niebuhr's classification in the main but with some modifications:[3]

---

2. H. Richard Niebuhr, *Christ and Culture*, Harper, 1951.
3. Charles H. Kraft, *Christianity in Culture, A Study in Dynamic Biblical*

1. God against culture (Niebuhr's 1)

2. God in culture (Niebuhr's 2)

3. Christ above culture:

   a. Above and unconcerned (Deism);

   b. Synthetic (Niebuhr's 3, Thomas Aquinas);

   c. Dualistic (Niebuhr's 4, Luther);

   d. Conversion (Niebuhr's 5, Augustine, Calvin, Wesley);

   e. God-above-but-through culture

Kraft seems to opt for the last answer. "Though God exists totally outside of culture while humans exist totally within culture, God chooses the cultural milieu in which humans are immersed as the arena of his interaction with people." "God is absolute and infinite. Yet he has freely chosen to employ human culture and at major points to limit himself to the capacities of culture in his interaction with people."[4] I would heartily recommend his book to the evangelical majority of our fellow Chinese Christians, most of whom take a rather rigid exclusivist view.

Let me give two more examples from the Catholic side, not exactly on Christ and culture, but on Christ and non-Christian religions, (which may be seen as components of culture, just as Christianity is taken as a cultural phenomenon by most Chinese scholars). First, I have in mind Paul Knitter.[5] Knitter has the merit of reducing all theological reflections on this subject to four patterns:

1. Christ against religions (culture), hostility towards "paganism," dominating in nearly all the history of Christianity, "*extra ecclesiam nulla salus*";

2. Christ within religions, possibility of salvation also for non-Christians within religions, (Karl Rahner and Edward Schillebeeckx);

3. Christ above religions (culture). Other religions have an independent validity: "Even if Christ is not the exclusive cause of saving grace, yet He remains above all religions and all peoples." (Hans Kung, Claude Geffre);

4. Unitive pluralism or "the coincidence of opposites." "Each religion is unique and decisive for its followers; but it is also of universal importance." It is neither exclusive (against) or inclusive (within or above), but is

---

Theologizing in Cross-Cultural Perspective, Orbis, 1979, Chapter 6.

4. Ibid., (pp. 114, 115)

5. Paul Knitter, *No Other Names? A Critical Survey of Christian Attitudes Toward the World Religions*, Orbis, 1985. Cf. Also John Hick and Paul Knitter, *The Myth of Christian Uniqueness, Toward a Pluralistic Theology of Religions*, Orbis, 1987.

"essentially related to other religions," so "perhaps . . . other revealers and saviours are as important as Jesus of Nazareth."

Another Catholic theologian, RaimundoPannikar, reaches the same conclusion by making a distinction between the Christ-Logos and the historical Jesus. There is more in the Christ-Logos than there is in the historical Jesus, so that the Logos can appear in different but real ways in other religions and historical figures outside of Jesus of Nazareth.[6]

Perhaps I may add here that Bishop K.H. Ting's essay "The Cosmic Christ"[7] hints at the same thing. His "Cosmic Christ" is synonymous with "the Christ-Logos." The theological implication of the Cosmic Christ in respect to our present issue is being slowly but gradually understood and accepted by an increasing number of Christians and theological workers in China now.

This much is enough as a background of theological reflections concerning this enduring problem. Perhaps the two Catholic theologians' views cited above are too radical for most Protestant Thinkers in China to endorse.

III. IN CHINA—HISTORICAL RETROSPECT

In the first part of this paper I have tried to compare two different circumstances: first, Christianity as a dominant cultural factor in the building up of a Christendom of so-called "Christian *civilization*" (as in Europe and North America from the fourth century to the present); with secondly, Christianity's encounter with older highly developed indigenous cultures in non-Christian countries. (Here I try to draw a hazy distinction between *culture* and *civilization*, the latter denoting an advanced level of scientific, technological development, usually with modern comforts and conveniences in urban societies.)[8] Whether Christianity is a *sine qua non*causal factor of the rise of modern western civilization or just a chance concomitant still remains to be settled.[9] The success of Christian conquests in the first

---

6. R. Pannikar, *The Unknown Christ of Hinduism*, Orbis, 1981.

7. K.H. Ting, "The Cosmic Christ," in *The Nanjing Theological Review*, Nos. 14/15, 1991.

8. These two terms are often used interchangeably both in Chinese and in English. "Culture" is usually translated wenhua 文化 and "civilization" as wenming 文明 in modern Chinese. My distinction is drawn from definitions one and seven of "civilization" in The Random House College Dictionary, rev. ed. 1973, p.246, b. The distinction may seem arbitrary, but I believe there are slightly different connotations.

9. See Christopher Dawson, *Religion and the Rise of Western Culture*, Image Books, 1958, and R. Hooykaas, *Religion and the Rise of Modern Science*, 1972. Chinese translations, 1989 and 1991, Sichuan People's Publishing House.

circumstance led many missionaries to develop a sense of superiority or "imperialism mentality" and to launch presumptuous "cultural invasions" under the name of evangelization. The not-so-successful attempts in the second circumstance have been so frustrating and perplexing as to force western missionaries to fall back to rethinking on this perennial problem of Christ and culture. The experience in China is a case in point.

We do not have sufficient materials to judge how the Syrian Nestorian missionaries in the seventh century attempted to deal with this problem. Perhaps all we can say is that they created a hodgepodge of Confucian, Buddhist and Taoist terminologies and transliterations in rendering the Nestorian Christian tradition (scripture, doctrine and history) into the Chinese language without trying seriously to adapt to the Chinese context or to accommodate to the content or essence of the then flowering Chinese culture, leaving an impression of syncretism. Anyway Nestorian Christianity lasted only about two hundred years, disappearing in the ninth century.[10]

Under the Mongols in the thirteenth and fourteenth centuries, Christianity, both in its Nestorian and Catholic forms, fared no better. With the political and military support of the Mongol rulers, who were themselves caught in the dilemma of whether to adapt the powerful *Han* culture or develop a new mixture, Christianity was not prepared to face this problem seriously. Prof. Wang Weifan (王维藩) has written a "Preliminary Study of Christian Thought in Ancient China."[11] But one wishes to see more systematic and in-depth analysis from the perspective of acculturation based on more substantial and substantiated materials.

The Jesuits in the sixteenth century approached the problem in a new light. Matteo Ricci was the first to propose and put into practice the policy of accommodation. His threefold strategy of Christianity "complying with Confucianism" (stressing the similarities and parallelisms in both), "supplementing Confucianism" and "surpassing Confucianism" approximates a combination of the second and third answers of Niebuhr (and Kraft). His attempt to discover an "original Confucianism" (claiming that the original teaching of Confucius was monotheistic, only later distorted by the Neo-Confucianism of Zhu Xi (Chu His 朱熹) and his followers into a metaphysical atheism)[12] failed to win the support of modern scholarship. But

---

10. Kenneth S. Latourette suggested that Nestorianism arrived at a time when a special need for a new religion was felt, as contrasted with the situation in the Roman Empire in the early Christian centuries. *A History of Christian Missions in China*, S.P.C.K., 1929, p.58. But how can one say at what time a people may feel a need for a new religion?

11 *The Nanjing Theological Review*, No. 16, 1992, Nanjing.

12 *The True Meaning of the Lord of Heaven*, published in its final form in 1604.

Ricci's insistence on the necessity and significance of Christianity's coming to terms with traditional Chinese culture is praiseworthy. He would have opened a new and interesting chapter in our discussion were it not for the fact that the folly and conceit of Pope Clement XII (1704) caused Emperor Kangxi to ban Christianity (1721) with a stroke of the imperial brush. Catholic Christianity in China has so far not been able to redeem the cost of this historical mistake.

The story of the introduction of Protestant Christianity into China is too well known to need recounting. Most of the missionaries were too preoccupied with the saving of souls, and with their arrogant air of the superiority of western "Christian civilization" over heathenism, failed to take enough heed of the splendid Chinese traditional cultural heritage. To be fair, exceptions must be made of some missionary scholars such as James Legge and Timothy Richard. It may be too sweeping a judgment, but they were more interested in translating Chinese classics into English and introducing western scientific knowledge into China, and must be complimented for their contributions to cultural exchanges rather than real encounters. A great deal can be learned from in-depth studies of the experiences of the Catholic and Protestant missionaries and the responses of Chinese people, both positive and negative, during this period, and this can shed light on the problem of the Christ-Culture encounter.

The Bai Shang Di Jiao (拜上帝教)(Religion of Worshipping God) of Hong Xiuquan (洪秀全) during the Taiping Heavenly Kingdom of the mid-nineteenth century may be regarded as a real attempt at a rather radical accommodation of Christianity to Chinese traditional culture in a milieu of revolutionary upheaval. It had developed into a successful mass movement and won partial support of some missionaries at the beginning. Its eventual failure was due more to the military defeats suffered at the hands of the overwhelming Qing forces with the assistance of foreign invasive powers, in which a few western Christian missionaries were involved, rather than doctrinal deviations from "orthodoxy" or cultural incompatibility.

The real clash came in 1919 when Confucianism was criticized in the New Culture Movement, attacked as the root and bulwark of feudalism and condemned as the main cause of China's backwardness and weakness as a nation and as a people. In the revolutionary reckoning Christianity became a target because it had been used as a "1001 of cultural invasion." It was seen as a Trojan horse for sabotaging the New Culture Movement. The anti-Christian accusations in the 1920s called forth responses from some progressive Christian intellectuals who accepted many of the criticisms while at the same time they were spurred to seek a new ground for Christianity in the Chinese cultural soil. It was at this juncture that some outstanding

Christian scholars and theologians like Wang Zixing (王治心), Y.T. Wu (吴耀宗), T.C. Chao, and N.Z. Zia (谢扶雅), steeped in Confucian philosophy and classical literature, came to grapple with this problem. It was a time when such terms and concepts as acculturation, inculturation, and contextualization were not in much use or even available. Credit must be given to these scholars who made great contributions to accommodation by pointing out the similarities or parallelisms between Christianity and Confucianism, but they did not go much further than Ricci, and remained more elitist than popular. The church's Independence Movement (1901–1933) had more followers at the grassroots level, but was primarily aimed at self-support and self-administration in order to overturn Christianity's bad reputation as a tool of western imperialism, and did not take seriously the relation between Christ and Chinese culture. So-called indigenization was more a matter of outward forms and structure than thought content.

The 1930s and 40s were a period of political and social unrest. Civil warfare and the Japanese military invasion plunged the Chinese people into extreme poverty, instability and despair. It was in this context that a Christian religion of the American revivalistic type—one which stressed the penal substitution theory of redemption and salvation of individual souls, fleeing from this fallen, sinful and condemned world, looking towards the immediate second coming of Christ, and advocating a pietistic, sentimental and sometimes fanatical religiosity—found fertile soil. (John Sung was enjoying Billy Graham-type popularity in China at this time.) Theologically this was fundamentalist. Understandably Christianity of this type took an extreme exclusivist view toward non-Christian cultures of any kind. Church leaders of "mainline" affiliations and with more liberal theological backgrounds either took a compromising stance or were simply banned as "social gospellers" and readily lost ground. Some of them gathered under the banner of neo-orthodoxy and looked askance at secular or non-Christian cultures also. Kirkegaardian existentialism was looming on the horizon, but little understood. Hendrick Kraemer's *The Christian Message in a Non-Christian World* was found in the libraries of many a theological seminary.[13]

This brings us to the present era.

---

13. See my paper "The Task of Theological Construction in the Chinese Church," (part 2) in *The Nanjing Theological Review*, Nos. 14/15, 1991, English translation in *The Chinese Theological Review*: 1992.

IV. A PERIOD OF RAPID CHANGES

The second half of the twentieth century witnessed profound changes in several aspects related to our present concern. The phenomena of modernity are too well-known to need any elaboration: great disturbances, divisions and realignments in the world socioeconomic-political arena, the rise of Third World countries with self-assertive consciousness of national and cultural identity, rocketing scientific-technological advancements and the shrinking of the world into a global village,—all these have combined to usher in a new era of modernity, pluralism and secularism. The problem of Christ and culture must be considered against this backdrop with its complexity and interrelatedness. I shall concentrate on its relevance in the Chinese context.

The revolution of 1949 has completely changed the socio-economic-political structure in China. Under the leadership of the Chinese Communist Party and the People's Government, with Marxist theory of social revolution and dialectical materialism as a guideline, a series of social, economic and ideological reforms and reconstructions were successfully carried out and eventually won the support of the people, including many religious believers. The suspicion that under communist rule all religions would be treated as reactionary and sheer superstition to be suppressed and liquidated was gradually dispelled through the implementation of policies of the "united front" and religious freedom. Some people still took a "wait and see" attitude. In any case, all religions and their adherents found themselves in the position that, willy-nilly, they had to adjust themselves to the new situation. For Protestant Christians, this took the shape of the Three-Self Movement, under the prophetic leadership of Y.T. Wu, which through persuasion and appeals, finally consolidated a large majority of Protestant church leaders and members to make the adjustment. This proved to be a decisive step in changing the image and nature of Protestant Christianity from a "foreign religion" (*yang jiao*) to an essentially Chinese one. But this was just a beginning, and much remained to be done. Now freedom of religious belief is vouchsafed by the constitution as the policy of the Party and People's Government. In practice it is being implemented with various degrees of efficiency and success, with much left to be desired. Catholic and Protestant Christianity, together with the three other major religions, i.e., Buddhism, Islam and Taoism, enjoy legal and popular recognition on a status of parity.

During the last four decades Christianity in China has undergone tremendous changes. It has rid itself of the stigma of being an imported foreign religion utilized as a tool by western powers for aggression and cultural invasion. Protestant Christianity has severed the umbilical cord that once connected it with the "mother" missionary societies and gained independence and an identity of its own. Without depreciating the historical *raison d'être* and special contributions of denominations, but realizing the frailty of the fibrous roots with the main roots cut off, Protestantism in China has tried to transplant "potted flowers" (D.T. Niles' metaphor) into Chinese soil, and to cultivate a multiflorous garden with a more or less unified pattern or design. We call this a "uniting church" of "post-denominational unity" on a conciliar basis. The soil is Chinese culture; the sunlight and rain are God's blessings and the guidance of the Holy Spirit; and the air is the modern Chinese milieu. We are fully aware of the immaturity and shortcomings of our experiments, and the many difficulties and problems before us. So far this approach has borne positive results, and reflects the desire and attempts "to build the church well in a socialist society with Chinese characteristics."[14]

A few digressive remarks on the meaning and content of the concept of "culture" and how it can be related to religion are perhaps in order. Culture is a very vague idea and not often precisely defined. H. Richard Niebuhr does not give us a concise definition, but describes some of its chief characteristics.[15] That culture and religion are closely related no one can dispute. It was Paul Tillich who advanced a theological theory of culture with the dictum "religion is the substance of culture, and culture the form of religion."[16] How these two (are there really two or just one including the other?) should be related remains a problem, especially in the Third World where indigenous religions and indigenous cultures are so intimately intertwined when they come to encounter Christianity and western culture. In the post-war era many attempts have been made to clarify this problem. C.S. Song (宋泉盛) in his article on "Culture" in the *Dictionary of the Ecumenical Movement* traces the course of development through the following stages:

(1) In the 1950s and 60s indigenization was widely advocated, and seemed to have enabled churches in the Third World to shed their foreignness. "But the change was largely of a structural and political nature. It was assumed that the Christian gospel would remain unchanged . . . Theologically, it was on the whole a matter of finding parallel indigenous religious and philosophical language and ideas and expressing the Christian truth in those terms." This was what Chinese theologians like T.C. Chao and N.Z. Zia had been doing. But again the word "indigenous" sounds hazy in

---

14. See my paper "Post Denominational Unity of the Chinese Protestant Church," presented at the IAHR Religion Conference, Beijing, April, 1992.

15. Niebuhr, 1951.

16. Paul Tillich, *Theology of Culture*, Robert C. Kimball, ed. Oxford University Press, 1959, Chinese translation, 1988.

a world where what was "indigenous" is being absorbed and assimilated and dissolved in modernity. Indigenization seems to leave out the "fourth dimension" of time and constant change. In the advance of time the formerly indigenous has undergone changes and become something different, though continuous with the original. Something more dynamic is missing in indigenization.

(2) In the late 1960s and early 70s, Shoki Coe (黄彰輝), then director of the WCC Program for Theological Education, proposed the now popular idea of contextualization, as focusing on the relation between text and context. This approach stresses "the careful study of the fit between the Christian Bible, the gospel, and the various cultural and religious settings to which Christian faith Addresses itself."[17]

This implies that the present is emphasized. It was not until the early 1980s that this idea was introduced to Chinese church and theologians to be tried out on a more conscious basis. Many Chinese theologians seem to prefer the concept of contextualization to "plain" indigenization.

(3) From the mid-1970s onward, acculturation and inculturation came to the fore. Both seek help from social sciences like anthropology, ethnology and the history of religions to assimilate more closely indigenous cultural factors to the expressions and understanding of the Christian faith. Acculturation means to adapt Christian practice to local culture, like using indigenous dress, architecture, music and fine arts in worship and liturgy, while "*inculturation* means the insertion of new values into one's heritage and world-view."[18] Some open-minded Chinese church leaders were enthusiastic about experimenting with these ideas in the last decade. "innovations." We find it difficult to "induce" or "seduce" second and third generation Christians (mainly in the cities) to accept and to like church music and Christian art in traditional Chinese styles. To them, to be Christian means to follow the western tradition. The indigenous has become alienated. The ghost of foreignness follows closely and refuses to be laid down. However, in rural areas and among most new converts we find less contamination by such alienation.

The distinction between indigenization, contextualization, acculturation and inculturation may be more academic than real. In fact they are

17. See Shoki Coe, "Contextualizing Theology," in *Third World Theologies* (ed. Gerald H. Anderson and Thomas F. Stransky; New York: Panlist/Eerdmans, 1976), pp. 19–24.

18. *Dictionary of the Ecumenical Movement*, p.506. See also One Faith, Many Cultures, Boston Theological Institute, Annual Series, vol. 2, 1988 (Orbis) Ruy O. Costa, "Introduction: Inculturation, Indigenization and Contextualization" and Max L. Stackhouse, "Contextualization, Contextuality and Contextualism," pp. ix-13.

very closely related and often used synonymously. But the observations of C.S. Song are helpful because they reflect the shift of emphasis in the last four decades in the Third World. In this paper I choose to use the concept *contextualization* to embrace the peculiarities of all four.

V. THE CONTEXT

I have pointed out the ambiguity in the use of the concepts *culture* and *indigeneity*. When we come to talk about Chinese indigenous culture the fogginess is multiplied. A library has been poured out on the subject. But one feels at a loss in trying to pinpoint the "quintessence" of *Chinese indigenous culture*. As the apt Chinese sayings go: "*renzhejianren, zhizhejianzhi*," and "*mozhongyishi*." ("The benevolent person sees benevolence while the wise one sees wisdom" and "there is no way of compromising and arriving at a consensus of right conclusion.") This is no place to quote authorities and make comparisons and selections. I choose to follow Richard Niebuhr by pointing out a few of the important characteristics of traditional Chinese culture with reference to their relation to religion.

(1) In the first place the Chinese mind was traditionally not accustomed to draw a line between culture and religion. The term *zongjiao* (宗教) as we understand it today as religion was absent in premodern literature. A near synonym could be traced to its Buddhist origin, which defined *zong* as "what was taught by Buddha himself" and *jiao* as "the teachings of his disciples." Etymologically *zong* means origin or source, and derivatively, tradition; and *jiao* means teaching, education or nurturing. Hence the idea of culture, as in *jiaohua* (教化), to teach, assimilate and change.[19] The present use of *zongjiao* as religion in the modern sense is an adaptation from the Japanese translation. One seeks in vain in the Confucian classics for the term *zongiiao* and the idea of religion. To try to dichotomize religion and culture and to clarify their interrelation often leads to confusion.

(2) Among the three main traditional Chinese religions, i.e., Confucianism (although many modern Chinese scholars argue that Confucianism is not a religion at all, but a system of ethical and educational philosophy), Taoism and Buddhism, there has long been a tendency to overlap, merge and interpenetrate. Confucianism is regarded almost unanimously as the dominant cultural factor. There were times when one of the other two grew stronger. But there has never been any state religion in China as there has in some other countries. The influences of these major three, supplemented

---

19. 《辞源》, see *Ciyuan*, a standard *Etymological Dictionary of Classical Chinese Terms*, compiled and published by Commercial Press in 1915.

by numerous *folk religions*, (which are usually combinations of heterodox or heteromorphic derivatives of the three, enjoying overwhelming popularity) are found to be in the blood and veins of traditional Chinese culture, often in a mixed way, both among the educated elite and the common people. Perhaps many people took an agnostic or indifferent attitude toward institutionalized religion. There were very few, if any, diehard, thoroughgoing rationalist atheists. But they were not immune to such cultural influences. Therefore, when we talk about traditional culture, we should bear in mind this compound nature. And when we talk about the indigenization of Christianity in China, if we confine ourselves to just pointing out the similarities and parallels of Christianity and Confucianism and/or Taoism and/or Buddhism in juxtaposition, there is a danger of forgetting the broad masses, who are also bearers of Chinese culture. This seems to be what many scholars and theologians have done and are doing.

(3) This leads us to the third consideration: the *non-exclusiveness* of Chinese religions. In religious matters the Chinese mind in general is one of tolerance, often tending towards syncretism. Instances of interreligious warfare and controversy have been only occasional. Many people hold that all religions aim at the well-being of individuals and all are helpful to "make men and women good." Even the agnostic and the indifferent often treat religious believers with smiling understanding and condone their practice of religion. It was only when western missionaries and fundamentalist Christian preachers who held an extreme exclusivist "no-other-name" view of salvation and looked down upon non-Christians as "pagan, heathen, fallen and condemned to hell" that enmity and resistance were aroused.

(4) Another characteristic Chinese mindset is "harmonizing opposites," such as heaven and earth, heaven and humanity, *yin* and *yang*, the cyclical series of dialectical derivations and counteractions of the *wuxing* (five elements), and so on and so forth, in a holistic cosmological and pragmatic oneness. This has already been elaborated upon by too many scholars, Chinese and foreign, to need any repetition or explanation. This characteristic can be found reflected in all Chinese religions, including the folk religions, in theology, beliefs, rituals and private practices; but is often neglected by professional theologians who excel at making minute differentiations and tracing origins.

(5) The humanistic, moralistic and practical features of traditional Chinese thought, emphasizing the value of moral cultivation and ethical duty and the heavenly (natural) law of retribution, have also been universally recognized. The Mencian doctrine of inborn goodness (cf. Christian doctrine of "original righteousness") of human nature, (as contrasted to the doctrines of "neutral nature" of Gaozi and "evil nature" of Xunzi), is

generally accepted. Hence the emphasis on education and free will. Linked to this is the absence of the idea of "original sin." To the Chinese mind sin often carries a legalistic or moral connotation, (crimes and immoral acts) rather than a sense of spiritual, existential or religious sinfulness. The etymological meaning of the Greek *harmatia*, missing the mark or breaching of relationship, is more easily understood and acceptable. We find in classical religious literature nothing like the great "Repentance Psalms" and *Confessions* of Augustine. This is why evangelical revivalists like John Sung had to begin evangelical meetings by stressing the sinfulness and fallenness of every individual (like Johnathan Edwards), and to arouse a deep, strong sense of remorse, contrition, and "lost-ness" before they could declare the gospel of grace, pardon and salvation. Usually we find ordinary people in the street rather averse to such an approach. To convince and convict the ordinary Chinese of his or her "original sin" and sinning against God is often difficult.

(6) We could also observe a difference in the eschatology in Chinese religions from that of the Judeo-Christian tradition. Confucianism emphasizes the this-worldly, the here and now, and tends to shun speculation on life after death and eternity. The classical idea of *datong* (the Realm of Great Harmony) is to be strived after in this world. Buddhism teaches the Western Paradise (*xitian*) but only for the devout religious few, who might attain it only after arduous and strenuous pursuit and trials, an idea more metaphorical than realistic. In vernacular satirical speech "*shang* (go up to) *xitian*" simply means "to die" or "to finish off" rather than to go to heaven. Taoism preaches a celestial, vividly anthropomorphic fairyland which is also not attainable by all the faithful, and often has very slight eschatological nuances. Hope lies in the present world, not in the far future. Popular Buddhist, Taoist and folk religions believe in transmigration and/or immediate judgment and punishment in hells (commonly believed to have eighteen layers, like limbo or purgatory), rather than eternal damnation. Taken all in all the Chinese mind puts great emphasis on the mundane life, the here and now, and cares very little about the end of history and the cosmos. The idea of eternity is often conceived more in terms of endless generations in this world, and lacks the dimension of transcendence.

(7) I might add another cultural characteristic related to religious life in China. I mean the irenic, gentle temperament and ethos of religious expression. One of the Confucian virtues is to keep to the mean, i.e., to try to maintain the "Golden Mean": everything in the appropriate order, relationship and proportion; avoiding excesses and extremes. Both Buddhism and Taoism place a high value on peace of mind and quietness in spiritual exercises. With the exception of some folk religions, Chinese people often

look askance at religious fanaticism. Chinese mysticism in general is of the meditative, not the ecstatic, obsessive or fantastic type. So in Chinese history one does not find so many frenetic religious movements comparable to the Crusades and witch-hunting in Europe, except for those connected with tribal or political causes, like peasants' revolts and uprisings. We also observe that modern religious charismatic movements have found only mild response in China.

I could continue with further observations, but these are enough to sketch a general profile of the *indigenous* Chinese cultural temperament or ethos with regard to religion. Again I want to stress that when we think of the *context* we have to use this just as a background and to look into what at present exercises the strongest influence on the entire population of China. Perhaps the Chinese people are not so traditional and indigenous in their way of thinking and feeling nowadays after all. I have mentioned the radical political, ideological and social changes of the last four decades. Now Confucianism is more often the target of criticism than an object of adulation. The current revival of interest in the study of Confucianism in mainland China (not as a religion) and of Neo-Confucianism (or more correctly "contemporary Neo-Confucianism") outside China seems confined to academic circles. The above-mentioned characteristics of indigenous Chinese culture still linger and can never be completely erased. Chinese still remain Chinese in a very real, general and subtle way, perhaps in what Jung calls the collective subconscious. But times have changed and so has the environment. Attitudes toward religion in general and Christianity in particular are undergoing significant modifications. Time and space do not allow me to dwell on this. I need only highlight some important changes in the present context, focusing on the last twelve years.

(1) We are in a new type of socialist society. People who are wont to gauge the present Chinese situation with the old meter used for socialism of the Soviet and Eastern European type often find themselves puzzled. For instance, the once heated controversy over the Marxist dictum of religion as the opiate of the people is abating. The famous Party Document No. 19 (1982), which is "the starting point and the landing point of the religious policy of the Chinese Communist Party," does not mention the word "opium" at all. An increasing number of scholars are discussing how religion can be adjusted so as to become compatible with socialism.[20] In many books on religious studies published in the last few years we find that overtones of dogmatic Marxist anti-religious clamor have been remarkably soft-pedaled.

---

20. See *Religious Problems in China During the Socialist Period*, LuoZhufeng (罗竹风), ed. Shanghai Academy of Social Sciences Publishing House, 1984.

(2) After a long underground hibernation during the Cultural Revolution, religion began to surface again. All five major religions, Buddhism, Taoism, Islam, Catholic and Protestant Christianity (counted as two different religions in China) are recording marked increases in their adherents. Protestantism is making the fastest advance, totaling over seven million, at a speed of about eight times the pre-liberation total in a decade. (This is a rather conservative estimate, yet large enough to trigger alarm in some government functionaries!)[21] But counted together with the 3.5 million Catholics, Christians still constitute less than one percent of the whole population, a tiny drop in an ocean of 1.2 billion. The general increase of religious believers after the Cultural Revolution calls for an explanation and has led many social scientists to theorize. This is no place to compare and evaluate the various answers advanced. All of these theories only explain the phenomenon in part. This is a rather complicated issue and we need more comprehensive investigation and scientific, unbiased analysis to substantiate the various answers. But to me the return of religious popularity is not very astonishing, but rather normalization of the abnormal. The "liquidation of religion" during the years of Cultural Revolution was itself an abnormality in an abnormal historical situation. The pent up religiosity of the populace, (here I mean the "natural" or "inborn" religious or spiritual aptitude or yearning of the masses), tends to burst with extraordinary force when pressure is suddenly released. In a certain sense and to some extent this is "overdoing in correcting a wrong," as the Chinese saying goes.

(3) Since most Protestants have come together under the China Christian Council (CCC) in a post-denominational unity, interdenominational dialogue is no longer necessary and attracts little interest. But there are several exclusivist "established sects" (like the Christian Assembly, usually known as the "Little Flock," the Seventh Day Adventists and the True Jesus Church, estimated to have a total of about four hundred thousand adherents) which prefer to stand aloof from the CCC. It seems impracticable to have any kind of dialogue with these groups, at least for the time being. By being sectarian and exclusivist they tend to confine themselves to minority groups, in spite of their proselytizing endeavors. This has caused grave concern on the part of many church leaders in China. The policy of the CCC is to adhere to the principle of mutual respect and render all possible service to these groups, with more love and patience, without prejudice or discrimination. The recent emergence and proliferation of a number of cults that bear little resemblance to Christianity, especially in the rural areas among

---

21. A group of scholars gathered in Beijing in the winters of 1990 and 1991 to study the phenomena of religious growth and concluded that the so-called "religious heat" had been much exaggerated.

the uneducated masses, have caused some alarm and bewilderment. (These pseudo/quasi-"Christian" groups should not be confused with the "meeting points," about twenty thousand in number. Most of the latter are under the pastoral care of, and maintain good relations with, the CCC.) This phenomenon of cult-breeding as a sub-culture requires separate study and cannot be treated in this paper. But to me it seems less startling and bewildering than what American "cult-watchers" see in California. New sects and cults and various sorts of deviations may emerge, merge, undergo changes and eventually disappear, as we often see in the history of all religions. So in my opinion they pose no grave threat to Protestant church unity today.[22]

Only a few Protestant theologians in China have shown interest in inter-faith dialogue. In practice it seems the time is not yet ripe. One of the reasons is that many evangelical church leaders who hold an exclusivist view are afraid of losing the "uniqueness" of Christ and Christianity. Leaders of other religions so far have shown little interest either. Academic discussions among non-believing scholars can hardly be considered as inter-faith dialogue.

(4) Believers in all religions are encouraged and admonished to live out their faiths in everyday life and do good works and make contributions to socialist construction as witnesses to their faiths and proof of their religious loyalty and their love for the country and the people. (May we think of these as a kind of Chinese "civil religion"?) The Christian slogan is "glorify God and benefit humanity." But we find many fundamentalist-pietists, though not openly opposed to such admonitions, still take a skeptical attitude toward this as a "religion of good works." They seem to forget or ignore the biblical teachings on social justice, peace and the integrity of creation, and regard them as "social gospel," too mundane and irrelevant to the salvation of the soul. As many foreign observers have pointed out, the majority of Chinese Christians are tending toward a type of pietistic, otherworldly "evangelicalism," and are more concerned with individual salvation and spiritual exercises, paying rather little attention to social issues.

(5) In academic circles we find a different picture. Many are being "liberated" from former rigid Marxist anti-religious views and are adopting a more objective, unbiased, scientific approach in their studies of religion. The study of religion, once taboo in China, is advancing by leaps and bounds. In the last ten years hundreds of books by foreign writers on religion, both general and specialized, have been introduced and translated into Chinese. Books on religion are often best sellers. An increasing number of scholars

---

22. See my paper "The Task of Theological Construction in the Chinese Church," (part 2) in *The Nanjing Theological Review*, Nos. 14/15, 1991, English translation in *The Chinese Theological Review*: 1992.

now take a more open and sympathetic attitude toward religion in general and Christianity in particular. There has emerged a sizable group of "culture Christians," who for some reason or other are not ready to be affiliated with the church and be known openly as committed Christians. But in private discussions and open forums they usually show unmistakable sympathy towards Christianity, and have become quite influential with readers.

(6) Last but not least, the global context must be taken into consideration. Under the present national policy of opening-up and reform, the Chinese church, having achieved her identity and independence, has developed many international contacts and relationships, and become a member of the family of world Christianity. We are widening our horizons to include more abundant and multifarious cross-cultural exchanges.

With the foregoing considerations as the cultural background and context, and keeping in mind the solutions described in section II of this paper, what actions shall we propose and what prospect can we visualize for the future of Christianity in China?

VI. THEOLOGICAL REORIENTATION

If Jesus Christ were born in China and lived and taught, died and was resurrected about five centuries before the common era, when Confucius and Lao Tzu had already exerted their strong influence on the Chinese people, what would Christianity and its subsequent developments be like today? J.A.T. Robinson has somewhere raised a similar question. This may seem an absurd and sacrilegious "if." Was it not God's decree that Jesus be born a Jew in Palestine at the appointed *Kairos* under the specific circumstances? By the same line of reasoning one would say that all subsequent developments of Christianity and Christian theologies were also decreed by God and could not be otherwise. The inference is absurd, and one would fall into a rigid mechanical historical determinism. No place would be left for human freedom and contingency. Creativity and variations would be ruled out. There would be no such thing as culture. *Incarnation* would be rid of its rich significance, meaning and value. But Christ came into the world and took on humanity, embracing all humankind, not just the Jews. If the Gospel is for all the world, to spread and reach all nations, contextualization and inculturation are inevitable. There should not be just one theology, but theologies of peoples and times. Theological reorientation and reconstruction have always been going oil (Paul Tillich and Gordon Kaufmann). The question is rather how this can and should be done in China.

I have found two books focusing on this problem very helpful. These are *Unfinished Encounter* by Bob Whyte and *Seeking the Common Ground* by Philip L. Wickeri.[23] Hans Kung's "Christian Theology's Responses" are also very illuminating and suggestive.[24] But it should fall upon Chinese Christians of today to undertake theological reorientation and response. So far we have not been able to face this challenge in a very conscious and systematic way. In the early 1950s one could observe a mass movement of very lively theological discussions in sermons and articles, as published in *TianFeng*. I tried to summarize the general trends of theological reorientation and reconstruction during that period in a paper published in the *Nanjing Theological Review* (No. 11). These efforts were interrupted by a period of peril from the "anti-rightist movement" to the end of the Cultural Revolution (1957–79). During this difficult time theological thinking seemed on the surface to be at a stand-still. However the painful experience did set many Christians to deep reflection and prepared the ground and material for further theological reconstruction. The last decade has witnessed the resurfacing and rapid development of church activities and theological florescence. As Dr. Gotthard Oblau, after studying hundreds of sermons preached and published in China in the last decade, notes:

"With my review of (mainly recent) sermons from China I hope to show basically two things. First: the theological orientation in today's Chinese churches is still very deeply shaped by the overwhelmingly evangelical or pietistic legacy of the western mission era. And second: despite the fact that most sermons appear to be orthodox and pietistic in style, and hence somewhat other-worldly and detached from public life in society, *they do sometimes, at least implicitly, grapple with challenges from the surrounding world, thereby providing a more or less unique Christian witness in China's present day context.*"[25]

Bishop K. H. Ting, confirming the preponderance of evangelicalism and fundamentalism in China today, also stresses the "need to take into account that somehow the Chinese context makes certain theological affirmations and accommodations unavoidable."[26]

---

23. Bob Whyte, *Unfinished Encounter: China and Christianity* (Collins, 1988); and Philip Wickeri, *Seeking the Common Ground: Protestant Christianity, the Three-Self Movement and China's United Front* (Orbis, 1988).

24. Julia Ching and Hans Kung, *Christianity and Chinese Religions* (Doubleday, 1988). Chinese translation, ShanlianXudian, 1990.

25. Gotthard Oblau, "Between Western Legacy and Contextual Challenges: Ordinary Theology in Chinese Protestant Sermons," unpublished paper presented at Chungchi College, Hong Kong, 1991. (Emphasis mine.)

26. K.H. Ting, "Chinese Christians' Approach to the Bible," *Nanjing Theological*

In the following I shall give in a very general way some salient shifts of emphases in theological reflections in China today.

In the doctrine of God, emphasis is put on love (agape) as God's essential nature, not just as one of God's many "attributes." Love is manifested in God's work of creation, providence, redemption and sanctification which runs through in an overlapping continuum, not as separable "stages," and all in relation to humankind and the whole universe. Without belittling God's transcendence, the stress is put on immanence. All that is true and good and beautiful comes from God as its ultimate source and reflects God's goodness and love and glory. God loves and cares for all humankind irrespective of their various religious traditions and disbelief. We are learning not to condemn but to appreciate and respect all the good works of people outside the Christian Church, and to regard them as also coming from God and out of God's all-encompassing Love through the Holy Spirit.

In Christology more attention is focused on the idea of the Cosmic Christ as taught by Paul in his Epistles to the Ephesians and Colossians. "Christ is the image of the invisible God, the firstborn of all creation; for in him all things in heaven and on earth were created, things visible and invisible, whether thrones or dominions or rulers or powers—allthings have been created through him and for him. He himself is before all things, and in him all things hold together" (Col. 1:15–17). "He has put all things under his feet and has made him the head over all things for the church, which is his body, the fullness of him that fills all in all" (Eph. 1:22–23). Christ is God incarnate in the union of God's perfect deity with perfect humanity so that through Him and in Him humankind can aspire to salvation and renewal in Him. His vicarious and exemplary suffering and sacrifice on the cross is the perfect manifestation of God's love, so that by accepting Christ as our Saviour we may be reconciled to God. The doctrines of incarnation and reconciliation should be understood in light of the doctrine of the Cosmic Christ.[27]

The Holy Spirit is conceived to be the all-pervading, all encompassing and all-powerful Spirit of God, acting from the very beginning of creation, down through all universal and human history until the final consummation. As the Spirit of God and the Cosmic Christ the Holy Spirit is not confined to the visible Church, but is ever present and working as universal "Life-Breeding Spirit" in the cosmos.[28]

Review, No. 13, 1990.

27. K.H. Ting, "The Cosmic Christ," in *The Nanjing Theological Review*, Nos. 14/15, 1991.

28. Wang Weifan, "The Life-Breeding Spirit," *Nanjing Theological Review*, Nos. 7/8, 1987.

In anthropology the doctrine of *imago dei*, marred but not entirely lost through the Fall, is often preached and taught. Emphasis is put on the absolute necessity and conditional possibility of redemption for its restoration. Humankind has been created as children of the loving God, and though fallen and sinful, are still worth saving. The doctrine of sin as preached from the pulpit still carries overtones of American revival meetings, and thus often fails to stir the hearts and souls of many young people brought up in a cultural tradition too humanistic, moralistic and pragmatic to grasp the depth of *sinfulness* in the religious and spiritual sense. The original meaning of *harmatia*, (missing the target) perhaps is more acceptable to the Chinese mind. We need a more convincing interpretation of the doctrine of "original sin," or might just relegate it to the realm of theological myth!

Christians are exhorted to practice spiritual exercises and piety. Faith is emphasized, but not in contradiction to Christian virtues and good works. In stressing the doctrine of sola fide and sola gratin care is taken to warn against the danger of antinomianism. The slogan "Glorify God and benefit humanity" has become a guiding principle. Conscientious attempts are being made to reconcile the seeming contradictions between faith and good works found in the teachings of Paul and James. Devotional life should be integrated with Christian love and righteousness.

We are rather weak in the doctrine of the Church. One of the reasons is, as Bishop Ting points out, that when China was a mission field, "Western missionary work put its emphasis mainly on extension and not so much on the building up of the church as the Body of Christ."[29] Another reason is that under the present condition of post-denominational unity, the former ecclesiological concepts and polities of various denominations have petered out and lost their hold among the congregations. We need to develop anew a Biblically valid and practicable ecclesiology, including the doctrine of sacraments. The newly adopted document *Church Order (For Trial Use)* is an attempt towards establishing a new doctrine of the church, though it appears to be practical rather than theological.

In eschatology many believers at the grass-roots level still cling to various premillennial "prophecies," and some even fall prey to fanatical aberrations. Yet we also observe that some fundamentalists who formerly took a staunch premillennial stance are conscientiously trying to shift to post-millenialism in order to make room for social improvements and development. Most liberal-minded Christians show no specific zeal in speculating on "the last things." Some theological students seem to be interested in Teilhard's

---

29. "Chinese Christians' Approach to the Bible."

"Omega point," JurgenMoltmann's theology of hope and Pannenberg's theology of history.

As we have torn down the "bamboo-screens" of isolation and come into contact with the wider world and learned more about contemporary theological trends outside of China, many students are opening their eyes and beginning to take an interest in social issues such as world peace, justice, the integrity of creation, etc. In Nanjing we offer courses on contemporary western theologies, Asian theologies, ecumenical theology, Chinese theology, and contextualization of theology, as well as series of lectures on liberation theology, feminist theology, process theology, theology of ecology, inter-faith dialogue, etc., in order to help students see the need for theological reorientation in the larger context of the global village of today.

The process of theological reorientation and reconstruction as sketched above has been gradual, and perhaps can only be observed among some theological-minded Christians. There have also been resistance and controversies. But that there are definite shifts of emphasis can he unmistakably detected in the sermons and articles appearing in *TianFeng*, the *Nanjing Theological Review* and other publications.

VII. THE FUTURE

A recent article written by a Chinese scholar of religion[30] has come to my attention. At the end of the article the author raised the question of the Future of Christianity in China, and speculated on three possibilities: he thinks it impossible that Christianity could win over the nation and convert the whole of China. Secondly, he thinks it unlikely that Christianity would entirely disappear like Nestorianism in the Tang Dynasty. With these two predictions I entirely agree. His third alternative, which he thinks most probable, that Christianity will for the foreseeable future remain a minority sub-culture, having little or negligible influence on the nation as a whole, needs further analysis. Admittedly Christianity in China is a very small, young and weak religion (only one percent of the whole population now), compared with Buddhism and Islam. It has a short history on Chinese soil: about four hundred years of Catholicism and less than two hundred years of Protestantism. Compared with two and a half millennia of Confucianism and Taoism, two thousand years of Buddhism, and thirteen hundred years of Islam, Christianity is just a teenager. Both Buddhism and Islam were also

---

30. Tang Yi (唐逸), "Chinese Christianity in Development," China Study Journal (China Study Program, CCBI) August, 1991. I will not here comment on certain observations made in the article with which I do not agree.

imported from the West, but both have been well acculturized and are no longer regarded as "foreign religions" by the Chinese people. It has only been since about four decades ago that Christianity has been able to rid itself of the stigma of "foreignness" and to take up in a more conscious way the challenge of contextualization. Yet the phenomenally rapid growth in the last decade, much faster than that of the other four religions, cannot he denied. 1 cannot go into the many explanations that have been advanced. Nor can I be content to say that this is because Christianity is superior to other religions, or is the *only true* religion, in a simplistic and taken-for-granted way.

Perhaps we could say that one of the reasons lies in the fact that Christianity is comparatively more flexible and liable (and viable) to accommodate itself to the changing cultures of a modern pluralistic and secular world. Just think of the rise of many denominations of Protestantism after the Reformation, their divergence and convergence, and of the many new "schools" of theology, and of the *aggiornamento* of post-conciliar Roman Catholicism! The Darwinian dictum of "survival of the fittest" also applies to religion. Protestantism in China has changed and is changing—making adjustments, accommodating, contextualizing, and inculturating, and trying to keep pace with the modern changing culture. Yet it remains Christian by remaining true to the unchanged "text," the Biblical Gospel of Jesus Christ. (I do not mean the other religions have not attempted to accommodate and keep up with cultural changes. That Buddhism has been thoroughly Sinicized and become "Chinese Buddhism" in the course of history and has become the most popular and influential religion is something we Christians should take note of.) But we are thinking of the future of Christianity in China. This brings us back to our central theme of Christ and culture.

Returning to the solutions of the problem of the relation of Christ to Culture in Section II of this paper, from what I have tried to argue above I would say that any type of extreme exclusivism (Christ against culture) is untenable and has no future. If Christianity is going to gain any hearing in the Chinese context today it has to forsake its traditional, "orthodox," "no-other-name" dogmatism. All exclusivisms in this pluralistic world will inevitably lead to self-isolation and shut themselves off in small, negligible enclaves of "minority sub-culture."

Therefore to most evangelical Chinese Christians I would highly recommend Charles Kraft's book as a mind-opener and corrective for their exclusivism. This is surely no easy task. The position of inclusivism, as propounded by Karl Rahner, with his "anonymous Christians," may be welcome by many liberal-minded Christians. But it still carries a tone of imperialism and makes it difficult to win the support or acquiescence of adherents of other religions. Why not "anonymous Buddhists or Muslims or Taoists"? The same may be said about the "Christ above culture" alternative. The self-claimed "uniqueness" of a religion is no proof of its "essential superiority" over others. "Each religion is unique and decisive for its followers."[31] But this does not necessarily lead to an "essential" or axiological relativism of religious truths. Christianity is unique to me and my own choice for personal commitment, but not necessarily for others who for various reasons prefer other choices. As a committed Christian I believe in and have chosen Christ as Saviour and Lord, not only for my individual self but also for the human community. Christ saves by transforming. The salvific efficacy of the Christian Gospel lies in its dynamic power to transform the lives of individuals and the community, *in and through culture*, because no one lives in a "cultureless" vacuum, not even the solitary hermit, and culture cannot be abstracted from its human and societal reality. The future of Christianity in China therefore depends upon whether it is able to show in practice its dynamic transforming power in the present pluralistic, secular and changing cultural context. This transformation must be through contextualization. And contextualization requires necessary accommodation or changes in the church herself, in the presentation of the Gospel, and in its theological structure and outward forms (rituals and organizations). In other words, Christianity itself must also be transformed if it is to play the role of transmitter of "Christ the transformer of culture." I have mentioned some of the structural changes of the Chinese church and its theological orientation and reconstruction. Perhaps these may partially account for the phenomena of rapid church growth and its increasing influence and attractiveness to educated and academic circles. The emergence of a growing number of "culture Christians," (or shall I say "cultured sympathizers and admirers of Christianity," the reverse of Schleirmacher's "cultured despisers" in nineteenth century Germany), in an atheistic society and overwhelming non-Christian religious environment, seems to me both encouraging and challenging indeed. The mandate to "run the church well," adopted last January in Beijing by the Fifth National Chinese Christian Conference will give a strong impetus to our fellow Chinese Christians. But we need to look beyond the boundary of the church and see Christianity in a wider perspective as a dynamic transforming force in the ever-changing culture of today's China.

Therefore, in response to Prof. Tan Yi's speculation about the future of Christianity in China I would like to quote with hearty agreement Dr.

---

31. Paul Knitter and John Hick, R. Panikkar, *The Unknown Christ of Hinduism*, Orbis, 1981.

Philip Wickeri's forecast in the excerpt of his article he has kindly shared with me: "Christianity will gain wider acceptance as a cultural and intellectual phenomenon in China, but this will not be accompanied by spiraling church growth."[32] As we come to realize the significance of the Biblical idea of incarnation "as a principle that *animates, directs and unifies the culture, transforming and remaking it so as to bring about a new creation*,"[33] and try to apply this principle by spelling out and living out the Christian message (text) in the particular Chinese cultural context of today (contextualization or incarnation in culture = inculturation). This optimistic prediction of Dr. Wickeri's may not just be utopian wishful thinking, but can serve as a dynamic challenge to us Christians in China. This is how I understand Prof. Wang Weifan's paper "*Verbocaro hic factum est.*" The *here* (hic) is of utmost importance. It means not just a locality, but has a rich connotation embracing place, time, culture, depth and momentum. Forty years after the publication of Richard Niebuhr's monumental book on this subject, may I present this paper as an illustration supporting his fifth alternative, i.e., "Christ the transformer of culture," by a Chinese Christian from the Chinese point of view.

---

32. Philip L. Wickeri, "Making Connections: Christianity and Culture in the Sino-American Dialogue," presented at the "Christianity and Culture: A Sino-Amercan Dialogue," conference, Columbia Theological Seminary, Oct., 1992.

33. I am using P. Arrupe's definition of *inculturation* as quoted by Nicholas Standaert in his article in *ChingFeng*, 34/4 Dec. 1991. This seems to be an excellent commentary on "Christ the transformer of culture."

Self-Propagation in the Light of the History of Christian Thought
(Nanjing, 1954)

BY CHEN ZEMIN

IN THE FOLLOWING ESSAY I want to discuss the theological question of three-self in the Chinese church today in light of the history of Christian thought, with an emphasis upon self-propagation.

To begin with, I would like to point out that three-self is not something we have created or invented, not some new idea or plan we have come up with. The three-self principle has its basis in the Bible and is a principle that has been adhered to by all churches throughout the 2000 year history of Christianity. One can say that nearly every religious organization has had a 'three-self' principle to a greater or lesser extent; otherwise they would not have lasted long. The term 'three-self, is not to be found in the Bible, but we know that the term 'trinity' is not to be found there either. The doctrine of the trinity, however, permeates the Bible. In the same way, this principle and spirit of three-self has a Biblical basis and theology as its theoretical grounds. We can see from church history or the history of Christian thought that three-self is a necessary principle.

The diametrical opposite of 'three-self' is 'three-other', that is, others support, others administer, others propagate. We speak of self-support, not 'standing on one's own feet,' because in Chinese this term has connotations of laying a foundation, of originating something, whereas the foundation of our church is Christ and not ourselves. We could not originate it, but we have a duty to support, establish and develop it. If any church wishes to exist for a long period of time, and wants, moreover, to develop, it cannot depend on other people for its financial support. We know that examples of this kind of situation can be found in the Bible as well. The churches of the New Testament all relied in principle on contributions from members. Naturally, they did not refuse assistance from other churches in times of difficulty.

However, we do not find any New Testament churches which relied entirely on support from other churches.

Self-administration means managing one's own church. In the New Testament, no local church saw its founder as the church's overlord, no matter who it was. When Paul founded a church, he also set up a supervisor (called a Bishop later in church history). When the church's foundation was solid, he went to another place. From then on, the supervisors, elders and administrators of that church ran the church. This is very natural. Paul never issued orders; he always exhorted others as equals. His role was that of an apostle of Christ, not that of a superior. So we can say that the churches of the New Testament were all self-administered.

Later the Catholic Church developed the papal system which in principle was a system of self-administration. The Catholic system uses the bishop as the head of a diocese or church. Theologically, the pope and other bishops were equals, but he was the head or convenor of equals. Later, the power of the pope grew, taking on a high degree of centralism or autocracy. But the bishop of each place still retained a certain independence, the pope was but the chief among many bishops, with the status or rights of a chief. The independence and initiative of the local churches was only limited and weakened by the papal system after a certain point in history, but historically the state of affairs in which the bishop is head has never been lacking or suspended. Today we find the trend toward autonomy throughout the Catholic Church to a greater or lesser extent and this trend is strengthening.

Before the religious reformation in 16th century Europe, there was already a trend toward autonomy on the part of the local churches. The clearest example of this is the Ultramontanist-Gallican controversy. Ultramontanism was a native Italian party, oriented "beyond the mountains," that is, beyond the Alps, toward the pope. Throughout history, most popes have been chosen from among the Italians. The party opposing them was called the Gallican party — Gallia being an ancient name for France. This party promoted independent powers for the French Catholic Church, that it should not be completely under the control of Rome. This was an expression of a local church seeking a definite initiative of its own and is not rare in church history. Another example would be the Hussite movement and Hussite wars prior to the Reformation. The local Czech church had a strong sense of national identity and demanded national independence and autonomy. Again, the main reason Henry the Eighth broke with Rome during the English Reformation of the 16th century was a fight for power of self rule. Of course the case was very complex, involving questions of marriage and rites, but the basic issue was England's unwillingness to be long under the jurisdiction of the pope. In the reformations in Germany,

France, Holland and so on on the European mainland, matters of theological thinking, liturgy and church order are all colored by nationalism. One of the three great principles of the religious reformation was the priesthood of all believers, that is to say that every believer has direct access to God and does not need the Catholic Church to act as intermediary. It follows then that the church established by the believers in each place should have the power of self-management. Therefore, as new churches developed following the reformation, many denominations were produced whose special feature was that they had thrown off the domination of the Roman Catholic Church. During the rise of nationalism in Europe from the 15th to the 16th century the principles of church order were closely linked to autonomy.

Since the schism between the western and eastern churches in the 11th century, the orthodox church has consistently emphasized the principle of autonomy. Today the 17 orthodox churches are all termed autocephalous (meaning that each church has its own head, that it controls itself), each church is in principle independent. Although the influence of churches like the Russian Orthodox Church or the Greek Orthodox Church is very great, they have no jurisdiction over the others. The Orthodox Church of Constantinople was once the head, but this was an honorary thing with no binding powers. These churches are basically distinguished in terms of national, state and geographic boundaries, so the principle of autonomy has continued to this day.

This question of autonomy touches upon that of ecclesiology, including issues such as the nature of the church, holy orders, organization, etc. There are generally three types of church order: the system of bishops, the system of elders and the congregational system. It is felt that a basis for all three types can be found in the Bible and that there is a theological basis as well. These forms have historical, social and cultural sources, and all are expressions of a certain level of the autonomy principle, but there are differences in the scope of autonomy and in the system of administration. Some are larger, some smaller. In the bishop system, the diocese is the administrative unit. For the presbytery system it is the presbytery, the session and finally the synod, in order of increasing size. The synod may cover several provinces or even a country. The congregational system in principle has a single congregation as an autonomous unit. All these systems follow the autonomy principle. Should the Chinese church today adopt one of these as a model of church order or create a new one? This is not a question to be hastily resolved, but should be decided on the basis of our historical conditions, the actual situation in our society and our cultural traditions. We must try to find a new road, one which has a theological foundation. In the past China was a mission field for foreign mission boards; all the different denominations came to proselytize in China. But the period of development for these denominations and organizations was relatively brief, their roots shallow, so we cannot choose one to be the model for our church structure without careful consideration. We ought to establish a church order appropriate to the actual conditions in our country and this requires consideration of many factors. For example, some western countries have experienced a relatively long historical period of capitalism so that their churches exist in a more or less bourgeois- democratic ideological milieu. A feudal way of thinking is deeply ingrained in the Chinese people, however, to the point where it has produced the tragedy of the Cultural Revolution. Therefore when we want to establish our system of church order, we cannot but take these factors into consideration. We must not be anxious to realize our goals, doing things carelessly as a result. What is even more important at present is that we safeguard unity and maintain mutual respect. We should manage our church ourselves. As for the method employed, we can explore this slowly.

Self-propagation does not mean propagating oneself, but undertaking the propagation of the gospel by oneself. Christianity has been a proselytizing religion from the beginning. Matthew 28:19 states: "Go therefore and make disciples of all nations, baptizing them in the name of the Father and of the Son and of the Holy Spirit." This verse of scripture has been called "The Great Commission." According to this great task given by Jesus, we all bear a special trust to spread the gospel everywhere under heaven. One who propagates the gospel is called a missionary. The apostle Paul was such a one and the Book of Acts is a record of his missionary journeys. We believe that the original Christianity was a missional religion, a religion with a mission to spread the gospel, but not a missionary religion. This means that it is a religion which does not rely solely on missionaries to evangelize. This distinction is seldom found in most writings. Our theology should be a missional theology, not a missionary one. This is due to the particular significance the term missionary has taken on; we do not want to use it. In the nineteenth and twentieth centuries, Christianity spread throughout the entire world, becoming a global religion. Naturally, this cannot be separated from the missionary movement. But should not the present task of continuing to spread the gospel in each country belong to the people of that country? Or should it be done by missionaries? Our views on this issue differ from those of certain people in Hong Kong and overseas. We believe that since it has been more than one hundred years since Christianity was brought to China, Chinese Christianity has already established itself and grown to maturity. From now on the mission enterprise in China should be borne to completion by Chinese Christians ourselves. Foreign missionaries should not supplant us.

Missionaries were active before the 16th century, but there was no missionary movement. In the apostolic age, Paul, Barnabas and others spread the gospel to every place. This was their mission activity but there was no missionary movement, no large-scale, organized, mass-type movement. In his 'A History of the Expansion of Christianity,' American church historian Latourette speaks of the historical process by which Christianity spread from Jerusalem outward to the rest of the world. He writes of the mission activities of the first person to go out to propagate the gospel and of how the missionary movement was later born.

In the period at the end of the 15th century and the beginning of the 16th, new geographical discoveries broadened the scope of this propagation. The feudal system in Europe was in ruins, giving rise to nascent capitalism and everyone was seeking markets, particularly some seafaring nations such as Spain, Portugal, Holland and England. One after another they expanded toward North America, Africa and Asia. This expansion marked the development of primitive capitalism, or the beginnings of colonialism. The missionary movement began at this time as well. Missionaries followed the businessmen and imperialist armies out. Some were the vanguard of the aggressors, some their backup force. Some were military advisors. Of course, some were genuinely engaged in propagating the gospel and we do not wish to negate this. But respecters of historical fact all recognize that the missionary movement was linked to colonial expansion. It was inseparable in terms of military ventures, commercial enterprise or culture.

The English writer C.S. Lewis has said that in propagating the gospel one should not be influenced by nor allow interference from anything that is not part of the essence of Christianity. The missionary movement really did spread the seed of the gospel everywhere, but at the same time, the missionaries brought their own cultural traditions, ideologies and lifestyles to the people of the mission field, making it very difficult for them to distinguish what in all this was truly the gospel. As people accepted the gospel, so at the same time, they accepted non-Christian 'weeds.' This situation is very similar to the weeds spoken of in the parable in Matthew 13. Of course, we do not want to fit every detail into the allegory, but the spirit of the parable is anchored in reality. The missionary movement could not avoid carrying with it some negative things. In the course of the twentieth century there has grown a definite perception of this fact in the hearts of the people of the mission fields (that is, in the third world), so they have put forward ideas of 'self-administration,' 'self-support,'and 'self-propagation.' If we continually rely on foreign missionaries to spread the gospel for us,the 'weeds' will increase. But of course in saying this, I do not mean to imply that all missionaries are bad people.

In the past China was a huge mission field, with great amounts of personnel and materiel invested by mission boards of every country. China was also the first country in which criticisms were levelled and resistance raised to the missionary movement. After the Opium War, Christianity was used as an instrument of aggression. The Chinese people were extremely sensitive to this and thus were produced many 'missionary cases' as well as the great Boxer Rebellion and the anti-imperialist and 'anti-Christian' movements in the period from 1916 to 1921. These circumstances were not to be found in other countries. During the twenties and thirties, the Chinese church put forward concepts of 'two-self' or 'four-self' in opposition to 'three-other.' At the time, the more enlightened missionaries endorsed these concepts but this independence movement of the Chinese church did not succeed because the 'wheat' was choked off by the 'weeds.' The 'fruit' was not properly set. All in all, the independence movement of the Chinese church achieved little prior to liberation. Following liberation, we went through a 'three-self reform movement,' and came to a clearer and clearer understanding that three-self was the road we should follow.

Today, the Three-Self Patriotic Movement of the Chinese Protestant church has aroused great response around the world. In Europe at first, some colonial mission organizations opposed Three-Self. But they gradually came to feel that there was a definite truth behind the three-self principle. For them, too, this was an opportunity for self-reflection, and they have now produced a number of books critiquing the missionary movements of the past. In the third world, in those churches called the 'backward churches' (the churches of Asia, Africa and Latin America) there is opposition to linking the missionary movement to colonial aggression as a tool of aggression and control in the third world. So we are not alone when we speak of three-self. Many churches have a 'three-self' movement, but they do not necessarily use our terminology.

At the 1980 meeting of the National China Christian Council in Nanjing, Principal Ting, in his "Retrospect and Prospect" address, said that since we had implemented self-administration, self-support and self-propagation to a certain extent, our task from now on should be to take stock of our experience, and, on the foundation of past achievements, go a step further in completing our mission to be "well-supported, well-run, and well-propagated."

In the remainder of my essay, I would like to focus on the question of self-propagation.

Self-propagation should include the two aspects of what is propagated and how propagation is carried on. I have said above that self-propagation is not the propagation of self, but the propagation of the gospel by oneself. That being the case, what gospel are we propagating? What is the content of evangelism? And how is it carried on? Seen from the vantage point of the history of Christian thought, this has been an issue from the very beginning of Christian propagation of the gospel. How will it be possible, in propagating the gospel in the soil of a new culture, to enable local people to understand and accept it? What should the evangelist do when the gospel conflicts with local culture? Is the answer complete rejection of the local culture, ideology and customs? Or compromise? The Catholic missionary Francis Xavier was the first to carry the gospel to Japan. He failed primarily because he did not understand oriental religion and culture. Matteo Ricci, who brought Catholicism to China during the same period, was more successful because his guiding principle was respect for and integration with Chinese culture. Later, during the K'angHsi period, Ricci was accused of surrendering to Chinese culture by the Franciscans, who insisted upon maintaining the whole spectrum of western Christianity in contradiction to traditional Chinese culture to the point where the K'angHsi emperor, in a fit of anger, threw them all out. Catholicism was thus nearly extinguished in China. This illustrates the fact that in bringing the gospel to a place, one cannot regard the indigenous culture as a complete enemy, as evil. This is a lesson of history.

When Christianity was spread throughout the Greek and Roman world in the first and second centuries, the issue of what was to be propagated and how had to be faced. The apostle Paul borrowed the language of Greek philosophy to spread the gospel and not only Paul, but the local bishops, were engaged in evangelism. When dealing with the question of how to enable people to accept Christianity they inevitably had to reflect the special characteristics and traditions of their own cultures in the context of self-propagation. Christian faith is a spiritual matter, inseparable from human thought and feeling. Each place has its own cultural traditions, which, along with the people's philosophy and original religion, possess its own national characteristics. Latin Christianity, for example, was colored by Latin civilization, while in the eastern churches, the Alexandrian and Antiochan schools reflected the national character of late Greek culture, that is Hellenistic civilization. Looking at the entire course of church history, each period reflected the dominant philosophy of the times. The philosophy of Augustine, for example, reflected the Platonism of the day, as well as the features of a period in which the slave system was crumbling in Europe, but feudalism was not yet established. Later when feudalism had reached its apogee, Europe entered the Middle Ages. At that time Aristotelianism was popular in Europe and all this was reflected in the scholastic theology of Thomas Aquinas. The eastern church, heir to Hellenistic civilization and eastern theological thinking, emphasized neo-platonism and mysticism. From the tenth century on, they blended into Slavic culture. The churches of the eastern orthodox tradition reflect these influences today.

Following the religious reformation of the 16th century, Christianity was integrated into the local cultural traditions, national characteristics and social conditions as it was being spread in western Europe. A detailed study shows that Germany, England, France, Italy, etc. all have different emphases in their propagation of the gospel. Of course Europe is a region both united and divided and it is very difficult to distinguish each country's special characteristics clearly. In a general way, however, they all possess European qualities. Many denominations and theologies appeared, due to the fact that each place has its own traditions, politics, economics and every kind of social factor, but all are still Christian. Throughout its development from the first century until its present status as a world religion, Christianity has not been one religion, but has had three major branches — eastern orthodox, Catholicism and many Protestant denominations. All have their own particular emphases, their own characteristics and colorations. This has made Christianity all the richer, the more in accord with the needs of the people in each place, the easier for people of all nations to accept. It would be inconceivable were Christianity to have been from the beginning a kind of unchanging, set model. From a theological point of view, the revelation of God in history has been apprehended and responded to in different ways by different peoples. This has enriched Christianity the more and illustrates its universality (catholicity). Churches in English speaking countries call this 'unity in variety', both one and diversified. It is an historical necessity.

How then can the Chinese church today propagate well? Have any special theological features or experiences emerged out of the tortuous course of the past 39 years? We always meet with this question, whether visiting abroad or receiving foreign visitors at home, and we feel that it is a very important one. At times we do not know where to begin in discussing it. Although in contacts with foreign friends we always take it up to some extent, we do not discuss it very systematically because of time constraints. We really need to spend time taking stock and setting in order; we should become systematic in our treatment of this question. But the whole issue may still be quite vague in our minds. There have been and still are quite a few Christians in our church whose concern focuses on the two questions belief/unbelief and spirituality/unspirituality. They divide all humanity into two parts: one Christian, the other non-Christian. They further divide the

Christians into two groups: one spiritual, the other not. Is not this too simplistic and self-centered? How then shall we deal with these questions? We do notconsider belief to be a matter of belief in certain doctrines. Thematter is not only one of belief in doctrines but of faith orcommitment — a commitment of one's whole life to God, to Christ.This is a theological explanation, for when we speak of belief vsunbelief, we must broaden our thinking a bit. We must not berestricted by a literal understanding of doctrine. What is spirituality?What is unspirituality? 'Ling (灵)' and 'jingshen (精神)' in Chinese both meansspiritual. The term 'shuling (属灵)' indicates the value of a person's spirituallife, with spirituality being expressed in every aspect of one's life. Human life has a rich spiritual side as well as a material one. Christianity seeks to resolve many problems of this spiritual side andthis naturally involves the whole of human life. Thus, the scope ofspirituality is broad and we should not limit it to certain narrow andsubjective emotions, or to a certain type of religious quest. Questionsof belief/unbelief and spirituality/unspirituality are questions whichour Chinese theological circles must resolve. If we were to confineall Christian gospel and doctrine to these two questions, however,and use our understanding of them as a standard by which to judge others, we would be too narrow and our Christian theology too simple, which would be extremely detrimental to our desire to 'systematize.'

    In the past, some people used these two sets of opposites as the boundary line between the fundamentalist or evangelical school and the modernist school or liberal theology, causing many ruptures and pointless disputes. In taking stock now of our thirty plus years of experience, it can be said that if contemporary Chinese theology has a special characteristic, it is to have overcome denominationalism, by which we mean endless divisive controversies and mutual attacks. In the Chinese term for denomination (zongpai) the first character (zong宗) refers to a source handed down which at a certain point is shaped into a group of adherents, as if we were to say Luther 'zong,'Calvin 'zong,' Anglican 'zong,' Wesley 'zong' and so on. The second character (pai 派) encompasses the ego-centric exclusivity of the small group or faction. To overcome denominationalism, we must overcome both 'zong' and 'pai.' We have taken some mainstream denominations of the past as well as some very exclusivist denominations of the past such as the Little Flock, theTrue Jesus Church, the Real True Jesus Church, etc. and step by step, united them. Our theological thinking should transcend denominationalism, promote church unity, mutual respect, mutual learning and mutual enrichment. Only in this way can we speak of systematizing our theological thinking. The system must be very broad and rich in content, including both the Biblical truth of "in many and various ways God spoke of old to our fathers by the prophets...(and) has spoken to us by a Son" (that is, Jesus Christ) and the exposition of Biblical truth by philosophers and theologians of church history. These are the treasures of the rich tradition we inherit. We must also include here the comprehension, understanding and experience of Biblical truth in our own spiritual lives. It should possess both breadth and depth as well as encompass our own national characteristics, which are extremely rich and varied. It should by no means be restricted to a narrow perspective or be allowed to ossify. To put it simply, it must be rooted in both Christ and China, a union of Christian and Chinese. Only in this way can it help us Chinese Christians as we witness to the gospel among the broad masses of our people. And only then can it contribute to the catholicity of the ecumenical Christian church.

At the same time, our theology should include a method of approach to non-Christian cultures, moralities, etc. What value have they as far as we are concerned? How shall we approach the realities of life I society? We should practice mutual respect both within the church and, outside it, toward other religions. Last semester we held a class here at the seminary entitled 'Introduction to World Religions,' which gave everyone the opportunity to understand something of other faiths. We did not treat them as entirely heresy or superstition. We are willing to listen to and understand whatever they have that we regard as of value. This can be called 'dialogue,' although it is an incomplete one.

Everyone has studied 'Systematic Theology,' which includes our concept of God, Christology, concept of humanity, salvation theory, eschatology, ecclesiology, etc. We make choices about what to absorb from the theological views of each denomination on the basis of our understanding. We also have our own viewpoint. Take for example our view of God. Is God the God of all humanity or of Christianity? We say that God is the God of all humanity.

When we apply religion in our lives do we think of the fact that God is also the God of the other and that God is the Lord of Creation? When we speak of the providence of God, we are not only referring to providence for Christians but for all humanity; this is a point we emphasize. We do not agree with duality or plurality of sources. We feel that all truth, goodness and beauty come from God, so at the seminary we frequently discuss how we should deal with the truth, goodness and beauty which exists outside the church. Actually the problems we meet with or discuss are not only Chinese problems. They have long been discussed overseas and many foreign friends have broken out of the circle of belief/unbelief.

Again, take Christology as an example. An American friend posed a question on his last visit, one he had often raised before: "How do you shape your Christology?" By which he meant, you already have a Christology, how did you arrive at it? Principal Ting has spoken in a number of essays of the Cosmic Christ, a concept based on the exposition of Christ's nature in the first chapter of Colossians and the second chapter of Philippians, Christ's role in creation and salvation and his future role in the final completion. All this concerns the entire cosmos. The Chinese term for cosmos (yuzhou) is composed of two characters also. The first, 'yu 宇,' means above and below, the four directions. It is infinite. The second, 'zhou 宙,' means for all time, so 'yuzhou' means all time and space, or Christ is always and everywhere present. Such a Christology is extremely broad.

Again, consider the understanding of humanity as an example. What is humanity in the eyes of God? Is it completely corrupt or does it have value? Is it worthy of salvation by God? We are also very concerned with this question. When we speak of the 'doctrine of salvation,' what, after all, do we mean by salvation? Some think that going up to heaven when one dies instead of down to hell is salvation. If we bring such a limited understanding to what it means to be saved, then our vision is too narrow. We believe that the significance of God's saving act is far broader than saving us from hell. Otherwise it would be enough to believe in God only as we near death. Whether or not we had believed during our lives, how we lived those lives, would be unimportant. But this is not how we see it.

Should our theology be this-worldly or not? Should it be concerned for and affirm the real world (while criticizing, transforming and judging) or shall we consider spiritual life to have no connection with the real world? At present, we are looking for ways to make the rituals, liturgy, music, art and literature of our church more Chinese, more indigenous in character. There is naturally a lot of resistance to this, mainly due to force of habit, by which I mean the kind of thinking characterized by the worship of things foreign found in the church in the past: the idea that only what was foreign was orthodox. As you all know, we have made some attempts at indigenization in the area of sacred music, but in some places, this too has met with resistance. There is a feeling that these are 'minor tunes,' not sacred songs, and some are unwilling to sing them. This requires reflection and reform on our part. We need to raise our standards, both in terms of quantity and quality. Our forms of worship, liturgy music, art, etc. can all be instruments of evangelism and we must all redouble our efforts in these areas, making them more consonant with the Chinese situation. Only then will they win approval from Christians and acceptance from non-Christians in China.

Chinese Protestants account for only 0.3–0.4% of the whole population. If we do not identify ourselves with the broad mass of the Chinese people, then we cannot bring the gospel to them. We, like everyone else, are patriotic. This is political identification. We, like everyone else, all accept the essence of the national culture. This is cultural identification. If we want to bring our most precious possessions to them, then it is from this basis of identification that we must work, before they will be willing to accept it. The gospel itself is a "stumbling block" for people. They have never been happy to listen to it. If we add to this some 'foreign matter,' then we make it even more difficult for people. We should find those areas where we speak a common language. These are things we should keep in mind when we consider our thirty years' experience of theological exploration, indigenous and contextual theology. We should also be familiar with trends in European, American and third world theology. We are more sympathetic to liberation theology from which we can draw concrete lessons. The Minjung theology of South Korea is also a branch of liberation theology worthy of our consideration.

Those of you who are to graduate, no matter what kind of church you are to work in, must take as your own task the establishment and development of Chinese theology. The churches of the whole world are watching you. What you do will be better than what we older generation have done. Rev. Y.T. Wu and the elder generation opened this way to us. If it were not the will of God, it could not have been done. According to the laws of history, one generation succeeds another and surpasses it. Thus, we cherish a tremendous hope for your generation.

Nanjing Theological Review, June, 1985, p.1.
Originally an address delivered to the student body,
Nanjing Theological Seminary,
translated by Janice Wickeri

Y. T. Wu
A Prophetic Theologian
(Beijing, November 27, 1993)

Chen Zemin

Y. T. Wu [Wu Yaozong] (1893–1979) was a leading figure in the Three-Self Patriotic Movement from its inception until the Cultural Revolution. He served the YMCA as editor-in-chief at the Association Press in Shanghai during the 1940s and founded the Protestant magazine, then a weekly, TianFeng. In November this year, the China Christian Council and the Three-Self Movement held a centennial commemoration of his birth.

HISTORICAL SKETCH

A complete biography or a chronology of Y.T. Wu's life has yet to be written. According to Mr. ShenDerong's *Profile*, beginning from the time that Mr. Wu became a Christian, we can divide his life into four periods:

1) From his introduction to Christianity (1911), baptism into the Christian Church (1918, at age 25),and the beginning of his work with the YMCA (1920) until he went to the United States for advanced studies (1924–1927), he was in what was then Peiping (Beijing). At this time he was influenced by the concept of reconciliation.[1] He produced over twenty articles in *Truth*, propounding Christianity and reconciliation. During his third year of overseas studies, he studied theology and philosophy at both Union Theological Seminary of New York and Columbia University, and was confirmed in his advocacy of reconciliation. After his return to China, he worked in the campus division of the YMCA, served as chair of the Fellowship of Reconciliation and

---

[1] Translator's Note: The Chinese rendering of this term means literally "By Love Alone."

as editor of the Chinese version of the *Reconciliation* journal. During this time (1931–1937) he authored over twenty articles in *Reconciliation*. Afterwards, he began to doubt "unarmed resistance" (pacifism), wrestled with the problem in his thinking for four years, and finally rejected it. In 1937 he resigned the chair of the Fellowship of Reconciliation. In 1934 he published *The Social Gospel* in Shanghai, which was a collection of his writings from 1931–1934 (altogether eighteen articles), representing his religious, theological, and socio-political thinking after 1918 and prior to changing his views on reconciliation.

2) In late 1937 and early 1938, he returned to the United States and Europe, and studied for six months at Union Theological Seminary in New York. After returning to China, he worked in the publications department of the national YMCA in Shanghai. He joined the "YY1 Society," and actively promoted patriotic progressive thinking. In Changsha 长沙 and Hankou 汉口, he became acquainted with XuTeli 徐特立, Zhou En-lai, and others. He travelled to India and visited with Gandhi. From 1939 to 1941 he travelled throughout China to promote resistance against Japan. From late 1941 through May of 1946 he was in Chengdu 成都, working on literary propagation. He joined the "YY2 Society." Heestablished the United Christian Publishing Society, and initiated *TianFeng Monthly* and the series *Christian Collection* (1942). In 1943 he published *No One Has Seen God*. He was an active participant in anti-Chiang Kai Shek democratic progressive activities. In June of 1946 he returned to Shanghai and published "The Contemporary Tragedy of Christianity" in *TianFeng* in the Spring of 1948. In May of the same year he was forced to resign as head of the *TianFeng* Society. In late 1949 he published *Darkness and Light*, a collection of fifty-three articles written during the previous seven years, representing his religious and socio-political thinking.

3) From 1949–1966 he actively joined in the Three-Self Patriotic Movement, and made immeasurable contributions to the reform and building up of the Chinese Church. He actively participated in many political activities, and published many articles in *TianFeng*. In addition, he made many speeches. However, materials from this period are limited.

4) Because materials after the Cultural Revolution are limited, it is difficult to form any judgement.

After he joined the Christian Church, during a period of sixty years, Y.T. Wu made innumerable speeches and wrote a great number of articles, only a small portion of which were published or have been preserved. I would like to suggest that the CCC and TSPM make the effort to produce a complete and in-depth biography.

A PROPHETIC THEOLOGIAN

There is no disputing the fact that Mr. Wu played a prophetic role, or that he was an advocate of the China Christian Three-Self Patriotic Movement, who openedup a new path for the Christian Church in a New China in the process of construction. However, there are inevitably some who raise doubts, criticisms, or reproach on theological or religious grounds. I would like to make some preliminary comments about such criticisms, but due to the constraints of time and resources, these may be superficial. I hope they will lead to a more fruitful exchange of views among a broader group, and would welcome all comments.

Theologically Mr. Wu has been criticized in four respects: 1) his espousal of reconciliation; 2) as an advocate of the social gospel; 3) for his liberal theology or "modernism" or "YMCA theology"; he has been branded as "unspiritual, or even as an "unbeliever"; 4) Consequently, he is not a theologian. To avoid bias, we must take a comprehensive and fair view of such criticisms, studying and testing without preconceptions, basing our views on Mr. Wu's entire lifetime of contributions and undertakings, his entire corpus of speeches and writings (or at least the most important ones), his background, his conduct and tangible accomplishments, and the influence he exerted.

First, we must state that Mr. Wu as a person was extremely just, reliable, and forthright. What he said was of a piece with what he believed and thought. One can perceive his conduct and innermost heart from his speeches and writings. His heart was without deceit. His talk and his walk were one; indeed his walk bore out his talk. He did not cover up his faith, his thinking, or his point of view. He had the courage to insist on what he felt to be right, but also to correct what he perceived to be his mistakes. His entire life was one of forging ahead. Thus, we must understand that in evaluating Mr. Wu, it is most important to measure his conduct, work, undertakings, and influence, rather than base our view primarily on his thought (especially his religious or theological thought). We must realize that his conduct was guided by his thought (including his religious and theological thought and his socio-political thought).

On the basis of what Mr. Wu himself said, his thinking underwent two major changes during his lifetime. One was his acceptance of Christianity.

This was the most fundamental change, and determined his perspectives on life and the world, which did not subsequently change. The second occurred during the later stages of the War of Resistance against Japan, when he "accepted the anti-religious theories of social science, and combined materialist thinking with religious faith." These two fundamental changes happened during the first period and the beginning of the second, referred to above. However, the second change was not a denial of his Christian faith, but rather deepened and developed it.[2] Even in 1979, at the end of his life he believed in Christianity, loved the Church, and even asked, in spite of illness, to attend the thanksgiving service marking the opening of Muen Church 沐恩堂 in Shanghai.

RECONCILIATION

Reconciliation was a form of pacifist thinking current at the time of the First World War. It considered love to be the highest principle in dealing with people or events, and opposed the use of military force to solve conflicts or struggles in society. This indeed has a basis in Scripture (e.g., 1 & 2 John and 1 Corinthians 13). From the point of view of faith, this is completely "orthodox." However, as a principle of social ethics, on a practical everyday level, it is not easily accomplished. It calls for very difficult choices in the conflict between the ideal and the real, and it calls for great sacrifice. Once Mr. Wu accepted Christianity, he felt he should be a genuine, consistent Christian. He needed great courage and commitment in order to live according to the Sermon on the Mount. At this time an English Quaker missionary in Beijing, Henry T. Hodgkin, initiated a "Fellowship of Reconciliation." Mr. Wu and some other Christians joined this organization, and contributed their devout and eloquent abilities by writing many articles, including editorials, news stories, discussions, and replies for the Fellowship's periodical *Reconciliation* (from the first issue in 1931 through 1935, there were a total of 17 issues). Reading these articles today we cannot but affirm and deeply admire Mr. Wu's thorough-going commitment of faith and his grounding in Scripture and theology. This was the time when Japanese imperialism was invading China, and vast areas of the northeastern and northern China came bit by bit under occupation. Countless millions of our compatriots suffered humiliation and massacre. In the face of this national distress, with patriotic compatriots increasingly pursuing a war of resistance, he still maintained his ideal of reconciliation, pursuing peaceful non-cooperation as a way to save the country. The conflict between the two approaches, however, began

2 Wu, Y.T. *No One Has Seen God*, 2nd. Edition, 1947, appendices A and B.

a long-standing and bitter strugglein Mr. Wu's heart. From the early 1920s to 1931 (Sep.18, Mukden Incident), 1932 (Shanghai Incident on Jan.28), and 1937 (the War of Resistance against Japan), Mr. Wu moved from pure reconciliation to non-cooperation with the Japanese, to a theoretical reconciliation, to actions that supported military opposition in the War of Resistance, to active participation with every kind of patriot in the movement to resist the Japanese and save the nation from extinction, to the use of military force for the sake of love that does not transgress the spirit of reconciliation, to singing the praises of military force to oppose aggression.In the end, he completed a long and difficult process of changing his political thinking (and also his theological thinking).[3]

In 1937 he resolutely resigned his position as head of the Fellowship of Reconciliation. However, this for him simply confirmed his faith in Jesus' teaching about love as the most important feature and the highest principle of the doctrine and faith of Christianity. How to express this principle of love in the face of brutal realities is the major question of Christian ethics. After Mr. Wu accepted Christianity, he perceived a sublime concept, a lofty principle in Scripture, and especially in Jesus' teaching, deeds, and suffering sacrifice. Throughout his life, Mr. Wu dedicated himself to the struggle for this concept and principle. During this time he faced many challenges, including the War of Resistance against Japan, the Second World War, the Anti- Chiang Democratic Struggle, the war of liberation, and a whole series of political struggles after liberation. . . He transformed his thinking from the principle of pacifism to accepting the Marxist-Leninist philosophy of struggle. He was convinced that in terms of purpose and basic thinking Christianity and Marxism-Leninism were one and could be reconciled, even if not in terms of the methods and theory of struggle. In terms of theory and theology, there must be a refined and reasonable explanation, and there must be a corresponding expression in terms of deeds. Throughout all of this, he was faithful to his religious faith and to what he felt to be truth. He did not violate the divine mandate of patriotism, nor did he transgress the mandate given him concerning God, Church, society, or nation. During decades of social disruption, he continued to forge ahead, revising his understanding of struggle as a method. Even up till the time of his death, he did not set aside his ideal and conviction of love. After the1950s, his effort to rouse the Christians of China to reform the church of China was based on this conviction and concept. There are too few theologians with this kind of wisdom and the courage to maintain their convictions, to do what should be done both theoretically and practically, and to make reasonable

---

3 Cf. ShenDerong, "Wu Yaozong and Reconciliation," 1989.

adjustments. (This reminds me of the young theologian in the Germany of the 1940s who gave his life in the struggle against Hitler, namely Dietrich Bonhoeffer!) Therefore, to say that Mr. Wu was a prophetic theologian is no exaggeration. (Later many things happened that no one could control or change; nor were they things he hoped for or should be held responsible for.)

THE SOCIAL GOSPEL

Mr. Wu's *The Social Gospel* was published in September of 1934 (Shanghai YMCA Publishers). It pulled together eighteen articles written between 1930 and 1934. This was just at the time when he was in the process of rejecting the unarmed resistance principle of reconciliation, during his transition toward acceptance of the Marxist theory of revolutionary class struggle, which he compared to Jesus' Sermon on the Mount. He was seeking a way to combine a love of country and a love of church, a way to remain faithful to the concept of reconciliation, while reforming society. At this time, he still held fast to his idealof reconciliation.[4] But both conceptually and practically, he retained aclose link between war and struggle and the problems of society.[5] Although this is not a systematic work.[6] its central idea is where Chinese Christianity should be heading.[7] The entire book takes its name from the opening article, "The Meaning of the Social Gospel." This has led to many misunderstandings, and provided a basis for many attacks and groundless slander.

The Social Gospel was a popular movement in North American Christian theology for some thirty years, in the late 19th and early 20th centuries. Its purpose was based on Jesus' teaching about the kingdom of God in the Scriptures, namely to correct the "spiritual gospel" prevalent in North American churches, i.e., the idea that only personal salvation is important, to the neglect of the social significance of the gospel. The message of the "social gospel" both continues the tradition of the Old Testament prophets, and is based on the teachings of Jesus himself. Theologically it is completely

---

4 W, Y.T. *The Social Gospel*, 1934, the tenth essay, "The Shanghai Incident and the Idea of Reconciliation"; the eleventh essay, "Reconciliation Amid the Drumbeats"; the thirteenth essay, "Reconciliation and Social Reform."

5 Ibid. The third essay, "China's Crisis and the International Situation"; the eighth essay, "Voluntary Army in the Northeast Army of Volunteers and Us"; the fourth essay, "The Prerequisite for a Way Out for Youth"; and the sixth essay, "Concerning Marriage and Love."

6 Ibid. The preface.

7 Ibid. The fifteenth and sixteenth essays, "Our Mission Today."

authentic, and hermeneutically it is beyond challenge. Mr. Wu in his first article ("The Meaning of the Social Gospel") discussed this concept in great detail, and made use of the Rauschenbusch's understanding of it. This was a contemporary bugle call for prophets in evil times. Today, some sixty years later, in the society and church of China, this still has a very important and practical significance. Christianity is fundamentally incarnational, concerned with society, and is not simply concerned only with the salvation ofindividual souls or with a mystical religious devotion. (If Christianity had been like the gnosticism that spread along the coasts of the Mediterranean in the first and second centuries, offering individual salvation and denying this mortal world, going to the extreme of excluding other teachings, it would likely have faded from history early on, with no chance of growing, as it has today, into the largest of world faiths.) Mr. Wu certainly never denied that Christianity changes individuals, or that it is a gospel of salvation for individual souls. He followed up his first article with the second, "Social Gospel and Personal Gospel." He emphasized that "the basic power of religious life comes from the personal gospel." He used Jesus' own words to explain that the personal gospel is "a form of clarity of consciousness, spiritual harmony, inner liberation, and the power of potentiality." The personal gospel is "the seed of life." This kind of life must flower and bear fruit in one's actual situation, which then becomes the "social gospel." Thus, social gospel and personal gospel are two sides of the same coin. Personal gospel and social gospel each should lead to the other in an ongoing cycle. He quoted Harry Emerson Fosdick: "Social gospel and personal gospel are like the ends of the Hudson River Tunnel. If you go in this end, you come out that end. If you go in that end, you come out this one. But there's only one tunnel."

The social gospel was a corrective movement at the beginning of the present century, and is not in itself a complete system of theology. At the time, it had affinities with the "liberal theology" of North America. After the Second World War, in the face of the brutal realities of history, the dreams of some proponents of the "social gospel" to improve society came to naught. "Liberal theology" was criticized and declared bankrupt by "Neo-orthodoxy." During the chaotic decades after the war, there appeared around the world a personal gospel and a "charismatic movement," which characterized the upsurging "Revival of Evangelical Religion." Since the 1970s many foreign "evangelical" groups emphasize only salvation to the neglect of the social origins of sin; this is one-sided and incomplete. There have appeared "neo-evangelicals" who have placed more emphasis on concern for society, and whose theological orientation is a bit more open. This is precisely the "cycle" that Mr. Wu spoke of Liberation theology, which began in Latin America and has influenced the entire third world, can be seen from one viewpoint to be precisely this "cycle," as it develops, "flowers and bears fruit" in the new historical conditions of society. Because of the decades of difficulties that the church in China endured, and because for a long period it was cut off from the outside world, and was indeed rather isolated, the mentality and theological viewpoint of most believers was captured in the outlook of the 50s and 60s, which was characterized by fundamentalism, unconcern about the world, personal salvation, and hostility to other denominations. Others were affected by the anti-communist propaganda both before and after liberation, and so could not understand, or even opposed, the Three-Self Patriotic Movement initiated by Mr, Wu. They consequently used Mr. Wu's *The Social Gospel*, written some sixty years earlier, as the basis for attacking him. If this was not done from ignorance, then it must have been done out of prejudice. I hope such people take a bit of time to read this small book carefully and with open minds, placing it in its contemporary social context. If so, they might be able to hear the voice of a prophet.

CONCEPT OF GOD

Ten years after the publication of *The Social Gospel* Mr. Wu wrote another small book, *No One Has Seen God* (early 1943, Chengdu), elucidating his views of religion and God. He went twice to the United States (1924–1927, 1936–1937) to study theology and philosophy at Union Theological Seminary in New York and at Columbia University. These were the times when the struggle between "fundamentalism" and "modernism" was at its most heated and nearly at an end. This struggle was in reality the conflict between fideism and rationalism, the debate about how, in the new historical situation and social environment, to use reason and modern scientific concepts to introduce and explain Christian faith and doctrine to the educated class. Union Theological Seminary in New York was a bastion of "modernism" and "liberal theology." Mr. Wu was himself a thoughtful person, with inclinations to the rational, ready to accept progressive thinking, and an activist who combined knowledge and action. His choice of Union Theological Seminary and his being influenced by this theological trend was no chance, and certainly was not "something he had no choice in." The view of religion and of God explicated in his *No One Has Seen God* simply reflected his established ideas. After his return to China, the growing educated class was caught up in the May Fourth Movement, there was "anti-Christian" influence, liberation thinking, seeking for freedom, and a yearning for truth. These were times when many educated young people, in times of national distress, were unsure of the future and without hope, but continued to seek truth and a viable future. The influence of Marxism-Leninism was growing daily. The anti-religious thinking presented a great challenge to religion. In Chengdu Mr. Wu met a large number of patriotic educated young people who had been exiled to western China. He used rational concepts and deep wisdom to introduce and explain the faith and truth of Christianity to them. Some people who have seen nothing more than the title of the book, and have not had time to read it carefully, conclude that this is a book that promotes atheism. In reality, Mr. Wu is simply using the Bible to explain the existence of God: in words from St. John's Gospel, "the only Son, who is in the bosom of the Father, he has made him known," and from 1 John "if we love one another, God's love abides in us." The entire book does not merely explicate the Biblical view of God, or Jesus' view of God; it also uses the concepts of philosophers, namely how to experience God on the basis of true feelings, beauty, or good experiences. He also discusses the problems of truth, of the meaning of life, and of materialism and socialism. Even more noteworthy is the length at which he discusses the meaning and effect of prayer. Mr. Wu not only sincerely believed in God, but also communicated regularly with God in prayer. "Prayer is harmony, light, and strength." (Mr. Wu's understanding and practice of prayer should be the topic of another study.) Of more value still is the fact that when Mr. Wu talks about the existence of God or about faith in God, it is not just idle talk. He expressed his faith and lived his faith in the midst of his life and work. We can say that Mr. Wu's entire life was built on his religious faith. Those who say Mr. Wu had no faith are those who espouse the judgement of him as an "unbeliever," "not a theologian." Reading the book would do them no harm. I suspect that the faith of many critics cannot approach the depth and strength of Mr. Wu's faith, nor does their "theological thinking" approach the brilliance of his.

It was not Mr. Wu's intention to establish a complete system of theology. He sought to bring faith and practice into harmony. He was involved in the midst of an intense and real struggle, which did not allow time for him to develop his theological thinking into a complete system. At the conclusion of this book, he wrote "I have many more years to go in my heart—and another book, *What is Christianity*? This should be a somewhat longer and more systematic study. By contrast, this present small study is only one part of that future work; in terms of systematic thinking, this is a prelude or miniature of that book." Later, historical developments demanded that Mr. Wu devote more time and effort to more crucial immediate struggles and undertakings. His vision far surpassed the limits of seminary lectures, classes, or writings. As a result, he was not able to complete this longer writing. This duty he left for the next generation of theologians.

CONCLUSION

During the intense struggles of the chaotic years, Mr. Wu wrote yet another book, *Darkness and Light* (1949, Shanghai), another collection of articles. We do not have time here to analyze the contents in detail. Very briefly, this book reflects Mr. Wu's mental struggle during the difficult passage of China and the Church in China from darkness into light. Mr. Wu was not satisfied being an abstruse, conjectural, pedantic theologian. He was rather a brave and wise prophetic theologian who devoted himself to bringing together faith, ideology, and life. The prophets of the Bible and of history have always been thus. If we were to feel that because Mr. Wu did not produce several major books of systematic theology or was not a theological specialist, he therefore was not a theologian, we would not understand Mr. Wu. That would show that our vision is too nearsighted and we are too narrow-minded. Those who from their own fundamentalist perspective feel that Mr. Wu was a "liberal theologian" or a "non-believer," simply demonstrate their own ignorance and self-pride. Their slanderous attacks do not in the least damage Mr. Wu's noble vision or his great accomplishments. We should maintain mutual respect in matters of faith and theological thinking, and hopefully not stir up useless "theological conflict" on the occasion of Mr. Wu's centennial.

Perhaps we should add a few other words here. Mr. Wu's theology leaned toward the rational and the practical. At the same time, he placed great emphasis on religious feelings. He emphasized personal devotion, prayer, and mystical experience. This is a religious feeling that surpasses the rational and the practical, and expressed his continued concern for the building up of the church after the 1950s, his fellowship with, love of, and help for coworkers whose theological outlooks differed from his, and his particularly strong feelings for a just society and politics. We can rightly say that this is the highest form of a prophetic religious feeling, and is completely different from the kind of "spiritual experience" that is content with a personal feeling of "ecstasy."

When we study the life and thought of Mr. Wu, we need to study the whole picture, objectively, historically (on the basis of the development of the contemporary social-political context). In order to reach a fair conclusion, we must proceed in a spirit of mutual respect, without denominational prejudice, and without taking things out of context.

Nanjing Theological Review, No. 19 (December, 1993), pp. 1–5.
Translated by Henry Rowold.

Protestant Christianity in China
Facing the Challenges of Modernization
(Beijing, April 1992)

Chen Zemin

MODERNITY AND MODERNIZATION BELONG to the category of time, and are therefore historical terms used with relative connotations. Chinese modern history, according to most historians, dates from the beginning of the twentieth century,[1] about one century after the introduction of Protestant Christianity into China.[2] The role of Christianity in the modernization of China is a debated topic among scholars and historians. As we all know, the primary purpose of the missionary enterprise was to evangelize, not to modernize China. Perhaps it was either because many early missionaries had failed to make a clear distinction between the essence of the gospel and Western "modernized" civilization, which they believed to be "more advanced" than traditional Chinese "pagan" culture, or because some had intentionally introduced cultural reformative measures deployed as a kind of Trojan horse, that the missionary movement in China did, in effect, have some share in bringing about the modernization of China during the period of about one hundred years between the Opium Wars and the establishment of the People's Republic. Some positive influences such as reforming the public educational system by setting up Christian schools and universities, introducing and disseminating Western medical and scientific technological knowledge and democratic ideas, promoting equal rights for women, and criticizing and abolishing certain feudal-superstitious practices have been generally affirmed and often cited as evidence of the contributions of the Christian church.

---

1 Most historians take the May Fourth Movement (1919) as the milestone marking the beginning landmark of Chinese modernization.
2 From Robert Morrison's arrival in China in 1807.

But in making such an evaluation we must keep three things in mind. First, such arguments are often impressionistic and too generalized, lacking scientific, quantitative, comparative analyses, and have been too often advanced for apologetic purposes rather than as objective sociological investigations. Secondly, with the collapse of the corrupt Qing Dynasty, the growth of the Reform Movement in the 1890s, the establishment of the Republic of China in 1911, and the May Fourth Movement in 1919, China was already inevitably and irreversibly on the way to modernization, whether with or without the "promoting" or "accelerating" influence of the church. Thirdly, most important of all, modernization is a complex and very complicated concept and procedure. It involves many phases or dimensions: economic, political, technological, social, cultural and spiritual. Speaking of modernization as a process of social historical development, the first two dimensions, i.e., material (or economic) and political factors, are more fundamental and decisive, while the other dimensions are more or less derivative and complementary, and only in a dialectical way reflect and react as superstructures upon the substructure. It is industrialization, commercialization and modern means of communication that lay the foundation and lead the way to modernization and change the cultural and spiritual milieu of a society. The arguments of Max Weber[3] and his friend Ernst Troeltsch[4], strong as they seem, have not settled the debate on which is determinative, the economic or the spiritual. The church's primary concern is spiritual blessedness, and only indirectly the improvement of material life. Most Christians in China adopt an other-worldly contemptuous attitude toward material life and often are skeptical of modernization. When we talk about modernization it is never very convincing to exaggerate the role and contribution of the Christian church or to expect too much from her.

Our theme today is not so much a historical evaluation as a discussion of the relationship between Christianity and modernization in present-day China. The content of the concept of modernization today is quite different from that of fifty to one hundred years ago. China had been modernized to a certain degree, as measured by certain standards and compared to pre-modern China before that. But when we say modernization now we mean and expect something quite different. The modern of the past has become pre-modem (Dr. Gotthard Oblau had spoken of the Cistercian Order as a model of modernization in the Middle Ages). The modern of the present is verging on and facing the challenges of post-modernity (I am looking

3. Max Weber, 1905. *The Protestant Ethic and the Spirit of Capitalism*, English version (New York: Scribner, 1930).

4. Ernst Troeltsch, 1913. *The Social Teachings of the Christian Church*, English version (London: Allen and Unwin, 1931).

forward to learning from the wisdom of three speakers later this afternoon). Modernity is like an ever receding goal and we are caught in the dilemma of pressing forward and catching up with modernity or staying still in complacency (under the pretext of "defending eternal truths"), and lagging behind in the perpetual flux of time and changes.

Christianity as a historical religion has always faced the danger of being out-dated. The Protestant church in China is a case in point. It is both easy and difficult to understand what modernization means today in China. Easy because it is everywhere when you open your eyes and ears. The whole country is brimming over with enthusiasm for modernity. One feels the rhythm of advances every week and month. Difficult because it infiltrates all phases of life –economic, political, technological, social, cultural, and spiritual—and all are supposed to be stamped with the label CHINESE. Now how is Protestant Christianity in China to be related to the overwhelming phenomena and processes of modernization?

We must begin from what it is and where it finds itself. I can only mention a few points that seem important to me.

1) It is young, and yet very old. Protestant Christianity has a history of less than two hundred years in China. Compared with Confucianism, Taoism and Buddhism, and even with Islam and Catholicism, it is but a teenager. Being young, it has not yet taken root in the soil of Chinese indigenous culture. But it claims to have the heritage of an old religion, at least as old as Confucianism (some have tried to trace it back to the time of Moses, which is even older). Being young, it was more susceptible to cultural changes in the last century. Being old, it is heavily bent with the burdens of conservatism, and shows a strong resistance to change.

2) It is alien in origin, form and matter. The unfortunate association of Christianity with the colonialism and imperialism of the foreign powers during the first century after its introduction into China has left a sense of hostility in the masses of Chinese people. The reluctance on the part of most church leaders and believers to change traditional foreign rituals for new and indigenous forms is another barrier. The Chinese Christian Three-Self Patriotic Movement has tried to get rid of the stigma of foreignness and make the church really Chinese. It has been successful to a certain extent. But the idea has not yet been accepted by a large number of Christians who take a skeptical attitude toward the movement. The narrow exclusivist view of salvation rooted in fundamentalist orthodox theology which shuts out all "non-believers" from the gospel will eventually lead to the self-isolation and alienation of the Christian church from the broad masses of the people, and keep the church in a sort of cultural enclave.

3) It is small and backward. Although the church has been growing rapidly in the last two decades, it remains a tiny minority of less than one percent of the total population. Most of the increase of believers is in the rural areas and among the less educated and poor strata. A large number of them are quickly attracted to Christianity by the preaching of "cheap grace."[5] A lack of proper Christian education and pastoral care often results in beliefs and practices bordering on feudal superstitions. So as the church grows quantitatively, the cultural and theological profile has become more and more backward and retrogressive, in a direction against modernization.

4) It is a uniting church, yet there are signs of centrifugal tendencies and disintegration. In a post-denominational stage, the Protestant church is still in the process of uniting. The China Christian Council (CCC) is not yet a united church in the ecclesiological sense. The three types of church polity of most mainline denominations (i.e., Episcopalianism, Presbyterianism and Congregationalism) can no longer be applied without important modification. The church needs a new ecclesiology and a new polity. The relation between national, provincial, and municipal Christian Councils and local congregations has never been clearly defined. Furthermore, in the last decade the development of some autonomous sectarian groups[6] has become more and more of a threat to the uniting church (CCC). The lack of competent leaders, especially within the middle-aged bracket on the national and provincial levels, is a danger which may result in a crisis in the near future. Modernization requires a balanced and mutually complementary form of structure between strong centralized leadership and efficient local autonomy. The aim is unity with variety, not uniformity. It is a kind of unity with certain flexibility to accommodate the pluralistic developments in modernization, but not anarchy. The exact form it will take still remains to be worked out.

5) In self-support there are also problems and difficulties. Generally speaking, for most of the larger churches in the cities or "developing areas" self-support is not much of a problem. But most rural churches are poor and dependent upon unpaid or partially paid "voluntary" church workers. The traditional teaching of the church is not to worry about the material needs of life but to have faith in God (Matt. 6:19, 25–33). In China, the Calvinist doctrine of predestination seems to have little to do with the spirit of capitalism! The church is generally short of personnel to handle financial matters. There was once even a controversy among Christians over whether

---

5. I borrow the term from Dietrich Bonhoeffer's *The Cost of Discipleship*, (New York: MacMillan, 1959).

6. I borrow the term from Troeltsch's *The Social Teachings of the Christian Church*.

it is Christian to get rich. Experiments in business enterprises have been tried by some churches in the name of self-support. As far as I know not many have been very successful. In present-day China the central task of modernization is economic development. But this is just where the church finds herself impotent. Christian churches have been encouraged by the government to make contributions in this area, including "inducing foreign capital" or setting up "joint enterprises." The response has not been too enthusiastic, probably due to lack of expertise or for theological reasons. On the other hand, there are foreign individuals, organizations or "foundations" offering large amounts of funds as contributions or investments to churches and seminaries to modernize. Such offers may become so alluring and hard to resist that sometimes the Three-Self principle seems to be at risk.

6) In theological construction and self-propagation I want to make three observations. First, a large number of preachers adhere to traditional "orthodox teachings" of the church (which are mainly Western in origin, conservative or fundamentalist in content and tend to be revivalist or charismatic in form and style). They regard modernization and contextualization (acculturation or "sinicization") as unorthodox, dangerous or heretical, and take an indifferent, skeptical or even hostile attitude toward all innovative attempts to modernize and contextualize. Secondly, some theologians tend to take the generally accepted view that modernization means Westernization, and to equate modern theology with western modern theology alone. They show little interest in indigenization or "sinicization." Thirdly, there are those who think of contextualization only in historical or traditional terms (such as those who take Confucianism or neo-Confucianism as the sine qua non element of indigenization). I think all these three groups of people are one-sided in their theology. They fail to understand the "tripartite" or "Trinitarian" character of the message of the Christian Gospel to be presented to Chinese people in a modern age. We need to work out a kind of theology that is Christian and at the same time appealing to modem Chinese minds.

7) The emergence of a group of so-called "culture Christians" in the last decade deserves serious study.[7] They are young intellectuals who are attracted to and have become interested in Christianity through literature, the fine arts, philosophy, history and other cultural and social disciplines. Their influence within academic circles has been mounting in recent years, although there is no way of making quantitative surveys because most of them are not willing to identify themselves with the organized church. Or, to put it the other way round, the church is not ready to open her doors to

---

7. Dr. Li Pingye 李平晔 has a very well written article analyzing this unprecedented and important phenomenon. I am thankful to her for letting me read her paper three months ago. I agree with her observations and conclusion.

them, or to make herself attractive to them. They could be a real asset to the church in meeting the challenges of modernization. But the church seems to be unaware of their existence and significance.

I think the above seven points are enough to give a picture of how and where the Chinese Protestant church finds herself in this time of social change and modernization. It does not require much imagination to foresee that twenty years from now China will be very, very different. The present eighty percent "rural area" with its eighty percent "agricultural population" will become industrialized, urbanized, commercialized with concomitant changes in education and in cultural and spiritual life. In cities the changes may be even more striking and rapid. The church cannot stand still and be unaffected by these tremendous changes. Not all changes brought about by modernization are "good" by the standard of Christianity.[8]

Now the question of how Christianity is related to modernization may be answered in three ways. The first is what contribution can the church make to help "realize the aims of modernization"? Of course the church by nature is unable to do much in the economic, political, technological dimensions. Perhaps some would say that it is in the cultural, moral, aesthetic, and spiritual fields that the church is expected to make her special contributions. My answer is that as the church is (as I have characterized it above) both young and conservative, foreign, small and backward, in danger of falling apart, not self-supporting, and lacking a theology to gird and equip herself to bear witnesses to the Christian gospel in a modernized China, it is more important and useful to leave this question unanswered, and to turn to the second question. How can the church change herself through "self-building" in order to catch up with the whole country and to accommodate the ideas and ideals of modernization? No matter whether one likes it or not, modernization is bound to happen, and it poses the church with threatening challenges.

If the church is going to survive, and to make life more abundant to the world as Christ has promised (John 10:10), then we need something like the ressourcement and aggiornamento[9] of the post-conciliar Catholic Church. So instead of talking highly and bragging about what the Protestant Church can do or should do to modernize, it seems to me we must first take a good and honest look at the Protestant Church in China as she is now, and try to meet the challenges and seek change for a real renewal.

8. I am expecting to learn from Mr. Martin Conway's speech, "Is Modernization a Good Thing?"

9 These are the aims of Vatican II. Ressourcement means renewal through return to sources, and aggiornamento means renewal through relevance. In both, "renewal" is the key word.

It is only after that, not before that, that we can try to answer the third question: how can we take Christianity as a norm or standard to assess, evaluate and pass judgements on the results of modernization, or to offer some guiding principles for modernization? I will leave this third question for others to answer.

Faith's Journey
Foreword to *Love Never Ends*
(Nanjing, January 1998)

Chen Zemin

IT IS A GREAT pleasure as well as an honor for me to read all of the selections in *Love Never Ends* before the volume went to press. I have known Bishop Ting since 1939, during the early days of the war against Japan. He had graduated from St. John's University in Shanghai and was serving as a Student Secretary in charge of student work with the Shanghai YMCA. I was studying in Shanghai University at the time and during the summer vacation I was assigned to do field work in the Shanghai YMCA, where he was my advisor. A hard worker, diligent in study, poised and dignified, but enthusiastic and affable as well, he made a deep impression on me. Later I studied at Nanjing Theological Seminary, which had moved to Shanghai during the war. Bishop Ting had received his B.D. from St. John's, and was serving as pastor of the Church of Our Savior of the Chung Hua Sheng Kung Hui 中华圣公会 (The Chinese Anglican Church) and the Shanghai Community Church. He frequently came to Nanjing Seminary library to read and borrow books, and I often went to Community Church to hear him preach. At that time nearly half of China had fallen into the hands of the Japanese, and Shanghai was cut off like an "isolated island." In that difficult and dangerous environment, he was earnest in his pastoral care among church members and students, while at the same time continuing conscientious research in theology. I knew him as a man who did theology not by fleeing reality for some theological ivory tower, ignoring the world while pursuing his own academic and moral cultivation, but rather by seeking ways in which Christian faith and teaching could be combined with the cause of national salvation and social transformation. This was reflected in his frequent admonition to students when he became Principal of the

Seminary: "In doing theology, one should not distance oneself from political reality; some times theology is more subtle politics."

After victory over the Japanese, Bishop Ting was invited to be a secretary of the Canadian Student Christian Movement, where he made friends with some progressive Western Christians (see "In Memory of Rev. Alan Eccleston," the Foreword to the newedition of *Christian Missions and the Judgement of God* and "In Memory of Rev. Edward Hewlitt Johnson"). He did graduate studies at Columbia University and Union Seminary in New York, where he gained a deeper appreciation of theology as an ideology and worldview that might serve either progressive or reactionary politics. From 1948–51, he served as a secretary of the World Student Christian Federation in Geneva, where some of his colleagues were progressives sympathetic to the Chinese revolution. This happened to be at the very time of the Liberation War in China, when Chinese Christianity was facing a life and death choice— whether to follow the progressive path of patriotism, or to shore up the backward forces of reaction. Many prominent Western Christians, with their anti-Soviet, anti-Communist prejudices, were harsh in their assessment of the new China, but Bishop Ting paid no heed to the "well-intentioned" advice of "friends." He and his wife, Siu-mayKuo 郭秀梅, returned with their son to Shanghai, where he became involved in the Christian anti-imperialist patriotic movement and headed up the Christian Literature Society 广学会 as General Secretary.

In 1951, as the Chinese Christian patriotic movement further developed and intensified, 12 Protestant theological seminaries in east China joined together to become Nanjing Union Theological Seminary, with Bishop Ting as Principal, a post he has held right up to the present. In the over 40 years I have been privileged to work with him, I have learned a great deal under his guidance;in particular, how to work in the church, do theology and carry on theological education inthe complicated environment of socialist new China. For several decades h6 has been a true leader of Protestant Churches inChina (as Chairperson of the National Committee of the Three- Self Patriotic Movement and President of the China Christian Council from 1980–1997, both positions he retired from with the titles of Honorary Chairperson and Honorary President, January 1, 1997). From 1979 to the present, he was VicePresident of Nanjing University and Head of the Center for Religious Studies, Nanjing University. He was Vice-Chairperson of the 5th and 6th Jiangsu 江苏 Provincial People's Political Consultative Conference, and a Vice-Chairperson of the 7th, 8th and 9th National People's Political Consultative Conference. In this past nearly half century, while busily engaged in a variety of church activities, academic research and educational work, as well as social and political activities, he has written a number of important essays, some of which have been published (eight appear in *Theological Writings from Nanjing Seminary*, and several of these are included here), while many have been lost. Included in this volume are some 80 pieces selected and edited by the Bishop himself. With the exception of six earlier ones, all are post-Cultural-Revolution works, most of which are published here for the first time. Bishop Ting is a man of strong commitment, lofty ideals and great enterprise. As a Christian leader of China, his life has been closely linked with the destiny of the Chinese Church. What he had probed and pondered during different periods and phases in the past half-century reflected the problems, challenges and responses of the Chinese Church. In a sense, his quests and thought in religious issues are reflections of the church's deliberation on her destiny and future during these periods. Hence the publication of this volume is of great historical significance and relevance to the Church in China.

Bishop Ting has also written many essays in English, some of which have been newly translated into Chinese for this collection (referring to the Chinese edition—ed.). Some have been published in English overseas, such as those in *No Longer Strangers: Selected Writings of Bishop K.H. Ting* (Raymond Whitehead, ed., Orbis Books, 1989) and in the Chinese Theological Review (published by the Foundation for Theological Education in Southeast Asia). Volume 10 (1995) of the *Chinese Theological Review* was a festschrift honoring Bishop Ting's 80th birthday and included many essays by friends at home and abroad. Bishop Ting is a well-known figure in world Christianity, recognized as the main spokesman for and theologian of contemporary Chinese Christianity. This collection of his writings has been made for readers in Christian and academic circles in China. An English edition is being published simultaneously by the Yilin 译林 Press.

The contents of the volume can be classified by subject matter as follows: 1) speeches made during overseas visits; 2) religious policy and religious studies; 3) Three-Self and running the church well; 4) theological lectures and sermons; 5) memorials, congratulations, prefaces, etc.

Since the Third Plenum (1978) of the Eleventh Congress of the CPC, the Party and government have been summing up their historical experience—correct and incorrect— in religious questions, clarifying the Party's basic viewpoint and policy, and rectifying the errors of the "Great Proletarian Cultural Revolution." Bishop Ting, as a member of the Commission on Constitutional Revision of the National People's Congress, was involved in the 1982 revision of the Constitution. In three articles in this volume Bishop Ting explicates the United Front policy and religious policy of the Party according to his own understanding. This is the foundation and basis of religious work and church work in the new period of opening-up and reform.

In the field of academic studies of religion, there was also a need to eradicate the influence of extreme leftist thought and to return to order. Up until the mid-eighties, there was a debate among Chinese academic circles on the so-called "Third Opium War." Some people had maintained a rigid stance insisting on the concept of "religion as opiate." Bishop Ting took an active part in this debate, opposing this view on scientific and historical grounds, and with an attitude of seeking truth from facts, giving a balanced critique of the notion that "religion is the opiate of the people." He put forward the view that the rich moral and ethical content of religion can be brought into harmony with socialism. Two longer pieces included here, "Recent Developments inthe Study of Religion" (with Wang Weifan 汪维藩, 1989) and "*An Introduction to Religion under Socialism in China*"(1988)can serve as summaries of this debate. Since then, there has been much more mutual understanding and common language and friendshipbetween religious and academic circles. We are very pleased to see that old taboos have been broken and great successes scored in the study of religion in China today.

In the past 20 years, Bishop Ting has devoted most of his time and energy to the work of building up the Chinese Church. The focus of his work during these years has been on maintaining the correct direction of Three-Self patriotism, strengthening and developing the achievements of Three-Self, bringing Three-Self patriotism to bear fruits in making the Chinese church well-run and effecting the transition from "three-self" (self-governing, self-supporting, self-propagating) to "three well" (well-governed, well-supported and doing the work of propagation well). Following the further implementation of the religious policy nationwide, the Chinese Church has developed very rapidly and the number of believers and church organizations has multiplied. Because pastoral care of believers and education work has not been able to keep pace with this growth, many problems and difficulties have arisen in local churches. In some places the understanding and implementation of religious policy by local cadres has been problematic. Some problems also exist within the church in terms of understanding and practice in the areas of enlarging unity and making the church well-run. Chinese Christianity is in a "post-denominational" stage that began in 1980 with the establishment of the China Christian Council. The "two bodies," the Three-Self Patriotic Movement Committee of Protestant Churches in China (est. 1954) and the China Christian Council, form the national "patriotic organizations" of the Chinese Protestant Church, and function to guide thinking, organization and church administration. Bishop Ting, a man of lofty and penetrating vision and great openness of heart, has made important proposals on mutual respect according to the three-self principle (in doctrine, liturgy and church polity), enlarging unity, "re-ordering the relationship" and running the church well. He advocates seeking greater unity with those, church bodies which are not associated with the Three-Self organization by relying on love, service and understanding. In the ten pieces included here that deal with these subjects, his magnanimity, sincerity andearnestness are evident.

Upwards of half the essays in this collection, in content and length, are theological. Over 30 of these were originally intended as sermons. Bishop Ting has always had a very high regard for self-propagation and theological studies. "Theology is the church in the act of thinking. A church that does not think is stagnant and dogmatic; it is a prison of the spirit. A religion that does not speak of theology is crude and primitive. A religion which does not apply reason to problems is unreasonable." The kind of theological thinking Bishop Ting advocates is one which considers how to bring faith and the realities of life together, a theory both rational and with transcendent power. It is neither the mysterious and abstruse subjectivity of the scholastics nor the preserve of "professional theologians" shut away in their studies. In one essay he writes of the "theological mass movement" of Chinese Christianity in the early 1950s, a time when the masses of believers themselves raised many theological questions which still have great significance today.

Bishop Ting has on many occasions spoken of the relationship between the ecumenicity (universality) and localness (particularity) of Christianity. He proposed that the Chinese Church should have its own theology. At the present stage, "Our theology has as a matter of course been constrained by history and the universal church, but it is not a copy, it is the thinking of Chinese Christians ourselves about the problems of the Chinese Church." At present we have not yet constructed or proposed a comparatively systematic or complete theology. We begin with the reality of where we are, and attempt to bring together Christian faith, traditional Chinese culture and special ethnic characteristics. Chinese society today is changing rapidly in a time of openness and reform. We must not raise demands for systematization prematurely in doing "contextualized theology," for, if we do, we will fall into the old ways of plagiarizing or aping traditional Western theology. For decades, from reading the Bible to faith in practice, Chinese Christianity has indeed seen much "new light," and has been engaged in doing theology. In many essays in this volume, Bishop Ting offers valuable, creative views of a breakthrough nature on fundamental theological issues, and selects concepts from modern Western theology for our consideration, adapting it for our use. All this canserve as guides for the future development of Chinese theology. For example, with regard to the Bible (See "Chinese Christians' Approach to the Bible") he refers to the fruits of contemporary Western biblical studies, avoiding pedantic debates and dogmatic "biblicism" of the quoting-out-of- context type. In accord with Chinese Christians' fervent love of the Bible and respect for biblical authority, he convincingly lays down a "biblical foundation" for a whole range of theological theses. In considering our concept of God (see "God is Love," "One Chinese Christian's View of God," etc.) he attests that God's most essential attribute is love; other attributes, such as holiness and righteousness, derive from this love which created all things and embraces all things. He disperses the metaphysical fog and avoids the logical contradictions of traditional Western theology, enhancing the sense of human feeling and warmth, which makes these ideas more easily understood and accepted by Chinese people. His christology posits the "Cosmic Christ" as an extension of "God is Love," absorbing the "process theology" of Whitehead and Teilhard de Chardin's evolutionary thinking, taking creation, providence, redemption and sanctification of the cosmos to its ultimate consummation, all as the whole process of God's work through Christ. He bypasses the thousand-year-old controversy around the Chalcedonian definition of the perfect deity and perfect humanity of Christ, and corrects the one-sidedness and narrowness of dwelling solely on his work of redemption in traditional christology. In theological study, there have long been two different approaches: creation-centered and redemption-centered. The former is usually more open and can easily accommodate all sorts of progressive thought and social changes, while the latter is often susceptible to a narrow exclusivism. In "Creation and Redemption," Bishop Ting handles this question very well, alerting us to and providing a corrective for the tendency in Chinese churches today to stress redemption while undervaluing creation. On human nature, Bishop Ting points to the concept in Chinese culture of the "innate goodness of human nature." He contrasts this with the Christian concept of original sin, reminding us that "humans are made in the image of God," and are "unfinished creations of God," "coworkers with God in the work of creation," while also pointing out the necessity of God's saving grace and emphasizing the possibility of human responsibility and development.

    I cannot elaborate all these at length here. But these brief indications can be used as the loci to construct a theological system—a *loci theologici*. If we substantiate and connect these loci, it is not difficult to glimpse the framework of a new system of Chinese theology. Bishop Ting explains his points brilliantly in compelling and easily understood language, more appealing to people than abstruse theological jargon. Further, in many of his essays, he writes of how we are to deal with all the truth, goodness and beauty we encounter outside Christianity. What about atheists? Or the teaching that "believers cannot be yoked together with unbelievers?" He provides answers to these perplexing questions. At the same time he introduces current topics in international theological circles, such as the movement for unity in the ecumenical church, international peace and social justice, liberation theology, feminist theology, eco-theology, etc., all of which serve to broaden theological students' horizons. This volume enlivens theological reflection, challenges theological construction in the Chinese Church and clarifies the way forward. Its publication is a significant milestone in the history of Chinese theology and should be required reading for Chinese theological students.

In the last decade or so, Chinese intellectual circles have become more open toward the study of religion and theology than at any other time. Many friends outside the church have expressed understanding and sympathy toward Christianity. They have even contributed to the field in translating, writing and publishing many high quality works related to Christian theology. These make theological studies in the church, or the sermons preached from the pulpit, seem backward and conservative in comparison. Many intellectuals have been unwilling to be in touch with or to be involved in the church for this reason. Bishop Ting coined the phrase "culture Christians" to describe these people, and although both within and outside the church there are still differing understandings and critiques of this issue, it is an expression of faith which should engender a positive response. Those of us within the church should ponder how to actively raise our own level, liberate our thinking, find a more common language with intellectuals in general, and encourage dialogue. These are issues that touch on whether Christianity in China will be able to break the bonds of being seen as a "sub-culture" and move forward together with all Chinese people. I hope the publication of this book will be noted and welcomed by intellectuals and help them to gain a deeper understanding of Chinese Christianity today.

In K.H. Ting, *Love Never Ends*. Nanjing: Yilin Press, 2000, 1–8.
Dr. Chen Zemin retired from his positions as Vice-Principal and Professor of Systematic Theology at Nanjing Seminary in 2002. He is a Vice-Director of the TSPM/CCC Advisory Committee and a member of the 7th Standing Committee of the TSPM.

Bishop K. H. Ting's *Love Never Ends* is available from: Foundation for Theological Education in SouthEast Asia
Dr. Marvin D. Hoff, Executive Director
21236 Barth Pond Lane
Crest Hill, IL 60435
e-mail: ftehoff@earthlink.net
US$30 postpaid

Address on the "Celebration of the First Publication of 'God is Love'"[1]
(Shanghai, December 14, 2004)

I FEEL GREATLY HONORED to be granted an opportunity to speak on thishappy and solemn occasion of "Celebrating the First Publication" ofanother new edition of the English version of *Collected Writings of Bishop K. H. Ting*, under the new title "*GOD IS LOVE*," published by CCMI (Cook Communications Ministries International). I have known Bishop Ting since 1939, and have been fortunate to be his student and later his co-workerat Nanjing Union Theological Seminary, where he is the President for all these fifty-two years. On behalf of all the faculty, students and alumni/ae, who all look on him as our beloved mentor, I want to express our hearty congratulations, sincere prayers and best wishes for his good health, longevity, and ever growing far-reaching influence in the Chinese Christian Church.

Over two thirds of his life is synchronized with the rebirth anddevelopment of the Christian Church in China. While busily engaged in a variety of church responsibilities, academic research and educational administrative work, as well as social and political activities, he haswritten over one hundred important essays, addresses, sermons andarticles. Bishop Ting is a man of strong commitment, lofty ideals and great enterprise. As a Christian leader of China, his life has been closelylinked with the destiny of the Chinese Church. What he had probed and pondered during different periods and phases in the past half-century reflected the problems, challenges and responses of the Chinese Church. In a sense, his quests and thought in religious issues are reflections of the church's deliberation on her destiny and future during these periods. The publication of his works is therefore an important phase ofthe achievements of the Church in China.

In order to do justice to the present new edition of *GOD IS LOVE*, may I briefly innumerate the previous publications of Bishop Ting's works.

---

1. Dec. 14, 2004. Shanghai. (2004年12月14日)在《神就是爱》首发式上发言（未定）稿

Address on the "Celebration of the First Publication of 'God is Love'"   211

(1) First, *No Longer Strangers—Selected Writings of L H. Ting*, edited by Raymond L. Whitehead, in English, Orbis Books, Maryknoll, 1989, including 47 articles written prior to the date of publication.

(2) *Selected Writings of Ding Guangxun*《丁光训文集》, in Chinese, edited by the author himself, including 82 articles written before 1997, and a Foreword by me, Yiling Press, 1998.

(3)《天风甘雨》, ("Ding Guangxun, Leader of Christianity in China"), in Chinese, including 21 essays and a list of 78 articles. Nanjing University Press, 2001.

(4) *LOVE NEVER ENDS—Papers by L H. Ting*, in English, ed. and tr. by Janice Wickeri, including 79 articles, edited and arranged in chronological order. Yiling Press, 2000,

(5) Five booklets containing 57 articles published by CCC/TSPM in Chinese, 2000, under five topics: "On the Bible," "On God," "On Christ," "On Three-self and Church Construction," and "On Theological Reconstruction."

(6) *A Chinese Contribution to Ecumenical Theology*, in English, ed. by Philip and Janice Wickeri, Geneva Risk Books, 2001.

So there are three editions in Chinese and three in English. Of the three English editions, the Orbis edition of 1989 and the Geneva edition of 2001, I presume, do not have a wide circulation. The Yiling edition (*Love Never Ends*, 2000) was published in China, so is not easily accessible in America. Since there have been much concern, discussion, misinformation, misinterpretation and misunderstanding in respect to the present situation of the church in China, it is of paramount importance that Bishop Ting's writings, especially those on his theological thinking, on how to build the church well, and on "theological reconstruction," be made accessible to Christian friends in the West. Hence the publication of the present new edition by CCMI is a great contribution of historical significance and relevance to the Church in China.

In this connection I wish to make a few observations:

(1) This is the latest and most complete and updated collection of Bishop Ting's writings, including fourteen articles heretofore unpublished in English. Those written in the last five years (since 2000) are of special importance in helping us understand the ever—progressive thinking of Bishop Ting concerning the course of future development of the Chinese Church.

(2) Gratitude should be extended to our good friend Janice Wickeri for her faithful work of translating all the articles included in both this edition and the Yiling edition (of 2000) from the original Chinese.

(3) The name of the book is changed from *LOVE NEVER ENDS* (of the Yiling edition) to *GOD IS LOVE* in the present edition. Both are biblical and can be found in the original Chinese titles of respective articles in the

collection. While the rhetorical emphatic use of double negative is stressed in the former, the latter seems more straightforward and all-embracing.

(4)The titles of many articles have been changed and reworded, and the order re-arranged into five sections, with an appendix and an epilogue. This may be done with an intention to make the book more acceptable to many readers in America, but somehow it tends to present the articles out of context. As I have pointed in the beginning, Bishop Ting's life has been closely linked with the destiny of the Chinese Church. His thought and writings during different periods and phases in the past half-century reflected the problems, challenges and responses of the Chinese Church. To read Bishop Ting's writings out of historic-social context may sometimes lead to misunderstanding and miss the thrust and significance of the messages.

(5)After all, we all want to hail that an up-dated complete, authentic, unadulterated English version of Bishop Ting's writings is now presented by a well-known Christian publisher Cook Communications Ministries International, as a major contribution to the Chinese Christian Church. May I quote from "A Note from the Publisher": There is reasonto hope for a better relationship between our great nations and a mutual sharing and support of believers for Christ and His Kingdom."

". . . What does it matter: Just this, that Christ is proclaimed in every way. . . . in that I rejoice. Yes, and I will continue to rejoice!" (Phil. 1:15–18, NRSV).

. . . . . .

To conclude, I venture to make a small suggestion, that when the book is going to be distributed in China, may the jacket be discarded. The front matter is marred by a stripe of gloomy tincture of mystical vagueness. Scrutinizing eyes can detect a significant cartographical omission. Let the untainted brilliance of the theme GOD IS LOVE shine out!

www.ingramcontent.com/pod-product-compliance
Lightning Source LLC
Chambersburg PA
CBHW070252230426
43664CB00014B/2511